MW00327780

DISPATCHES FROM PAKISTAN

MADIHA R. TAHIR
QALANDAR BUX MEMON
VIJAY PRASHAD

Editors

Dispatches *from* Pakistan

University of Minnesota Press
Minneapolis
London

First published by LeftWord Books (www.leftword.com), New Delhi, India, in October 2012. LeftWord Books is a division of Naya Rasta Publishers Pvg. Ltd.

Individual essays copyright 2012 by the respective authors

This collection copyright 2012 LeftWord Books

First published in the United States in 2014 by the University of Minnesota Press

All rights reserved. No part of this publication may be reproduced, stored in a retrieval system, or transmitted, in any form or by any means, electronic, mechanical, photocopying, recording, or otherwise, without the prior written permission of the publisher.

Published by the University of Minnesota Press
111 Third Avenue South, Suite 290
Minneapolis, MN 55401-2520
http://www.upress.umn.edu

LIBRARY OF CONGRESS CATALOGING-IN-PUBLICATION DATA
Dispatches from Pakistan / Madiha R. Tahir, Qalandar Bux Memon, and Vijay Prashad, editors.
Originally published: New Delhi : LeftWord Books, 2012.
Includes bibliographical references and index.
ISBN 978-0-8166-9223-1 (hc: acid-free paper)
ISBN 978-0-8166-9224-8 (pb: acid-free paper)
1. Pakistan—Politics and government. 2. Pakistan—Foreign relations. I. Tahir, Madiha R., editor of compilation. II. Memon, Qalandar Bux, editor of compilation. III. Prashad, Vijay, editor of compilation.
DS384.D57 2014
954.9105'3—dc23

2014001728

Printed in the United States of America on acid-free paper
The University of Minnesota is an equal-opportunity educator and employer.

20 19 18 17 16 15 14   10 9 8 7 6 5 4 3 2 1

Contents

What Does Pakistan Mean?
Pakistan ka Matlab Kya?

HABIB JALIB

Roti, kapda aur dawa
Ghar rehne ko chhota sa
Muft mujhe talim dila
Mein bhi Musalmaan hoon wallah
Pakistan ka matlab kya
La Ilaha Illalah . . .

Amrika se mang na bhik
Mat kar logon ki tazhik
Rok na jamhoori tehrik
Chhod na azadi ki rah
Pakistan ka matlab hai kya
La Ilaha Illalah . . .

Khet waderon se le lo
Milen luteron se le lo
Mulk andheron se le lo
Rahe na koi Alijah
Pakistan ka matlab kya
La Ilaha Illalah . . .

Sarhad, Sindh, Baluchistan
Teenon hain Panjab ki jaan
Aur Bangal hai sab ki aan
Aai na un ke lab par aah
Pakistan ka matlab kya
La Ilaha Illalah . . .

Baat yehi hai bunyadi
Ghasib ki ho barbadi
Haq kehte hain haq agah
Pakistan ka matlab kya
La Ilaha Illalah . . .

Bread, clothes, and medicine
A little house to live in
Free education given to me.
I have always been a Muslim.
What does Pakistan mean?
There is no God, but God.

Do not beg for American alms.
Do not mock the people.
Do not stop the democratic struggle.
Do not abandon the road to freedom.
What does Pakistan mean?
There is no God . . .

Confiscate the landlords' fields.
Confiscate the robbers' mills.
Redeem the country from the blind.
Don't let the vermin remain.
What does Pakistan mean?
There is no God . . .

The Frontier, Sind, Baluchistan:
These three are dearest to Punjab.
Bengal is their splendor.
No anguish among them.
What does Pakistan mean?
There is no God . . .

This is the basic thing:
Ruination for the liars.
Those who have seen the Truth speak rightly.
What does Pakistan mean?
There is no God . . .

Translated by Vijay Prashad and Raza Mir

Introduction
Pakistan's Futures

MADIHA R. TAHIR, QALANDAR BUX MEMON,
AND VIJAY PRASHAD

Main Zinda Hun

Main ahbi Zinda Hun
Tum ne sang bari ki
Mere pekar ko
Diwarow ke qalib men chuna
Nagon se daswaya
Salibon per charhaya
Zehr pilwaya
Jalaya
Phir bhi main sach ki tarh painda hun
Main zinda hun

Mere Chehra, meri Ankhen, mer bazu
Mere lab
Zinda hain sab
Main shahab-e-shab
Hazaron bar
Tuta aur bikhra
Phir bhi main raqsinda-o-rakhinda hun

I Am Alive

I am still alive.
You stoned me
Entombed me
Crucified me
Poisoned me
Burned me
Yet, like the truth
I am alive, eternal

My face, my eyes, my arms
My lips
Are all alive;
I, the meteor of the night
A thousand times
shattered and scattered,
Yet I go on dancing, shining.

—Ahmad Faraz

PAKISTANIS ARE ALIVE. Sold by governments who should save them, killed by secret agencies who should guard them, bombed by American drones, "structurally adjusted" into starvation, beaten, rendered, tortured and disappeared, and yet, inscrutably, immutably, even joyously, they are still alive. In other places, other times, that may not be much. In Pakistan, that's an extraordinary feat. It is, after all, a place so thoroughly reviled that the world watched pitilessly as a quarter of the country drowned in summer 2010 in one of the worst floods in memory. The great deluge swallowed up lands and homes and livelihoods, but the international response was deplorably tepid. Pakistanis, the world seemed to say, were bad Muslims, and if some of them were destroyed, so much the better. It's a country used to living on its own charity, by its own wits. That's what it did. Students, bankers, and businessmen started flood drives. Government workers donated their paychecks for flood relief. Neighborhoods hired trucks to send food and medicine to the affected. There wasn't a street without flood relief work. For those of us who were in America when Hurricane Katrina ravaged Louisiana, the contrast was marked. Pakistanis do not wait for their government to help. They do not wait for the international community to help. They know they will die waiting.

Survival is a technique, living is an art, and Pakistanis have become masters at both.

Despite what the media may tell you, they also don't bother much with what the world thinks of them. There's too much else to do: lives to give birth to, lessons to learn, a living to make, food to cook, rolling blackouts to endure, friends to see, unions to build, prayers to offer, gifts to receive, loves to start, arguments to finish, and the night to live through. The explosions in the distance are just the staccato soundtrack.

It's a life that can produce daily frustrations. The lack of adequate water, electricity, education, or legal rights and protections can contribute to the lure of the jihadi or the junta, but there are other possibilities. With a population that's quite energetic and young—69 percent of Pakistanis are below age 30—the multitude is exploring other avenues, other ways of living, other futures.

Dispatches from Pakistan is an account of those other futures grounded in the particulars of an uncomfortable present. It is a book about Pakistani grit.

Hope is in the details.

PAKISTAN IS ONE OF THOSE CURIOUS PLACES about which everyone has an opinion, whether they have been there or not, studied about it or not. While some valuable work is starting to become available, major scholarly accounts have thus far largely concerned themselves with history from above, that is, official politics. Mainstream journalism has followed suit. Written by those reporters who delight in their token access and acquaintance with political celebrities, such journalism does little to explain the logic of Pakistani life except as oddity or contradiction. Finally, autobiographies by retired diplomats, bureaucrats, and army generals are often only outmatched in their bloated self-regard by the memoirs of the scions of political dynasties—we're looking at you, Bhuttos—who use them to air personal rivalries. Where then are the voices of the rest?

Dispatches from Pakistan is an attempt to account for the voices of the multitude. That task, immediately, presents problems. First, there is everything the global audience thinks it knows about Pakistan, that is, its obsession with Islamism, its propensity for terror, and so on. Those, too, are obstacles. Should one engage with these tiresome narratives to explain, yet again, how particular interests and ideologies undergird such depictions of Pakistan? That task is necessary but, we must admit, exasperating. Those who had hoped to follow and to write about alternative strands of Pakistani life that are overtly unconnected with the reasons the country is in the news have been reduced to calling out the same tired assumptions that underwrite dominant tales.

If figuring out how to write against the excessive force of certain accounts of Pakistan is one issue, discussing topics for which the audience has no maps is another. The figure of the Islamist, for example, scores starring roles in Pakistan, while the laboring worker, the secular separatist, and the socialist intellectual only manage bit parts—if at all.

And finally, there is the delicate and volatile problem of language and nuance. How does one carry, for instance, the cadence of impassioned speeches at peasant meetings or the indelible humor of trucker poetry from their local linguistic homes—Sindhi, Punjabi, Urdu, Pashto, Balochi—to the global vernacular, English? Translation across these linguistic and geographic borders becomes a double act. The first consists of language. The second grapples with how to make the local legible to the global without destroying the fragile, granular details that, in fact, invest the local with its meaning.

Dispatches from Pakistan is thus a kind of straddling act across boundaries—geographic, linguistic, and narrative. It aspires to enter the conversation about Pakistan on those issues that make the headlines, but more than that it endeavors to introduce the reader to the less-covered dimensions of Pakistani life, to its potential for other lives, its promise of hopeful revolutions. The essays in this book move from a poetry society in Gilgit to an army barrack in Punjab, from the hopes of a Pakistani politician in Karachi to the ruthless acquisition of land in Balochistan. In the process, they stay close to the bone, trying to uncover the complex skeleton of Pakistani society.

Such a task is never completed in one book alone, but this is our effort to recover, at least partially, Pakistan's *inquilabi* undercurrents and its hopeful overtones. It's our attempt to map the determined Pakistani spirit that, despite imperial designs to crucify it, goes on dancing and shining.

Several Dawns over the Indus
Three Maps

ZAHRA MALKANI

MAPS ARE NOT PERFECT COPIES of what lies on the ground. They are re-presentations, explorations: they harbor feelings as much as lines and curves.

The first map, with English writing in stencil, names Pakistan's largest administrative areas: Khyber Pukhtunkhwa, Punjab, Balochistan, and Sindh. The names leak across borders, following the trails of the people in their extended homelands: the Baloch cross into Iran, the Sindhis into India. These are historical boundaries, not identical to political ones.

The second map juxtaposes the outline maps of Balochistan and Bangladesh. They are about the same size. Will they have the same fate?

The third map, in pencil, shows the swollen Indus and its tributaries. They connect the entire region and, when they choose, flood the plains and displace the people. Below the map is a verse by Shah Abdul Latif Bhittai. It was originally written in Sindhi and is from his *Shah Jo Risalo*.

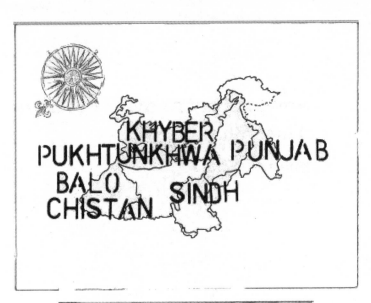

Zahra Malkani

Where with violence waters flow and beasts abound
Where even through sailors, waters depth cannot be found,
Where furious beasts of water howl and roar,
Where whole boats are sunk without a trace,
Not a sign, no piece of their board remains:
Where from whirlpools mysterious, none ever come back,
There, lord, to those who cannot swim render thy help.

— *Shah Abdul Latif Bhittai*

New Wine in Old Bottles

AASIM SAJJAD AKHTAR

FOLLOWING THE SENSATIONAL DISCOVERY of Osama bin Laden in the garrison town of Abbotabad in May 2011, it has become more difficult than ever to write about Pakistan without digressing into superficial narratives about religious militancy, the machinations of the country's military, and the vagaries of regional geopolitics. It is true that much of what is projected about Pakistan—or not, as the case may be—can be explained by the fact that mainstream politics is so deeply riven by intrigue. Pakistan is easily misunderstood thanks to the ethnocentrism that runs through much "analysis" that originates in western metropolises, whose writers seem obsessed with the motivation of actors in the current Great Game being played out in Pakistan and neighboring Afghanistan. There is indeed a strangely positive fascination with the secretive and often brutal conduct of Pakistan's security apparatus.

Pakistan's ruling bloc, for its part, is just as prone as its imperial patrons to project simplistic narratives. Yet, conspiracy theories exist because conspiracies do take place, even if the prototypical "foreign hand" theories cultivated by the military establishment and its loyal lackeys in the media and academy dominate over more subversive narratives. I believe that it is only possible to make sense of the complex wrangling of "great men" by probing the tremendous social change that has and continues to take place across the length and breadth of the Pakistani social formation. Relatedly, rationalizing the Pakistani military's apparent duplicity in dealing with its erstwhile protégés requires some serious thinking about the sociological bases of the state. My objective in this essay is to provide insight into the political economy of change and the ideological and social polarizations in Pakistan. In doing so I hope to show why certain intellectual trends predominate. The political economy of war and neoliberalism, and a deeply embedded system of patronage, needs to be understood if meaningful explanations are to be forged for why Pakistan is a hotbed of religious militancy, why a seemingly divided and militarized state remains powerful, and why substantive political transformation is unlikely in the short run.

"The Unplanned Revolution"

A handful of Pakistani scholars have been attempting over the course of many years to counter the perception that Pakistani society has changed little in the more than six decades since the end of colonial rule. This perception is propagated widely by the urban, educated elite in its caricaturing of the rural "masses" and the omnipresent "feudal" lord. A static social structure produces an intrinsically "corrupt" political leadership, constituted primarily of the all-powerful "feudals." The dissident view posits that the old "feudal" incumbents are increasingly challenged by the commercial nouveau-riche, the social formation is no longer primarily rural, and labor and capital are both highly mobile.[1]

I concur that the deepening of capitalism in society has forever changed patterns of social and political exchange, and what is emerging on the other side is a picture of both extreme differentiation and ever more ruthless competition for what are considered scarce economic and political resources. The manipulations of the state—and particularly the military—and piecemeal political realignments that have taken place to accommodate new contenders for power have polarized politics along ethnic and religious lines. Those who talk class politics, having always found it hard to establish their niche within Pakistan, are now struggling to be heard in a society wracked by sectarian and ethnic conflict.

This state of affairs—widening social (including class) chasms, no-holds-barred competition in the battle for political and economic resources, and increasingly incongruous and conflict-ridden politics—has intensified in the past decade. I believe that there are a few important factors that underlie this increased polarization that have also helped consolidate the broad secular trends of urbanization, enhanced labor and capital mobility, and the expansion of a commercial middle class.

It is now well established that the reaction of western governments and international financial institutions (IFIs) to the September 11 attacks has had great bearing on Pakistan's polity, economy, and society. However, there has been near silence—both within the popular media and in scholarly circles—on what might be called the "political economy of war." In short, an already huge underground smuggling economy that has thrived on the Pakistan–Afghanistan border for the best part of three decades has been given a massive fillip by the intensification of armed conflict on both sides of the border. One of the major outcomes is that Pakistani society has been flooded with cash: add to this the major inflow of remittance money from rich Pakistanis following 9/11, an investment binge on the part of Gulf states, and the rapid financial liberalization enforced by the IFIs, and it becomes clear that the winds of change are gusting harder and faster than ever before.

The Political Economy of War

By definition, details of the underground economy are underspecified. In my estimation, there have been only a handful of efforts to outline its sociological and political economy bases. Indeed the little information in the public realm deals mostly with heroin smuggling and gunrunning.[2] In recent times it has become common knowledge that Pakistani businessmen smuggle wheat, petrol, and a host of consumer goods into Afghanistan, where profit margins are exponentially greater. More generally informalization in Pakistan has not been the subject of any major academic work or policy focus, despite the fact that it is becoming a favorite topic of sociologists, economists, and historians throughout the world.[3] As such much of what I suggest here is based on anecdotal information that needs to be built upon through more systematic study.

The underground economy in Pakistan features a close nexus between state functionaries, suppliers of goods, transporters, and merchant-traders. On the Pakistan–Afghanistan border at Chaman (Balochistan), for example, there is open sale and purchase of guns, cars, and electrical equipment under the watchful eye of border security. In the north, massive amounts of weapons and contraband come into the country via the Federally Administered Tribal Areas (FATA). These goods are transported across the border and then into Pakistan's urban centers in huge oil tankers and dumper trucks. According to the World Drug Report 2010, in 2009 approximately 150 metric tons of heroin were smuggled through Pakistan to destinations further west. Thus Pakistan is the world's biggest heroin trafficking country after its neighbor Afghanistan.[4]

The most popular destination of the drugs and guns coming into Pakistan from its western borders is the country's biggest metropolis, Karachi, from where most of the goods are exported out of the country to western metropolises while some circulate within the city and surrounding urban centers. Crucially Karachi's transport industry is dominated by Pakhtuns, a reflection of the close link between the almost 40–year war that has ravaged Pakhtun society and the burgeoning countrywide underground economy that has been produced by this war.[5]

Karachi is home to numerous conflicts, including ethnic and sectarian ones, which have ebbed and flowed over the years; in recent times these conflicts have once again reared their ugly head. The free flow of sophisticated weaponry into the city has given impetus to turf wars between warring gangs that contend for all manner of political and economic resources. Bloody competition over urban real estate has become particularly intense in the past decade, a reflection both of the continuing urban explosion and of wider structural changes wrought by the forces of neoliberal globalization.[6]

Pakistan as Laboratory of Neoliberalism

If Pakistan is awash with cash that has followed the intensification of a four-decade political economy of war, then it has also functioned in the past decade as a virtual laboratory for neoliberalism. While it is not possible to specify the scale of the underground economy, it is well known that tens of billions of dollars of official aid have flowed into the country since 9/11. Perhaps more important, the IFIs' insistence on radical financial liberalization has precipitated a windfall of low-interest credit for an urban middle class taken in by the glitter of consumer capitalism. Added to these easy loans has been the large amount of remittances sent home by (mostly) rich Pakistanis residing in western countries. Much of this cash has been put into circulation in high-return, high-risk sectors such as real estate and the stock market—in short, a "hot" capital binge with investors allowed free entry and exit.[7] The investment of remittance monies in real estate to a large extent explains the amazing rise in the price of land.[8]

The dramatic inflow of cash into the country during the Musharraf period (1999–2008) explains the speculative growth bubble that was formed. Predictably, this bubble burst spectacularly due both to the internal contradictions of the IMF-championed neoliberal growth strategy and the rise of food and oil prices on the world market (along with other exogenous shocks). Yet the economy remains flooded with cash, mostly in the hands of the super-rich but also circulating freely among middle-class consumers, as well as the trader-merchant segments. As I have already pointed out, much of this cash cannot be formally accounted for, and even where drugs and contraband are not the goods being traded, the trader-merchant lobby has fended off government attempts to survey and take account of their enterprises.

Even outside the upwardly mobile segments of society capital has penetrated deep into relatively remote regions of the country, thanks in large part to the mobile phone revolution. A host of foreign companies—mostly Arab but also China Mobile—have invested heavily in the telecommunications sector. The result has been a remarkable explosion of mobile phone coverage and usage. There are now also dozens of private TV channels operating in the country, making tens of millions of working people into a captive audience and further enhancing the scope of the consumer capitalist movement. That labor has become even more flexible and informalized in this same period proves just how perverse the logic of capital is; it lures and seduces, even while exclusion and oppression intensify.

The Historical Bloc Reconstituted

It is only by recognizing the profound changes that continue to take place in Pakistani society that one can truly make sense of the state—what it is, who it represents, and how it conducts itself—along with other elements of the ruling strata. The Pakistani state—like most other postcolonial variants—has long been characterized as the exclusive preserve of a small oligarchy that reflects continuity from the colonial period.[9] Yet while it is undoubtedly true that the "steel frame" (civilian and military bureaucracies) and propertied classes enfranchised by the British Raj remain powerful, it is also true that widespread social changes and the cynical use of Islam by the oligarchy have eroded its insularity. The social classes from which the civilian and military bureaucracies are recruited have become much more diverse and, as I will show presently, the changing composition of the services—and the military in particular—has been accompanied by the emergence of new contenders of power from within a rapidly changing society.

Writing in 1974, Eqbal Ahmad demonstrated amazing prescience in profiling the changing class composition of the military and civilian bureaucracies.[10] He suggested that the "old" westernized upper strata would gradually become a minority due to the rise of a much more overtly religious element, with sociological roots in the middle peasantry and urban petty bourgeoisie. It is a measure of his analytical acumen that Ahmad was able to outline during the Bhutto years (1971–77) a sociological trend that would be consolidated later during the Zia dictatorship (1978–88) in the shape of "Islamization."

Mainstream writers such as Stephen P. Cohen and Charles Kennedy confirmed toward the end of the Zia years that the insularity of the "steel frame" had been permanently shattered. This change in the class composition of the services was coeval with differing political trajectories for the military and bureaucracy. The military had been forever politicized, particularly in the wake of the humiliation of 1971, and was ready to assert itself as the arbiter in Pakistan's fractious political game. The bureaucracy, once the wellspring of policy and power, was no longer ambitious or coherent, and was subject to the whim of its military overlords and only chance encounters with elected politicians.[11]

Importantly, the gradual erosion of the secular, westernized elite's political and social influence can be explained at least in part by this elite's voluntary retreat.[12] The populist upheavals of the decade 1967–77 forced the elite onto the back foot, both politically and economically. A number of previously powerful families moved their capital abroad, while withdrawing from the formal political sphere. This same elite quietly welcomed the Zia takeover, if only because the military regime was committed to rolling back the politics of class. Yet it remained deeply uncomfortable throughout the 11-year dictatorship with the real and perceived consequences of "Islamization." In short, the elite was torn between its liberal, secular disposition and its real class concerns. The result was an intensified alienation from society and the creation of elite ghettoes.[13]

Quite predictably, this self-imposed estrangement ensured that the elite's worst fears became a self-fulfilling prophecy. The Afghan war became a window to a new Pakistan, one in which the security apparatus became virtually indistinguishable from the "non-state" right-wing militants that, at the time, were favorites of the "Free World." I have attempted above to demonstrate the political and economic impacts of this globalized "jihad" over the past few decades. The withering away of the westernized elite's cultural hegemony was the other profound consequence of the state's chosen policy vortex.

It is important to note here that there was no wholesale takeover of state institutions by lower-middle class conservatives; insofar as a not insignificant cultural transformation of the public sphere did take place, this cannot be attributed solely to the personal preferences of those who staffed the services, and the military in particular. Indeed, state patronage of the religious right—which extended both to nonstate militants and political parties such as the Jamaa't-e-Islami (JI)—has been a secular policy trend since at least 1970.[14]

Of course it is now obvious that almost four decades of state-sponsorship of the religious right has facilitated an unambiguous cultural change. But too much emphasis—both within scholarly circles and the popular media—is placed on the "cultural" and "political" in abstraction from the "economic." The burgeoning "real" economy is peopled by a teeming commercial class that has fully imbibed the official religiosity of the Zia-ist state, and therefore developed a symbiotic link with the religio-ideological establishment represented by parties such as the JI and the myriad *ulama* formations.

In contrast to the "old" propertied classes, this relatively new commercial class is "nativized" in much the same way as the post-1970s entrants into the services.[15] Its lineage can be traced, in the first instance, to the economic modernization of the 1960s (including the Green Revolution), which facilitated a boom in the secondary and tertiary sectors of the agrarian economy. The resultant mushrooming growth of small towns along major thoroughfares such as the Grand Trunk Road provided further impetus to small enterprises in trading, transport, and construction. The political economy of war has permanently consolidated the economic and political power of these commercial segments.

In suggesting that these segments enjoy a symbiotic link with the religio-ideological establishment, I am arguing against a simplistic separation of religious militancy and the ostensibly parliamentary religious parties. Additionally, notwithstanding the right's incessant rhetoric against imperialism, it has evinced no discomfort with neoliberal economics: during the Muttahida-Majlis-e-Amal's (MMA) time in government in the then North West Frontier Province (now called Khyber Pakhtunkhwa, KPK) between 2002 and 2008, multiple cooperation agreements were signed with the international financial institutions; more so, in fact, than any other provincial government or that at the center. Finally, the religious right has slowly but surely established some semblance of autonomy from the state, due to the regular supply of monies from external patrons in the Middle East sheikdoms. This state-level support has been supplemented by regular cash transfers from the upper-middle class diaspora in Europe and North America and other first-world regions; this diaspora has been taken in by the right's setting up of innumerable "welfare" organizations that purportedly meet people's needs where the (bureaucratic and inefficient) state has failed.[16]

To sum up, the reconstituted historical bloc is familiar yet different from the constellation of forces that ruled the roost until the 1970s. The military is still at the helm yet is now internally differentiated in terms of its class composition and ideological disposition. This institutional transformation has been coeval with the emergence of a "nativized" commercial class that is rooted in the informal economy and became politically influential due to state patronage during the Zia dictatorship. Finally the religious right has also become a claimant on power with an unspoken mandate to perform duties as a moral police. All of these constituencies are sociologically and politically interlinked, and generally share an interest in maintenance of established ideological and political hierarchies, but this does not necessarily mean that there exist no contradictions between them (even if these are primarily nonantagonistic in nature).

These contradictions have sharpened over the past decade, but the more serious contradictions have emerged between the "old" and "new" constituents of the historical bloc. The "old" does not simply refer to the westernized elite but also segments of the propertied classes represented in parties such as the Pakistan People's Party (PPP) and Awami National Party (ANP) that perceive an unwelcome encroachment on the part of the "nativized" segments.

The murder of the Governor of Punjab, Salman Taseer, by one of his own bodyguards in early 2011 is indicative of the fissures that threaten to undermine the structure of power. Taseer was in many ways the symbol of the westernized elite, a cynical businessman-cum-politician who had once been a genuine believer in social change. His death was mourned widely by many progressives, particularly as he was killed for taking up the cause of a poor Christian girl sentenced to death under the country's draconian Blasphemy Law. On the other hand his killer was celebrated openly by the religious right, while conservative elements within the services hardly shed a tear. Taseer had been Governor of Punjab in the later period of the Musharraf dictatorship and retained the post under the new PPP government. His politics and the various reactions to this

Aasim Sajjad Akhtar

death are a microcosm of the tensions within state and society that have become acute under the backdrop of imperialist war and right-wing militancy. Yet the uneasy tension between the old incumbents and the relatively new "vernacular interests" in the corridors of power will not necessarily result in rupture, not least of all because both segments continue to be represented within the military and bureaucracy.

Meanwhile all members of the historical bloc are implicated heavily in the political economy of war and committed to a cynical patronage politics that keeps the subordinate classes pliant, a trend that has been exacerbated by the consumer capitalist upheaval of the past decade.

This patronage politics—with deep roots in the colonial model of government—was given new impetus under the regime of General Zia ul Haq, following an upsurge of progressive politics in the preceding period (1967–77). Zia relied primarily on the military and its imperial patrons to prop up his rule, but he also inducted the commercial nouveau-riche into formal politics through local government and then eventually through nonparty provincial and national elections in 1985. Subordinate classes were compelled to buy into a regenerated patronage-based political order given the tremendous repression visited by the regime on organic working-class politics, their recourse to "big men" to cope with state and market compounding longstanding social hierarchies.

A consolidated politics of patronage has been symbiotic with the growth of the informal economy in an era of unending war and radical neoliberalism. The state appears to fragment, yet the structure of power remains resilient due to a dialectic of coercion and consent that breeds cynicism, fear, and alienation. State functionaries—both civilian and military—use their positions to facilitate accumulation, both for themselves and "new" propertied elements, with elements of the "old" surviving tenuously.[17]

Progressives at Loggerheads

As this incredibly complex political economy has played out, resistance to organized power has continued to emerge, and in some cases intensify. Other than classic examples of resistance to what David Harvey calls "accumulation by dispossession"—on the part of the rural landless, urban informal workers, and many others—ethnonational politics outside the Punjab has become more pronounced. The country's largest province of Balochistan is wracked by a low-intensity insurgency that has generated substantial support from a wide cross-section of Baloch society. Yet the machinations of the state have served their purpose. Ethnonationalists who have historically challenged the state's unitary character while retaining a staunch commitment to anti-imperialist politics have become increasingly distant from the left, with xenophobic tendencies intensifying accordingly.[18] Young people—now a majority of the population—have been brought up to despise politics and politicians. As elsewhere in the world, the non-governmental organization (NGO) revolution has served to legitimate post–Cold War intellectual and political trends rather than facilitate counterhegemony.

So even though the military's policy of instrumentalizing Islam to serve domestic control objectives and fuel an expansionist foreign policy has imploded spectacularly, the increasingly untenable situation is not being redressed, in large part because of the absence of a coherent and countrywide counterhegemonic political force. Instead of popular forces, it is Washington that is also mounting unprecedented pressure on General Headquarters (GHQ). However, the American Empire is least concerned with the welfare of Pakistan's people and it would be foolish for the latter to look to Washington to cut the military establishment down to size.

In a nutshell, then, even while divergent ideological and institutional tendencies become more acute within the ruling class, the shared stakes in the cynical political economy of war and neoliberalism preclude a conclusive rupture. While it would be remiss of me to avoid mention of the obvious tensions between the military establishment and mainstream political forces, and the fact that the former is clearly more culpable for the current impasse than the latter, it cannot be argued that the entire political class is doing anything more than negotiating for a greater stake within the existing system rather than seeking to transform it. The sympathizers of the PPP-led government argue that this is the only available strategy and one that will herald gradual change, but this hypothesis holds only if one is unwilling to build a more radical political alternative.

In the final analysis, speculation about the opaque tug-of-war within Pakistani corridors of power is unlikely to abate anytime soon. I have already asserted that there is an urgent need to undertake more detailed study of some of the issues I have outlined, and particularly the working of the actually existing economy. It is only in light of more concrete empirical evidence that the confusing narratives propounded by the establishment and its hangers-on can be definitively challenged.[19]

Having said this there are serious differences within progressive circles about the principal contradiction in the current conjuncture and appropriate political strategies therewith. I can identify at least three distinct strands of thinking and action. These are not mutually exclusive but in recent times have unfortunately appeared to be so.

First there are the "secularists." Mostly hailing from the urban upper-middle class, they argue that the most urgent task of progressives is to rally around the "anti-terrorism" cause. They tend to be alarmist due largely to their alienation from wider society and their inability to relate to the "religious" sentiments of ordinary working people. They view any kind of reference to western imperialism as playing into the hands of the religious right.

Second there are the ethnonationalists. Ethnonationalism has been the dominant form of resistance to the state and propertied classes throughout Pakistan's existence. As mentioned above, distrust among ethnonationalists of anything emanating from the Punjabi center has reached epic proportions. It is becoming increasingly difficult to convince ethnonationalists—particularly in Balochistan—that Pakistan's oppressed nationalities share a future with Punjab's working people.

The left rounds out the progressive intellectual spectrum. It has a long (and tortured) history, which is both cause of its continuing intellectual stagnancy but also a necessary springboard for regeneration. Opposed in principle neither to the secularists nor the ethnonationalists, the left is struggling—like its counterparts in many other areas of the world—to remake an anti-imperialist politics of class in the face of much more potent, and apparently immediate, politics of identity.

In particular the left has to move beyond superficial explanations for the spread of religious militancy and imperialist war, and, in totally different vein, increasing ethnic polarization. Until and unless the left is able to provide a clear and coherent analysis of the *structural* roots of the current imbroglio, and a workable politics that addresses the concerns of both the secularists and the ethnonationalists to boot, progressives will remain divided. The already serious structural contradictions that run rife through the polity, economy, and society will then only become more acute with little chance of a new progressive equilibrium being established.

Notes

1. Arif Hasan, *The Unplanned Revolution: Observations on the Process of Socio-Economic Change in Pakistan* (Karachi: City Press, 2002).

2. Eqbal Ahmad and Robert J. Barnett, "Bloody Games," in C. Bengelsdorf et al., ed., *The Selected Writings of Eqbal Ahmad* (New York: Columbia University Press, 2006); Ikramul Haq, "Pak-Afghan Drug Trade in Historical Perspective," *Asian Survey* 36:10 (1996).

3. For example, there is now a plethora of work on informalization in the Indian context, much of which has been published in *Economic and Political Weekly* (Mumbai). The importance of the informal economy in India is recognized across the board—even the government has taken initiatives (National Commission for Enterprises in the Unorganised Sector) to document and understand the multifarious aspects of informality.

4. United Nations Office of Drug Control (UNODC), *World Drug Report 2010*.

5. Dumper trucks in Karachi are controlled almost exclusively by Waziristanis. It is in the North and South Waziristan tribal agencies that the current war rages most ferociously, and, it must be said, opaquely. I should also note here that some of the available literature attributes much of the "kalashnikov" and drug culture that developed in Pakistan during and after the original Afghan war in the 1980s to the massive influx of Afghan refugees. See A. Z. Hilali, "Costs and Benefits of Afghan War for Pakistan," *Contemporary South Asia* 11:3 (2002). For the purposes of this essay, many refugees—on account of their Pakhtun ethnic roots—have become part and parcel of Pakistani society. Among the Pakhtuns involved in the transport industry is a substantial refugee component, both owners and workers.

6. See Arif Hasan, "Politics of Ethnicity," *Dawn,* June 25, 2010.

7. See Hisaya Oda, "Pakistani Migration to the United States: An Economic Perspective," *IDE Discussion Paper* 196 (2009).

8. The situation in the federal capital Islamabad merits attention. A decade ago most of the land on the outskirts of the city was either lying idle or used by hereditary owners for seasonal agriculture. With the dramatic influx of money, suburban and rural lands have been transformed into prime property, with values rising up to twentyfold. Previously modest families have become billionaires overnight, while real estate agents and revenue collectors have also secured a healthy share of the windfall rents available.

9. For the classic theorization by Hamza Alavi and an alternative interpretation, see Aasim Sajjad Akhtar, "Pakistan: Crisis of a Frontline State," *Journal of Contemporary Asia* 40:1 (2010).

10. Eqbal Ahmad, "Signposts to a Police State," *Journal of Contemporary Asia* 4 (1974).

11. Stephen P. Cohen, *The Pakistan Army* (Karachi: Oxford University Press, 1998); Charles Kennedy, *Bureaucracy in Pakistan* (Karachi: Oxford University Press, 1988).

12. At a more functional level, the English-educated elite is now far more attracted to the private corporate sphere, which guarantees much more lucrative employment/entrepreneurial opportunities as well as exposure to the so-called "global village."

13. This alienation can be traced back to the Zia period. See Arif Hasan, "The Roots of Elite Alienation," *Economic and Political Weekly*, 2–9 November 2002.

14. It was in the 1970 general election—the first in the country's history—that the military establishment decided to patronize "Islam-pasand" parties to counter the emergence of the "Taraqqi-pasand" parties (Pakistan People's Party, Awami League). See Hussain Haqqani, *Pakistan: Between Mosque and Military* (Washington: Carnegie Endowment for Peace, 2005).

15. Mustafa Kamal Pasha, "The 'Hyper-Extended' State: Civil Society and Democracy," in Rasul Bakhsh Rais, ed., *State, Society, and Democratic Change in Pakistan* (Karachi: Oxford University Press, 1997).

16. An example should suffice: after the devastating earthquake that hit the northwest of the country in October 2005, the most prominent relief work was undertaken by organizations such as the Al-Khidmat Foundation and Falah-e-Insaniat Foundation, welfare fronts for the Jamaʾt-e-Islami and Laskhar-e-Taiba respectively.

17. This is true of the "high" and "low" bureaucracies within the civil service, police, and military. Importantly, the distinct class and regional backgrounds of "high" and "low" bureaucrats produce a far less cohesive state than is often assumed.

Sudipta Kaviraj puts it thus: "Long-term historical memories and time tested ways of dealing with power of the political authority took their revenge on the modern state, bending the straight lines of rationalist liberal politics through a cultural refraction of administrative meaning." See Sudipta Kaviraj, "The Modern State in India," in S. Kaviraj and Martin Doornbos, eds., *Dynamics of State Formation: India and Europe Compared* (New Delhi: Manohar, 1977), 235.

18. See Aasim Sajjad Akhtar, "What Is Really Happening in Pakistan," *Economic and Political Weekly* 45:10, 10–11.

19. In recent times the official narrative has been remolded and the United States has been elevated to public enemy number one. Washington and New Delhi (with Tel Aviv also involved) are seen to be colluding to defang Pakistan. This flies in the face of the fact that, current tensions notwithstanding, Washington continues to be the militarized state's biggest benefactor in terms of economic and military aid.

Aasim Sajjad Akhtar

The Neoliberal Security State

SAADIA TOOR

Bhooke mar gaye main aur tu, loot ke le gaya GHQ
You and I are dying of hunger. The GHQ has looted everything.

—Slogan of the Anjuman-i Mazarin-i Punjab

BETWEEN 2001 AND 2003, 18 villages in the district of Okara in the Punjab were the focus of a violent crackdown by the paramilitary Pakistan Rangers.[1] Villagers, regardless of age or gender, were subjected to a campaign of sustained harassment, arbitrary arrest, detention, torture, and death. For roughly three months in 2002 and then again in 2003, the Rangers literally besieged these villages, blocking off all access roads and preventing the passage of food, medicine, and people to and from them.

At issue was the refusal of over a thousand tenant farmers in this region to sign a new contract with the military that changed the terms of their sharecropping agreement, transforming their status from tenants to lessees. The refusal was born of a very real and justified fear that this new contract rendered them vulnerable: the requirement of cash payment as opposed to harvest shares meant that a bad harvest could leave them indebted or unable to pay their "rent" while the change in their status would mean that they were no longer covered by the provisions of the Punjab Tenancy Act of 1887 under which they, as long-term cultivators, could not easily be evicted and could even potentially

19

claim ownership of the land. Under the Punjab Tenancy Act, ownership rights could be granted to farmers if they made the land cultivable. The Act made a distinction between "simple" versus "occupancy" tenants: simple tenants could be easily evicted while the eviction of occupancy tenants required a court decree. The villagers on the military farms were occupancy tenants. The farmers had, in fact, been unsuccessfully petitioning the government since the 1970s for ownership under the provisions of this Act. Aside from these issues, the new contract laid out a number of other conditions that were clearly designed to facilitate the eviction of farmers. For example, the contract "severely limited the use of natural resources by the lessee," including firewood and mud for building homes, requiring lessees to get permission from the military authorities.

The farms in Okara are part of 68,000 acres of agricultural land owned by the provincial government in the most fertile part of the Punjab (which is itself the breadbasket of the country). At the turn of the past century, the British introduced canal irrigation to the hitherto forested area, making it prized agricultural land. Although the colonial government had promised proprietary rights to migrant farmers from Eastern Punjab who had been brought in to help develop the area, it had retained control over a large portion of these "canal colonies" that contributed toward the creation of a landed elite in Punjab and Sind. The military farms in question had originally been under the control (but not ownership) of the British military at the time of Partition, following which the Pakistan Army had taken them over. The actual ownership of the land rested with the Punjab government, with the army being merely a lessee although it had been trying unsuccessfully to have the land transferred to itself.

In 2000, after the military changed the terms of the contract and tried to force the farmers to sign it, the latter organized themselves under the umbrella of Anjuman-i Mazarin-i Punjab (Association of Tenant Farmers of Punjab, henceforth AMP). In the early stages of the dispute, the farmers hoped to convince the military to leave their status as it was; they even agreed to the demand for cash payment. The military's intransigence, and its use of intimidation against the farmers, their families, and their supporters strengthened the farmers' resolve to fight the military and turned the AMP into a militant movement of almost a million. During the course of the conflict, it was discovered that the army had no legal claim to the land at all, even as a lessee, since the original lease that the British military had signed with the Punjab government had expired in 1943 and had never been renewed. Emboldened, the farmers refused to pay the military anything at all, and demanded ownership rights to the land, adopting the powerful cry *mulki ya maut!* (Ownership or death!). This brought on a wave of further and more intense repression by the army, with Okara becoming the epicenter of the confrontation between the military (via its vicious paramilitary force, the Pakistan Rangers[2]) and the AMP. Amazingly, the AMP not only managed to survive but grew in numbers and strength.

The AMP has become an enduring symbol of successful subaltern resistance to the most powerful institution in the country. Today the farmers (unofficially) control the majority of the land in the military farms and still steadfastly refuse to pay any rent. The army continues its harassment and the civilian government has reneged on promises made to the leadership, but the movement remains strong and undivided. In 2010, it commemorated a decade of militant struggle against the military and its feudal allies with a rally comprising 15,000 landless peasants that made its way in a "long march" from the Okara district to the Punjab Assembly building in the provincial capital of Lahore.

The AMP's struggle lies at the nexus of almost all the major issues that face Pakistan today. At a million strong, the AMP is the largest genuinely grassroots-based social movement in Pakistan's history and yet has no connection with Islam, jihad, or sectarian militancy. In fact, it is a movement that exemplifies solidarity across the religious divide since it is comprised of both Christians (who represent 40 percent of the farmers) and Muslims. The AMP also defies stereotypes of Pakistan (especially of the "backward" classes) with regard to gender; women have been at the forefront from its very beginning, leading marches and protests with their *thappas* (sticks used to beat the dirt out of clothes while washing) in the air, defying the repressive apparatus of the state despite being subjected to abduction, physical abuse, and torture.

Pakistan diyaan maujaan ee maujaan,
Jithe vekho faujaan ee faujaan

Pakistan is having such fun.
Everywhere you look, the army.

—*Ustaad Daman*

THE STORY OF THE AMP also underlines the central role of the Pakistani military in establishing a neoliberal security state. It should be abundantly clear by now that any effort to understand Pakistan's current problems—the fragility of democracy, the corruption of politics, the weakness of social and political institutions, and the issue of religious extremism and militancy—must begin and end with the Pakistani military establishment. The military dominates the state, society, and the economy, creating a predatory environment that works against the interest of ordinary Pakistanis as well as against peace and stability in the region.

The predatory nature of the military in Pakistan is starkly exposed in its relationship to land, which most Pakistanis were not even aware of until the confrontation between the tenants in Okara and the Rangers became national news. This is astounding when you consider that the military, as a corporate institution, is the single largest landowner in Pakistan of both urban real estate and rural agricultural land. This does not include the amount of land that is under the ownership of individual members of the military fraternity, especially officers (serving and retired). Given the economic, political, and symbolic power that land ownership confers in a primarily agricultural country like Pakistan, the military's relationship to land is the least understood and yet possibly most important aspect of its economic and political domination.[3] In fact, as Ayesha Siddiqa has pointed out, the military's behavior toward the tenants in Okara is of a piece with its general attitude toward the poor and disenfranchised, such as landless peasants, fisherfolk communities, or even those low in the military hierarchy such as ordinary soldiers.[4] Okara and other similar land grabs take place against the backdrop of an acute inequity in the distribution of land in Pakistan, where rural poverty is directly linked to a lack of access to land.[5] Issues of skewed patterns of land ownership, therefore, pertain directly to the Pakistani military's parasitic relationship to its people. It was significant that in 2003, at the very moment that the confrontation with the AMP reached its peak, the state shut the door on any possibility of future land reforms.[6]

The military's eagerness to change the terms of its contract with the tenants on the military farms reflected another aspect of the development of the neoliberal security state: the corporate control of agriculture in Pakistan. As an expert on tenancy law pointed out to Human Rights Watch, if the army was mainly interested in switching to cash payments rather than harvest share, the terms of the original contract allowed that change to be negotiated. Also, since the earnings from these military farms were "fairly paltry," the push to implement a new contract with its attendant conditionalities was clearly designed to make it easier to evict the tenants. In 2001, Musharraf's government passed a Corporate Farming Ordinance. Under the provisions of this ordinance, foreign firms were allowed to lease land in Pakistan for 50 years, extendable for another 49 years; the minimum amount of land they could lease was set at 1,500 acres. This ordinance, as well as follow-up efforts to woo foreign investors, has been analyzed as part of the "global land grab" whereby rich countries lease or buy land in poor countries in order to secure their food supplies in the future. In Pakistan, the state has wooed mainly Gulf States. In May 2009, for example, the Ministry of Investment decided to offer 1 million hectares of farmland for long-term investment or sale to foreigners—specifically, the Emirates Investment Group. That 2001–02 budget provided incentives to extend the advantages facilitated by the Corporate Farming Ordinance. Such initiatives were in line with global trends and with the Pakistani establishment's pro-liberalization stance that included the privatization of state enterprises, the removal of welfare subsidies and safety nets, and the levying of taxes that disproportionately burden the poor.

It is clear, however, that more than economic interests were at stake for the military in terms of its handling of the tenant revolt in Okara. The military's extensive ownership and control of land underwrites its vast patronage network, through which it rewards its own personnel but also co-opts politicians, media personnel, etc. Control over agricultural land is also a "resonant and enduring symbol of the powerful status of the military."[7]

Being the totalitarian institution that it is, the military was shocked at the temerity of the tenants who stood up to it, and was worried that the virus of revolt might spread if the movement were either accommodated or allowed to continue. The deployment of the Rangers and the brutal nature of the violence unleashed on the farmers and their families and supporters was thus a carefully considered strategy. It was also very much in line with the way in which the Pakistani military and its paramilitary forces deal with dissent or resistance.[8]

The stranglehold of the military over every aspect of Pakistani state and society has also contributed in large part to the transformation of Pakistan into a heavily indebted neoliberal security state, underwritten once again by the U.S.'s latest war in Afghanistan. It is worth noting, for example, that in every budget since independence, Pakistan's allocations and expenditure on defense have dwarfed those for development. Not only does this bloated defense expenditure divert money away from investment in other sectors, which might directly and indirectly improve the conditions of the poor, it also contributes in large part to the debt burden that tightens IMF and World Bank control over Pakistan's economy.

The new U.S. war in Afghanistan once again gave a military regime in Pakistan a new lease on life. The government of Pervez Musharraf, which had come to power in 1999 after deposing the then-Prime Minister Nawaz Sharif, had been fast losing legitimacy, and the Pakistani military was quick to use the Global War on Terror (GWoT) to consolidate its domestic power. The starkest example of this, and one that exemplifies the economic and political agenda of the neoliberal security state, is the occupation of Baluchistan. The military's fifth operation in Baluchistan was already underway when the GWoT was launched, but the latter provided a useful cover under which the military could initiate a full-scale occupation of the province. A long (and continuing) string of harassments, threats, arrests, torture, and disappearances designed to squash dissent and resistance was initiated, which, predictably, had the opposite effect of producing a new and even more determined Baloch insurgency. The number of those who disappeared in the province is estimated between fifteen hundred and four thousand people. The Western media's inability to parse the various forms of militancy in Pakistan proved extremely useful for the Pakistan army as it encouraged the discursive collapse of the resolutely secular Baloch insurgency with Islamist militancy while diverting funds allocated for dealing with the Taliban to suppressing the nationalists. The army also initiated a strategy of neutralizing Baloch nationalism through the infusion of Islamist ideology and the support of Islamist political groups via the intelligence agencies. This strategy has proven an overwhelming failure, as nationalist feelings remain high and have in fact become stronger as the military occupation of Balochistan has grown in size and intensity. Events such as the assassination (in August 2006) of Nawab Akbar Khan Bugti, a respected political figure and staunch Baloch nationalist, by the Pakistan military and the rape of a woman doctor by an army officer, and the consequent refusal of the army to either hand the officer over or prosecute him, further hardened the resolve of the nationalists.

This latest army operation in Baluchistan accompanied the launching of several high profile and lucrative "development projects" in the province (many in cooperation with the Chinese government), the most significant being the Gwadar Port Project and the proposed establishment of several new cantonments in resource-rich districts. Baluchistan is of immense importance for the military; it is a resource-rich and, given its borders with Iran and Afghanistan, a geopolitically strategic region. Despite its wealth of natural resources, however, Baluchistan is Pakistan's poorest province with the lowest social and human development indicators (this is saying something, given Pakistan's abysmal performance on human development indicators as a whole).

The Pakistani establishment's relationship with Baluchistan is colonial in the extreme. Baloch grievances with the center include the expropriation of the province's wealth, land grabs and the consequent loss of livelihood (the military often displaces or evicts locals when it occupies large tracts of land), and continued high unemployment in the face of large-scale projects as jobs generated are pointedly filled by the non-Baloch. Baluchistan is also the Pakistani state's nuclear weapons testing site of choice; the Chaghai hills that became part of mainstream nationalist lore as a symbol of the might of the Pakistani military following the explosion of nuclear devices in 1998 are located in Baluchistan. The testing was done without Baloch consent and certainly without any effort to shield the population from the effects of radiation.

Included among the military's investments in Baluchistan are three nuclear and chemical weapons testing sites, eight naval bases (not including the strategic port of Gwadar), six missile-testing ranges, seven air-force bases, and fifty-nine paramilitary facilities. Seven thousand acres of land were "acquired" recently for a new airport by the Pakistan Air Force, which is also eyeing seventy thousand acres along the Coastal Highway for a new weapons testing and firing range, and pressuring the local population to vacate the land. The military took advantage of the devastating floods of 2011 to illegally occupy even more land in Baluchistan. The extent of the irregularities surrounding the transfer of land in Baluchistan has been such that the Supreme Court of Pakistan took cognizance of it in October 2006. The navy's control of the Makran coast has made the coastal waters—with their rich fishing grounds—inaccessible to the local fishing community, severely impacting its livelihoods. Meanwhile, the navy has struck lucrative deals with international trawlers.

Ayesha Siddiqa has outlined the extent of the Pakistani military's economic empire, along with its implications for the well-being of the vast majority of Pakistanis and for Pakistan as a state. The Pakistani military dominates each and every aspect of the economy from agriculture to manufacturing to services and, unsurprisingly, jealously guards the information pertaining to this economic empire. This domination is based on the existence and proliferation of military-owned and operated enterprises such as agricultural farms, manufacturing companies producing everything from fertilizer to breakfast cereal, and commercial ventures such as military banks and real estate agencies. Indirect control is enabled by the ubiquitous presence of serving and retired military personnel in private and public enterprises, key government departments, and throughout the civil bureaucracy. This enables military enterprises as well as private enterprises run by (ex)military personnel to get privileged access to all possible perks, including foreign investment, government subsidies and monies, and infrastructure development at public expense.

Siddiqa has convincingly shown that, in direct contradiction to the claims of the military, the military's dominance of the Pakistani economy is more like a choke-hold, strangling initiative, encouraging patronage and cronyism, and producing large-scale distortions and inefficiencies. The military's domination of the economy has severe implications for the well-being of Pakistan's citizens, especially its most vulnerable. It has a negative impact, as one can imagine, on labor rights, given the number of private and semi-private enterprises run by ex-military men and their family members. Constant increases in military expenditure, especially in the context of structural adjustment, shortchange social welfare and development.

Its domination and manipulation of the political process even when it is not technically in charge, and its hold over the country's political leadership, breed authoritarianism, while through its double game with regard to religious extremism and militancy it actively produces instability. All these factors work against (and not by accident) any hope that democracy will take root in Pakistan. Under these circumstances, and given the clear and ample empirical evidence, it is difficult to argue that the Pakistani military can in any way be considered a savior, even of a small handful of liberal elites. The military is far from an agent of progressive social change or economic development in Pakistan; the claim that the Pakistani military can not only produce political and social stability but also somehow be an agent of democracy can only be the result of willful (indeed, willed) ignorance.

It is important to note that the Pakistani military's stranglehold over its people has been enabled over the past half a century by the material and moral support of the U.S. establishment, with military regimes such as Zia's and Musharraf's being given a new lease on life by the U.S.'s own military adventurism. Along the way, this support has been justified—by Cold War and establishment social scientists as well as key decision-makers in Washington, D.C.—on the premise that the military in third world societies generally or the Pakistani military in particular is a source of stability, development, and/or progress.[9] With political Islam replacing the Soviet Union as public enemy number one following the end of the Cold War, the United States continued to choose unrepresentative regimes, civilian or military, across the Muslim world purportedly because of their "secular" credentials, a premise that is belied by the case of the Pakistani military given its role in the creation and support of the Taliban in Afghanistan, of Kashmir-focused jihadi groups such as the infamous Lashkare-Taiba, and of sectarian outfits such as the Jaish-i-Muhammad and the Sipah-e-Sahaba.

The State of Progressive Politics

The story of the tenant uprising against the might of the military in Okara also highlights the state of progressive politics in Pakistan today. Although NGO activists did eventually get involved once the movement had made it to the headlines — sadly, with disastrous results for the movement — their absence from what was essentially the front line of the struggle of ordinary Pakistanis was no coincidence. Ironically, in its efforts to discredit the movement, the military establishment has taken the line that it is only an NGO initiative and not a genuine movement.

Major shifts occurred in the field of progressive politics in Pakistan in the 1990s. These were not unique to Pakistan and were the result of the emerging consolidation of a global neoliberal project ushered in by the break-up of the Soviet Union. This project had, like all global projects worth their salt, economic, political, intellectual, ideological, and cultural dimensions whose ultimate aim was the reorganization of the world in the interests of capital. The role of the Bretton Woods institutions and later the Washington Consensus in realizing this agenda is well known. With the fall of the Soviet Union, History itself was declared to have ended, and all alternatives to capitalism were smugly dismissed. Within academia, a liberal attack on Marxism (both as an analytical frame and as an emancipatory project) was launched with much fanfare. And crucially, for our story here, the World Bank began to promote non-governmental organizations as the antidote to the unwieldy (and implicitly, totalitarian) welfare state. An abstract discourse of "universal human rights" replaced real political engagement and mobilization.

In Pakistan, as elsewhere, the organizational and ideological decimation of the Left meant that liberal politics and values came to stand in for progressivism tout court. The NGO-ization of this liberal politics (with its focus on the priorities of international donors, preoccupation with the funding cycle, and bureaucratization) effectively divorced it from the real issues facing the majority of Pakistanis and rendered it a politically and culturally ineffective force within the national mainstream. For all intents and purposes, then, Pakistani liberals made themselves irrelevant to national politics and were unable to provide a counter to the rightward shifts that were rapidly changing the political, social, economic, and cultural landscape of the country.

The disconnect with people's issues was reflected in the fact that NGO liberals did not agitate against structural adjustment policies and programs in Pakistan, which consistently targeted the poorest and most vulnerable, nor did they see it fit to take on neoliberal globalization until international donors began to fund antiglobalization work. This was in stark contrast to the critiques of globalization that were emanating from the global South and the mobilizations against it that were building across the world. NGO "activists" also did not see it fit to connect with the people's struggles that had begun to emerge, such as the AMP, until these struggles became well known nationally and internationally, and especially not until donors began to notice them.

Not only did NGOs in Pakistan not resist neoliberal globalization, they often enabled it by taking on the state's social welfare responsibilities. The case of a well-known education NGO is illustrative. It actively bid to take over the running of government schools under the rubric of a "public–private partnership"; crucially, the state handed over the responsibility of running these public schools but did not relinquish control over the curriculum. As one of Pakistan's most respected feminist educationists, Rubina Saigol, told me, this not only enabled the state's retreat from its social welfare responsibilities (a major focus of structural adjustment policies), but also ensured a more efficient delivery of the state's retrogressive ideological agenda as coded into the national curriculum. Another, even more stark example was that of the overwhelming support given by NGOs to Musharraf's plan to devolve power to the local level in 2000–2001. The "devolution plan" sounded progressive but in fact was essentially in the same vein as Ayub's Basic Democracies and Zia's local bodies elections, designed to undermine national politics rather than devolve power to the people, and to consolidate central control over local governments rather than empower the latter. Not surprisingly, there was plenty of World Bank and other donor money for NGOs to participate in institutionalizing this plan. The idea of a 30 percent representation of women at all levels made it especially appealing to NGOs and international donors.

NGO liberals' endorsement of this devolution plan was not an anomaly, for they were, in fact, Musharraf's biggest supporters. It may seem paradoxical for those whose bread and butter (literally) is human rights and who were, in many cases, veterans of the anti-Zia movement to be openly supportive of a military dictatorship. The explanation lies in the shifts in the political priorities of Pakistani liberals from the Zia era onward, both in terms of their material interests and in terms of specific class-based anxieties.

Following Zia's regime, and especially after the Taliban takeover in Afghanistan in the 1990s, Pakistani liberals became increasingly obsessed with what they referred to as Talibanization—a catch-all term that included everything from state-led Islamization efforts to the rise in social conservatism and an increase in public displays of piety. As we have seen, the rightward shift in Pakistani politics, society, and culture did, in fact, continue after the literal and metaphorical demise of Zia. However, liberals focused on only one aspect of it—the rise of a militant and narrow version of Sunni Islam—while ignoring all the others, particularly the reactionary thrust of the state's economic agenda. Unfortunately, not only did the obsession with Talibanization not translate into any form of organized resistance at the social, political, or cultural level, but it also led Pakistani liberals in dangerous and fundamentally antiprogressive directions, a particularly egregious example of which was their open support for Musharraf's coup d'etat in 1999. The murder of Salman Taseer in January 2011 at the hands of a zealot has mobilized the liberal elite, but its attempts at responding to the tide of Sunni sectarianism reflects all the drawbacks of elite politics. The very fact that this mobilization happened in response to Taseer's murder as opposed to the pogroms against Christians and Ahmedis over the past few years is revealing.

The government of Nawaz Sharif was about to push through the controversial and draconian 15th Amendment to the Constitution, otherwise known as the Shariat Bill, and had been taking an increasingly aggressive stance vis-à-vis women's rights and human rights NGOs. Binyamin, the Punjab government's Minister of Social Welfare, had openly vilified these organizations, denouncing them as fifth columnists working to undermine Pakistan and Islam and serving the interests of Israel, India, and the West, and had explicitly begun threatening those who ran them. As a result, instead of condemning the overthrow of a democratically elected government by a military dictator, most NGO activists openly celebrated it as a release and welcomed the General as a savior.

Nighat Said Khan, a prominent women's rights activist from Lahore who had been singled out for special mention by Binyamin,[10] relates her shock at the proceedings of the meeting of the Joint Action Committee for Peace and Democracy (a Lahore-based alliance of thirty-six organizations and political parties) convened immediately following the coup:

> I assumed that all we would be doing was deciding the wording of our immediate resolution and working out our strategy. The reaction of a majority of the organizations was stunning. They supported the Military taking over—this despite the fact that the JAC was for democracy and most of them were familiar with the history of the military as an institution and its role in politics in Pakistan.

There was much excitement among the NGO elite at the fact that the NGO Bill that Nawaz Sharif's government had been trying to pass would not see the light of day. That this reaction indicated that they were "more interested in saving their NGOs than saving the nation" did not seem to register or matter, especially after Musharraf welcomed many of them into his government with open arms. In fact, so many NGO representatives joined the government in one capacity or another as ministers, advisors, members of task forces, and consultants, that it became popularly referred to as the "NGO government." The welcoming of the military as a savior by women's rights and human rights stalwarts reflected a mixture of historical amnesia, political confusion, and crass opportunism. Those who supported the coup justified their decision based on the General's liberal lifestyle, an argument that makes sense only if progressive politics in Pakistan can somehow be reduced to a rejection of Islamization, and political analysis to issues of an individual's lifestyle rather than an understanding of institutions. The widespread belief that the army was a progressive force that would save the country from Talibanization also reflected an ignorance of the military's role in creating and sustaining the very forces of the religious right wing that it was expected to protect the people from. Liberals were not the only ones to succumb to the charms of the General. Even the National Workers Party, led by veteran Leftist intellectual Abid Hassan Manto, joined the military alliance.

The attitudes of "civil society activists" mirrored those of the westernized liberal elite more generally. While they had been unable to identify with Zia's petty bourgeois conservatism and smug piousness, they saw in Musharraf's westernized lifestyle and his philosophy of "enlightened moderation" a reflection of themselves. The significant growth in GNP during the first few years following the start of the GWoT—a result of renewed aid from the U.S. and other donors, and of overseas Pakistanis repatriating their money and/or returning to Pakistan as the international climate grew more hostile toward Muslims and Pakistanis—further affirmed their faith in him as Pakistan's savior. Musharraf's abortive attempt to reform the Zina Ordinance (which sparked such a reaction from the Islamist parties that he had to backtrack even from the minor procedural change he had intended) and the passage of a Women's Protection Bill were seen as evidence of his progressive credentials, as was his plan to allocate a quota for reserved seats for women from the local to the national level.

Musharraf's liberal (i.e., westernized) lifestyle—signaled by the fact that he drank alcohol and had two pet pomeranians—and his official commitment to "enlightened moderation" reassured Pakistan's "lifestyle liberals" that they were safe from the Islamists under his watch. Their support essentially translated into turning a blind eye to the terror(s) that his regime unleashed on various groups, such as the tenants on the Okara military farms and the thousands of political activists from

Sarhad and Baluchistan that were disappeared by intelligence agencies. Even more remarkably the liberals said little about the crackdown on the peasantry in Hashtnagar in 2002. The military launched an attack on the legendary people's republic of Hashtnagar, an area comprising eight villages (*basht* means eight and *nagar* means settlement) that had been freed from landlord control in the late 1960s under the leadership of Afzal Bangash of the Mazdoor Kissan Party. The struggle of the Hashtnagar peasants against landlord control goes back to before Partition. In addition, many Pakistani liberals, including respected members of the human rights community, either explicitly or tacitly supported the U.S. attack on Afghanistan and the Pakistani military's role in it, and continue to support the violence visited on innocent civilians under cover of the GWoT through drone attacks and army operations.

Any notion that Musharraf was a champion of women's and minority rights should have been decisively shattered by his relationship with the MMA (the Mutahhida Majlis-i-Amal or United Assembly of Action, the alliance of right-wing political parties that won majorities in Sarhad and Baluchistan for the first time in Pakistan's history, albeit during a much-reviled election; the MMA quickly became popularly known as the Mullah–Military-Alliance). In January 2004, Musharraf essentially bartered away the rights of women and minorities when he made a deal with the MMA; the context was his bid for a "trust vote" from Parliament that would allow him to continue as President while maintaining his status as an active member of the military corps. The MMA only agreed to this once Musharraf assured them that he would not touch Islamic laws and provisions (especially the Hudood Ordinance). As Nighat Said Khan noted at the time, there was "not even a whimper from women Parliamentarians, women's organizations or individual women or the press . . . the silence was deafening."[11]

Interestingly, the same liberal intellectuals who had welcomed Musharraf and supported his regime joined the anti-Musharraf movement once it gathered momentum. The 2007 Lawyers Movement, as it came to be called because of the catalytic and leading role played by the legal fraternity, was a welcome respite from the stifling politics of the post-Zia period. The movement's focus on rule of law, while liberal, was refreshing in its support for democratic principles and its secular political idiom. The significant participation of young people from across the class divide was a hopeful sign that a new politically engaged progressive generation was emerging in Pakistan and made up for the movement's urban bias. Most significant of all, there appeared to be an emerging consciousness that the problem was not one individual but an institution, i.e., the army. The use of the poetry of Jalib and Faiz by activists connected this movement to Pakistan's earlier tradition of progressive politics.

However, this analysis was to be proved premature. It soon became clear that the liberals' obsession with Talibanization would continue to prove detrimental to democratic politics. The first indication of this came soon after the elections, when the new President, Asif Zardari, reneged on the PPP's promise to reinstate the Chief Justice of the Supreme Court as well as other judges who had been dismissed by Musharraf. This was particularly egregious given that it was Musharraf's dismissal of this Chief Justice that had catalyzed the Lawyers Movement to begin with, and whose reinstatement had been the movement's singular focus. When protests erupted, the government responded with sweeping raids and arrests of lawyers and their supporters; in the most astonishing move of all, in 2009 Zardari blockaded all approaches to the capital city of Islamabad with trailers in order to prevent the planned culmination of a "long march" in Islamabad.

Throughout this unfolding drama, which involved the display of explicitly authoritarian and antidemocratic tendencies by the newly-elected government of PPP, several prominent liberal intellectuals refused to support the democratic demands of the Lawyers Movement and stood fast behind Zardari. Their justification for this was the same as that of the PPP—that by demanding their democratic rights, from which the PPP itself had only recently profited, the Lawyers Movement was destabilizing the government and preparing the ground for either the military or religious extremists to take over.

Even if one were to buy this argument at face value, this essentially meant that Pakistani liberals were willing to tolerate authoritarianism of the most draconian sort as long as it was from a democratically elected civilian government that was led by a purported "secular" party. This liberal support of Zardari and the PPP did not diminish even after the shocking news that two of the ministers appointed by the leader of this "progressive" political party (with whom he also had close personal relationships) had a record of supporting customary forms of violence against women. Bijarani, a landlord from Sindh, had been accused of heading a jirga that "awarded" five girls, ranging in age from two to five, as compensation for the murder of a man; the case had been pending in front of the Supreme Court (which had issued orders for Bijarani's arrest) when Musharraf dismissed the judiciary. The other minister, Zehri, was a tribal leader and on record as having defended the practice of burying women alive as a "tribal tradition." He had been commenting on reports of a case in which three teenage girls had been killed in this fashion for daring to choose their own husbands. The stories had made national headlines, and many progressives (especially feminists) had strongly protested the appointments and demanded that the two ministers be dismissed, but to no avail. In the face of this, the liberal support for Zardari and the PPP is mystifying unless one recognizes that Pakistani liberal politics are essentially about the liberal elite's self-preservation, and the forms of violence that feudal elites visit on the weak and vulnerable under their "jurisdiction" do not pose the kind of immediate danger to the lifestyles of liberals in Pakistan that Talibanization does.[12]

As for the antimilitary sentiments that had appeared to be crystalizing during the anti-Musharraf movement, and which could be seen in the liberal support for the PPP, these dissipated overnight after the circulation of a video in April 2009, which claimed to show a young woman being flogged by the Taliban in Swat valley. The timing of this video's emergence was suspiciously convenient, given that the U.S. had just turned up the heat on the Pakistani military, demanding proof that it was actually fighting the Taliban. The video resulted in generating overwhelming support for the army's subsequent operation in Swat that displaced millions of Swatis, rehabilitating the army's image among liberals. So strong was the fear and anxiety generated by the video that this support did not diminish even in the face of overwhelming evidence that emerged soon after the military operation showing the army's reign of terror in Swat. Since that time, liberals have backed every military operation, as well as the expansion of the GWoT into Pakistan via drone attacks on the border areas, despite the clear evidence that drones are not the efficient "militant-killing" machines that they are promoted as being. Accompanying this unqualified liberal support for the U.S. and Pakistani militaries and the GWoT is an overt derisiveness toward a progressive antiwar position, especially toward anti-imperialist critique. In fact, even prominent liberal intellectuals in Pakistan collapse the anti-imperialism of the Left with the anti-Americanism of the right.

Another less direct but no less important way in which the liberal obsession with the "Taliban" feeds into the military's project of a neoliberal security state is reflected in the proliferation of "security talk," i.e., the tendency to couch the very real grievances and issues of the Pakistani people in the language of security, and specifically in terms of combating "Islamist militancy." The executive director of a major policy think-tank in Islamabad made the case for addressing the food security needs of tens of thousands of Pakistanis on the grounds that to not do so would be tantamount to handing the "Taliban" and other militant Islamists new recruits.[13] Ahmed Rashid, the quintessential liberal establishment intellectual, made the same argument when appealing for help for the victims of the recent devastating floods in Pakistan.[14] Needless to say, this equation between deprivation and religious extremism/militancy dehumanizes the poorest and most vulnerable.

What this liberal discourse reveals is a profound dissociation from—and even a distaste for—ordinary Pakistanis and their lives, hopes, dreams, and struggles, reflected in the abandonment of mass political work. Thankfully, the working people of Pakistan are not waiting for these elite progressives to initiate change but are building movements of their own and taking on the various aspects of the monstrous system that oppresses them. The AMP's courageous stand against the leviathan of the Pakistani military is an example of one such movement; the resurgence of working-class radicalism is the other part of this story.

The rise of left forces in the late 1960s, in particular a politically conscious working class and peasantry, had made the ruling classes understandably anxious. Therefore, as we saw earlier, there was a concerted effort by the state from the 1970s onward to defuse and dismantle these left-wing forces, especially the militant trade union movement. This was achieved through various means: the replacement of independent trade unions with PPP ones under Bhutto, the indiscriminate use of state violence against striking workers and the leadership of left-wing trade unions, and the outright co-optation of public sector unions under Zia. As a result, there was no meaningful resistance to IMF-imposed privatization when it began in the 1980s and even when it accelerated in the 1990s despite the fact that it resulted in massive lay-offs.

While Benazir Bhutto and Nawaz Sharif exhibited differing levels of enthusiasm for liberalization given their different constituencies, the IMF's program was most effectively implemented during the interim administrations in the 1990s; so obvious was this that they were openly referred to as "IMF administrations." The first of these was headed by Moeen Qureshi, an ex–vice president of the World Bank (derisively referred to as the "imported Prime Minister" given that prior to becoming the PM he had been living abroad for 25 years), and in the second another ex–vice president of the Bank (Shahid Javed Burki) was the economic advisor to the caretaker Prime Minister. Scholars have also pointed to the Punjabi-ization of liberalization under Nawaz Sharif, as non-Punjabi business groups were cut out of deals. The fact that most of the privatized units collapsed soon afterward only added to the misery of the working class. Private sector unions, meanwhile, were devastated by the informalization that came with the severe fragmentation of the production process, which had become the norm from the 1990s onward. Expressions of dissent or attempts at collective action on the part of workers were dealt with severely. Under Musharraf, strikes and go-slows were not just declared illegal but prosecuted in special courts under antiterrorism laws (passed under Nawaz Sharif's second administration in the late 1990s). Forming a trade union under the Musharraf government was tantamount to losing your job, since an application for a new union was immediately followed up by a list of workers being sent to the employer by the government for "verification."

At the same time, other IMF conditionalities led to the slashing of the already modest social sector, the ending of subsidies on basic necessities, and an increase in direct taxation. Needless to say, the military's budget and expenditure remained untouched. These measures put the burden of debt-repayment squarely on the shoulders of the working class and the poor while pulling the rug out from under their feet through privatization, downsizing, and informalization. It was hardly surprising, then, that the 1990s came to be characterized by rising poverty and inequality, a trend that has continued into the new millennium. As a result, rates of suicide and self-immolation among the working classes and the poor rose exponentially by the late 1990s.

The Musharraf regime continued to push through neoliberal policies, selling off public sector enterprises at a speed that was astonishing even for Pakistan, often well below their market value.[15] However, it was soon faced with increased resistance to privatization from a working class pushed to the brink and a newly revitalized (if still weak) left. The first such organized resistance came in 2005 from the workers of the state-owned Pakistan Telecommunications Limited (PTCL), which was slated for privatization. As a result of the hard work of a few politicized left workers, a Unions Action Committee was formed in March 2005 that launched a nationwide protest campaign, culminating in a massive meeting at the PTCL headquarters in Islamabad on May 25, 2005. Twelve thousand out of PTCL's sixty-two thousand workers came for the meeting from all over the country. The militant and uncompromising mood of the workers at the grassroots level kept the pressure on union leaders and a nationwide strike was called.

Soon after reaching an agreement with the union leadership, however, the government unleashed a wave of reprisals, arresting union leaders under the antiterrorism statute and declaring that the privatization of PTCL would go on as planned. Despite this setback, the mobilization of PTCL workers and the broad Anti-Privatization Alliance that came out of it marked an important turning point in the recent history of the Pakistani working class.

In the following years there has been an increase in the intensity and radicalism of working-class activism in Pakistan. From the sit-in strike of the workers of the premier Pearl Continental Hotels in Karachi in May 2010 (ongoing since 2001) to the standoff between the Gadani Ship-Breaking Democratic Workers Union and the Owners Association in June that same year, a new spirit of fearless rebellion is clearly evident among the working classes of Pakistan. Among the most salutary of developments on this front has been the establishment of the Labour Qaumi Movement (Labour National Movement) in the industrial Punjabi town of Faislabad in 2003 by power-loom workers attempting to unionize. Today the LQM boasts a strong membership spread across several sector offices staffed by full-time workers. A tragic mark of the success of the LQM has been the violence—both from the state and from owners—that its leadership and its members confront on a daily basis. In June 2010, gunmen entered the office of the LQM in Faislabad and killed two of its leading lights, Mustansar Randhawa and his brother. In response, Faislabad was confronted with the largest strike it had witnessed in recent history, as 100,000 workers took to the streets in protest.

These are the stories that never make it to the headlines of international newspapers—or even domestic ones. Yet, these are the mobilizations and movements that hold the most promise for Pakistan because, unlike the religious extremists or the liberal elite, they represent the hopes and aspirations of the vast majority of Pakistanis. It is therefore in their struggles that the real Pakistan exists and through their struggles that it has any hope of surviving and triumphing over the storms that threaten to engulf it.

It is fitting to close with these lines from Faiz:

Yehi junoon ka yehi tauq-o daar ka mausam
Yehi hai jabr, yehi ikhtiyaar ka mausam
Qafas hai bas mein tumhaare, tumhaare bas mein nahin
Chaman mein aatish-e gul ke nikhaar ka mausam
Bala se hum ne na dekha to aur dekhenge
Furogh-e gulshan-o saut-e hazaar ka mausam

This is the season of passion, yet also of the yoke and noose
This is the season of repression, yet also of agency and resistance
The cage may be in your control, but you have no power over
The season when the fiery rose blossoms in the garden
So what if we do not live to see it? There will be others who witness
The season of the flowering garden, of the nightingale's song.

Notes

1. This essay is a modified version of the Conclusion of Saadia Toor, *The State of Islam: Culture and Cold War Politics in Pakistan* (London: Pluto Press, 2011). It is reproduced with the express permission of Pluto Books. www.plutobooks.com.

2. For details, see "Soiled Hands: The Pakistan Army's Repression of the Punjab Farmers' Movement," *Human Rights Watch* 16:10 (July 2004), and Rubina Saigol, *Ownership or Death: Women and Tenant Struggles in Pakistani Punjab* (New Delhi: Rupa, 2004).

3. Human Rights Watch references the "long and sordid history of human rights abuses against civilians." "Soiled Hands," 15.

4. Ayesha Siddiqa details numerous examples of the brutal and rapacious way in which military and paramilitary forces have occupied land, evicting local communities, such as: (1) In 1977, the Rangers (a paramilitary border security force) took over four lakes in Sindh and leased out fishing rights to private interests in violation of provincial law, depriving the local fishing community of its livelihood; they later occupied 20 more lakes in Sindh. Within the same period, they also took over a significant stretch of the Sindh–Baluchistan coastline (purportedly to secure it from Indian threat), stopped local fisherfolk from fishing the waters off the coast, and sold the permits to large contractors, resulting in a decimation of the local fishing communities; (2) In the village of Nawazabad in Bahawalpur, hundreds of landless peasants were threatened with dire consequences unless they vacated state land on which they had lived for many years; and (3) The land of the small and poor village of Mubarik, Sindh, was completely taken over by the Pakistan Navy and its residents evicted. Ayesha Siddiqa, *Military Inc.: Inside Pakistan's Military Economy* (London: Pluto Press, 2007).

5. Ayesha Siddiqa reports a naval officer as saying "Why do landless peasants have greater rights over land? They do not deserve land just because they are poor," and quotes another military officer who believed that "there is no difference between allotment of land to poor people and the military. The armed forces personnel deserve to be given land as much as the poor landless peasants." Siddiqa, *Military Inc.,* 205.

6. Syed Akbar Zaidi and Syed Akbar, *Issues in Pakistan's Economy* (Karachi: Oxford University Press, 2005). The effects of land concentration on impoverishment go beyond the issues of control of and access to assets; land distribution has repercussions in terms of the abuse and exploitation that the poor are subject to in rural Pakistan. A Planning Commission report on poverty showed that the poor see land as an important source of power. Improved land access is linked to poverty alleviation in both the short and the long term, and women's access to land is of special importance.

7. Sultan Ahmed, "No Land Reforms Any More!" *Dawn*, 20 March 2003.

8. "Soiled Hands," 205.

9. Siddiqa outlines the use of brute force by the military and paramilitary forces to occupy land at will, often without compensation. *Military Inc.*, 186–205.

10. Siddiqa states that "Since 9/11 U.S. policymakers" generous statements endorsing Musharraf's apparent efforts to strengthen democracy were just one example of the mind-set that views non-western militaries as relatively more capable than civilian institutions." Siddiqa, *Military Inc.*, 18.

11. At a press conference in December 1998, Binyamin claimed, "The Institute of Women's Studies Lahore headed by Nighat Said Khan instigated people against the Shariah Bill and was promoting Jewish culture." Khan writes that "these comments were carried by all the newspapers, many on the front page. This was the beginning of a vicious campaign. On the 30th of December he went on to say 'The government will never allow these modern, westernized women to create a free society' and further, 'Strange organizations like the Women's Institute should not make him open his mouth because if he informs the nation about their activities, the people will burn down their bungalows and skin them alive where they teach their special studies.'" Nighat Said Khan, "Preface," in Nighat Said Khan, ed., *Up Against the State* (Lahore: ASR Publications, 2004), xviii.

12. My critique of liberals for their obsession with religious extremists should not, under any circumstances, be taken as an apologia for the latter. There is no doubt that their agenda is retrogressive and reactionary to the extreme.

13. Abid Suleri, "The Social Dimensions of Food Insecurity in Pakistan." Talk given at Hunger Pains: Pakistan's Food Insecurity, Woodrow Wilson Center for International Scholars, Washington, D.C., 3 June 2009.

14. Ahmed Rashid, "Pakistan Floods: An Emergency for the West," *The Telegraph*, 12 August 2010.

15. According to Aasim Sajjad Akhtar, over 160 PSEs were privatized in the fifteen years prior to the PTCL strike, of which 130 had collapsed, leaving hundreds of thousands of workers in the lurch. Aasim Sajjad Akhtar, "Privatization at Gunpoint," *Monthly Review* 57:5 (October 2005).

The Modern Mixed Political Economy of Pakistan

MALIHA SAFRI

THE POLITICAL ECONOMY OF PAKISTAN is Janus-faced. One face is feudal and pretends to look to the past, while the other is capitalist and attempts to ignore its twin. Both, however, are inextricably linked in the Pakistani context, existing side-by-side in the countryside, in the mines, and in the factories. They also operate together through democratic institutions, such as Parliament. According to the self-image of Pakistani capitalism—bolstered by the IMF and the World Bank—the zamindari or feudal system is allegedly the "really" exploitative one, while the capitalist system is more "progressive." But this illusion denies that both economic systems are two sides of the same coin.

The task of the critical thinker is to examine the class mix in Pakistan where zamindars (landlords) constitute only one form of the feudal economy that has today extended into manufacturing firms as well as the service sector. This includes brickmaking kilns, carpet manufacturing, glass bangle-making, porters, domestic work, and construction-related activities. By examining the research on nonagricultural occupations, we shall see that feudalism and capitalism constitute a spectrum in contemporary Pakistani society. Thus, Pakistani farms and firms only sometimes fall on the ideal ends (farms are feudal, firms are capitalistic).

More routinely, they fall somewhere in between. The dual political economy coexists with and contributes to a disturbing trend of ever-increasing inequality in Pakistan.

Zamindari from the Farms to the Firms

Many South Asian scholars and activists have reached some consensus that bonded labor, whether born through customary or cultural ties or through debt bondage, could be described as feudal or semi-feudal.[1] Along the grain of this new consensus comes very good empirical analysis on bonded labor in Pakistan. The International Labour Organization's (ILO) 2004 studies in a number of Pakistani provinces investigated the possible existence of bonded labor. These studies provide us with useful data to decide whether feudalism is dead or dying. All of the ILO studies revealed the widespread functioning of *peshgi* (i.e., debt bondage), the most common mechanism by which people become bonded laborers. In agriculture, *peshgi* is a relation in which a sharecropper receives an advance to maintain food consumption while crops are sown and harvested. When the harvest comes in, it often turns out that the borrower has more debt than at the start of the season. The magic of compound interest traps the laborers into long-term debt. Not only the tenant but his or her family is also "bonded" to the zamindar. Many borrowers reported that it was not they but their parents who took out the original loan (Arif 2004). Many *haris* (sharecropper tenants) today report being inherited by or sold to new zamindars along with the land (Hussein et al. 2004).[2]

Unfortunately, the 1992 Bonded Labour Abolition Act did not truly eradicate debt bondage: a 2004 survey of five districts in Sindh showed that 75 to 100 percent of all *haris* were indebted to the local zamindar and could not leave the district (Hussein et al. 2004).

Sharecroppers in Khyber-Pakhtunkhwa (KP) receive one-fifth of the crop under the *hatian* system (sharecropping), and the landlord appropriates the rest (Arif 2004). Sharecropping is the most common land tenure arrangement in Sindh, where sharecroppers can, at most, receive half of the output (Hussein et al. 2004). Gazdar et al. (2002)

report that less than 10 percent of the sharecroppers actually receive half the output. The rest—despite having that 50–50 arrangement—receive less because input costs are deducted at harvest time. Most tenants with a 50–50 contract actually received an average of 13 percent of the output because of high input costs and charges for tube-well usage; a large number reported receiving nothing at all.

The convention is for the landlord to take possession at harvest; in the case of cotton, for example, the zamindar takes possession of the entire crop at harvest and may or may not tell the *hari* what price it fetches. The price structure, the interest rate, and the accounting calculations are set by zamindars. While verbal work arrangements are made with male tenants informally, wives and children are expected to work in the field, tend livestock, and do chores when required by the landlord. After paying back loans for inputs, food rations, and medical expenses, *haris* can become indebted to landlords. Due to substantial illiteracy and the social and political connections of the landlord, legal challenges usually result in favor of the landlord. As there is no written proof that the landlord received his share, he can take the tenant to court to receive more than the contractual share. Other landlords use deceitful accounting to short-change sharecroppers.

Although sharecropping is on the decline, there has been a marked increase in usage of "permanent" agricultural workers who can also be subject to bonded labor. Wages for permanent workers can simply consist of two meals daily, and they are often required to live at the employer's house. There is no cash wage. Consequently, the system of indebtedness extends not only to sharecroppers but to permanent workers as well. Migrant permanent workers (laborers who come to work for decades on the same farm) can be forced to perform *begar,* where the laborer cultivates land parcels on a completely unpaid basis because they lack any social relationships and accumulated assets to put toward agricultural inputs. In fact, this kind of arrangement is common in nearly half of the Sindh province.

Large farms are considerably more likely to use permanent rather than casual labor. (In the system of casual labor, the wage relation is on a temporary seasonal basis and *peshgi* advances are so limited that long-term indebtedness does not routinely result.) In Punjab, over half of all farms larger than 150 acres primarily use permanent labor, with some districts almost solely relying on this kind of arrangement (Arif 2004). Not only, therefore, are sharecroppers potential bonded laborers, but so too are permanent wage laborers.

Usually, wage labor is automatically identified as a capitalist relation: where we see wages, we see capitalism, and vice versa. But in the Pakistani context, it's apparent that wage labor can be organized by feudal relations and debt bondage since "permanent" wage workers are no different from the classic bonded laborer. While leftists are ready to see forms of feudalism at play in sharecropping and capitalism in wage labor, relying on such a simple distinction is erroneous and dramatically underestimates the incidence of feudalism in Pakistan today.

Akbar Zaidi, a prominent Pakistani economist, has argued that those insisting on the prevalence of feudalism are relying on "clichés," that untrained political economists are deploying a "redundant concept" and conflating power with distinct modes of production (Zaidi 2008). Zaidi is both partially right and wrong in his denunciation: he is right in arguing against the prevalence of feudalism in agriculture, but as we can see from our snapshot of agriculture, feudalism continues to characterize agrarian relations for some significant portion of the rural population in Sindh, Khyber-Pakhtunkhwa (KP), Balochistan, and Punjab, which is both the heart of Pakistani politics as well as the center of the Green Revolution. According to the Pakistan Institute of Labour Education and Research (PILER), 8.6 million of the 22.8 million employed in agriculture nationwide experience some form of bonded labor (PILER 2000; Federal Bureau of Statistics 2008).[3]

However, feudalism does not end at agriculture. It also extends into manufacturing and services in rural and urban areas, involving millions of workers.

Studies have found widespread forms of classic debt bondage throughout the mining sector in Pakistan, with migrant workers more likely to be involved in *peshgi* (Saleem 2004). Miners attempting to escape are tracked down by the middleman labor agent (the *jorisar*, or the mate) and subsequently beaten and chained. In his assessment of

Pakistan's mining sector, International Labour Office analyst Saleem Ahmad relates that when asked what would happen if the workers ran away with the advance, a *jorisar* replied, "Where will he hide from us? We know him and his family. He will have to move to a different province" (Saleem 2004). Miners who wish to take leave to visit the home village must ensure that a family member remains in the mine during the absence. The system involving middlemen who are directly responsible for the repayment of the advances given to workers is common to both mining as well as brick kilns. In brick kilns in central and southern Punjab, debts of Rs 50,000 per family are routine for the "classic *pathera*" (brick worker) family. Afghans, however, become bonded for smaller sums of around Rs 3,000 or less (PILER 2004). While debt transfer to the next generation is seen only in the "worst case" mining scenarios, it was discovered in all the brick kilns visited by PILER in and just outside Hyderabad, Multan, Lahore, Rawalpindi, Peshawar, and Haripur.

Fieldwork interviews with workers, owners, and subcontractors in glass bangle-making in Hyderabad revealed that *peshgi* was widespread but devoid of the worst abuses common in agriculture. Despite *peshgi*, the Collective of Social Science Research (2004a) determined that extreme forms of bonded labor, where the next generation inherits debt, were present neither in glass bangle-making nor in tanneries. However, extreme forms of bonded labor, coinciding with abusive labor relations, were found in construction in small and large cities, such as Karachi and Lahore, with more intense forms of bondage in rural areas (Collective of Social Science Research 2004a).

Bonded labor is also widespread in domestic labor and in specific subsectors of begging. In the latter line of work, the strongest evidence of bonded labor was in the hijra communities.[4] On average, the guru appropriates half of the proceeds from begging for himself. He directs a quarter of that to communal household expenses and the remaining quarter is equally distributed across his fellow hijras. Hijras can also be sold from one guru to another (Collective for Social Science Research 2004b). In domestic labor, fieldwork in Lahore and Karachi as well as surrounding towns and villages revealed that employers originating from rural areas were more likely to engage in relations of bonded labor. Landed Sindhi families in Karachi routinely brought servants with them from the village who received no salary or in-kind payment to village-based parents (Collective for Social Science Research 2004b).

All research studies show that bonded labor is both a rural and an urban phenomenon, present in agriculture, manufacturing, and services. Hence, while Zaidi is correct to argue that feudalism is not the dominant mode of production in all of Pakistan, it is present in all economic sectors and dominant in specific Pakistani locations. Just because agriculture has fallen in terms of its contribution to the GDP does not mean that feudalism is dying. In fact, it is fascinating to trace how this distinct mode of production has arisen in work relations characterized originally by piecework, subcontracting, and wage contracts in non-agricultural industries.

The discussion above touches on a controversy among many Pakistani leftists and liberals. Many acknowledge that feudalism is alive and well culturally, socially, even legally, but they deny its existence in the economy. The material presented here provides sufficient proof that feudalism remains a part of the economic structure as well. But what are the social, political, and legal aspects of Pakistani feudalism? In agriculture and in rural areas, zamindars wield considerable political power, adjudicating legal disputes instead of the courts, or family disputes and other matters such as marriages. They can even determine who wins the local and national elections by promising votes to their candidates. The Bhutto family of Sindh, which has produced a political dynasty, is the best example of the intersection of feudalism and electoral power. Two journalists, Aryn Baker and Mirpur Bhutto, captured this intersection in a 2008 *Time* article on the cousin of Pakistan's former president and a politician in his own right, Mumtaz Ali Bhutto. They wrote:

> Bhutto says his tenants are free to vote for whomever they please—in fact he complains that despite all he has done for them some are still disloyal. But sharecroppers on other feudal properties speak of coercion. Ghulam Abbas, an unemployed villager in rural Dosera, Punjab province, describes a climate of fear on Election Day. "The feudals have their own cronies on every street. They know who is favouring whom. If they lose in any polling station they can figure out through this system and take revenge." Revenge can come in the form of false police cases, he says, or unfair prices at the mills, which are owned by the feudal lords. Bhutto agrees that these practices

have happened, and do happen, but, he's quick to add, not on his lands. "We don't need to do that here, people vote for us already. . . . If the courts functioned, I wouldn't have to arbitrate. I only do this because nobody else is. Otherwise I would be vacationing in Majorca."

Some landlords, like Mumtaz Ali Bhutto, stand for and win elections in provincial or national assemblies. One landlord in a provincial assembly audaciously rejected any increase in spending on education because he explained that his tenants would be unlikely to perform certain tasks, such as replacing hunting dogs on his weekly hunting forays, if they became skilled laborers less dependent on him (Talbot 2005). This also showcases a point that should not be missed: there is no reason to believe that democracy is incompatible with feudalism or would even uniformly act as a break on feudalism. In fact, feudal landlords have actively intervened in parliamentary debates on land reform since the inception of Pakistan, shaping the many different legislative acts to avoid strong negative impacts on themselves (Herring 1979).

Ever-Increasing Inequality in Pakistan

Zulfikar Bhutto's socialist economic rhetoric may have superficially targeted feudal landlords and elite industrial capitalists, but his policies were without teeth. Political scientist Ronald Herring has demonstrated how landlords used various loopholes to circumvent land redistribution, including transferring land to other family members or abruptly ending leases to avoid tenant claims. In fact, Herring's work demonstrates three central contradictions of Bhutto's policies: (1) that the land reforms affected very few landlords in Punjab and Sindh, where Bhutto's party, the Pakistan People's Party (PPP), was strongest, but attacked rebellious and nonconforming landlords in Balochistan and KP; (2) that smaller and medium-sized farms may have been more likely to be organized by feudal relations, and they were completely untouched by the land reforms' higher ceilings; and (3) the land reforms privileged and encouraged "entrepreneurial" land use over feudal land use. This last point shows us that land reforms were opposed only to a specific type of exploitation that may be characterized as feudal but encouraged capitalist exploitation.

And, while Bhutto's nationalization policies during the 1970s targeted the top twenty-two families who owned over half of Pakistan's industrial wealth along with a majority of its insurance funds and 80 percent of the country's bank assets, they were barely affected since the majority of their wealth went untouched (Rashid 1989). Nevertheless, worried about their assets, these families along with others in Pakistan's elite, organized a backlash to Bhutto's policies following his forcible removal from office. Subsequent politicians pushed for privatization of the country's national industries.[5]

Bhutto's own daughter, Benazir Bhutto, who would hold the prime minister's office more than once, became the first to embark on the policies of "liberalization, privatization, and deregulation" with the aid of the same British consultants that Margaret Thatcher had used during British privatization. Bhutto also had the dubious distinction of signing Pakistan's first structural adjustment package with the IMF and the World Bank in the 1980s.[6] Following Bhutto, Nawaz Sharif's government followed suit and carried out the privatization of two banks.[7]

Proceeds from the privatization under Sharif were split between defense spending and repayment of foreign loans, such as the IMF loans taken out under Benazir's first term. By the time General Pervez Musharraf came to power in October 1999 in a bloodless coup, most of the money from privatizations was going toward repayment of loans (Tariq 2008). In other words, where economic policy is concerned, it has not mattered whether there was a military dictator or a democratically elected prime minister.

The results are to be expected. Unemployment has risen, and poverty and inequality have worsened. Talat Anwar (2003) notes that expenditures have been falling for the already-poor lowest 40 percent of the population, but rising for the top 20 percent from 1984 onward. Subsidies for flour and *ghee* were removed under the technocrat Moeen Qureshi's caretaker administration in 1993, further depressing the living standards for the poorest. In 1990, one in five families was living below the poverty line in Pakistan, and by 2000 this had risen to one in three families (Social Policy and Development Centre Karachi 2000). The World Bank itself has noted that "indeed, assistance packages appeared to do little but increase the country's debt burden" (World Bank 2006). Inequality is the inevitable result of paltry government expenditures on social services. Although Benazir Bhutto was heavy on populist rhetoric, she did not raise spending on education or on development. Her government, as well as Nawaz Sharif's and General Musharraf's later on, roughly split over 60 percent of government expenditures on debt servicing and military expenses, leaving little room for anything else.[8]

Conclusion

When feudalism in the South Asian context is under discussion, some mistakenly connect it to a system of "corruption." Instead, we should think of a dual political economy in operation where feudalism is not a crony form of economy that is "worse" than capitalism, or even less democratic. Both are exploitative economic forms in which workers produce surplus or profit that is appropriated and distributed by others. Both zamindars and capitalists have made unique claims on the Pakistani state to provide suitable conditions for themselves. Feudal landlords have their demands (for instance, their opposition to agricultural income tax or land redistribution), and small, medium, and large capitalists voice their demands (access to cheap credit from national banks, or underpriced bids for state-owned firms). It is by focusing on the commonality between the two economic forms that workers and citizens have the best chance to avoid the crippling contradictions of ineffectual economic policies and reforms that have thus far identified exploitation only in feudalism, and not in capitalism.

Notes

1. See Prakash (1990) for a sophisticated analysis of freedom, reciprocity, and bonded labor in colonial India.

2. The practice of transferring bonded labor brings up a controversial point: does the sale of the worker mean the presence of feudalism, or of slavery? Anti-slavery activists define slavery as the commodification of people as private property, while others in the Marxian scholarly tradition (such as E.P. Thompson's analysis

of southern U.S. sharecropping in the post–Civil War era) classify systems of debt peonage resulting from sharecropping as feudal. See Kayatekin (1996) for an insightful Marxian analysis of the various forms and theorizations of sharecropping.

3. Out of a total labor force aged ten and over, of 51.78 million, roughly 44 percent are employed in agriculture, 20 percent in industry, and 35 percent in services (Federal Bureau of Statistics 2008).

4. The hijra community is made up of "third sex" individuals (self-identifying as neither men nor women) and has a long history in South Asia dating back at least 4000 years. Their most frequent occupations are as ceremonial dancers and singers at weddings, births, and festivals; sex workers; and beggars; most live in close-knit all-hijra communities with a head guru who leads a group of disciples.

5. For instance, Nawaz Sharif comes from one of the 22 families whose property was partially nationalized by Bhutto; in the case of the Sharifs, the Ittefaq foundry was nationalized in 1972, and returned to them in 1981 by Zia. Sharif would enter the political system as Zia's chief minister of Punjab, and carried out the privatizations in a notoriously nontransparent manner, using favoritism and personal connections to decide the winning bidders rather than highest prices (Talbot 2005).

6. "Liberalization" and "deregulation" refer to a variety of strategies: allowing the exchange rate and interest rates to be determined by markets, the elimination of quotas and other trade barriers, and elimination/ minimization of direct price controls and subsidies, etc. In general, both refer to a decreasing role for the government and an increasing role for the "free market." Privatization refers to the sale of state-owned industries to private firms.

7. State-owned banks were reporting a loan recovery rate of less than 8 percent in the first quarter of 1990 (Talbot 2005). However, Sharif was certainly not the only one to use financial credit to political advantage this would be true of all heads of state.

8. In a ranking of 117 top global spenders on the military, Pakistan ranks ninth, despite being one of the poorest countries. Such a measure is even more dramatic when compared with a ranking of health care spending in the poorest 34 economies, where Pakistan ranks 34th, helping us to see how military expenditures displace, or "crowd out," social service expenditures on education, health, sanitation, irrigation networks, etc.

Works Cited

Anwar, Talat. "Trends in Inequality in Pakistan 1998–99 and 2001–02." *The Pakistan Development Review* 42:4 (2003).

Arif, G. M. "Bonded Labour in Agriculture: A Rapid Assessment in Punjab and

Northwest Frontier Province, Pakistan." Working Paper, International Labour Office, Geneva, March 2004.

Baker, Aryn, and Mirpur Bhutto. "Landowner Power in Pakistan Election." *Time,* 13 February 2008.

Collective for Social Science Research, Karachi. "A Rapid Assessment of Bonded Labour in Hazardous Industries in Pakistan: Glass Bangle-Making, Tanneries, and Construction." Working Paper, International Labour Office, Geneva, March 2004.

Federal Bureau of Statistics, Government of Pakistan, Statistics Division. *Pakistan Labour Force Survey, 2007–2008.*

Gazdar, Haris, Ayesha Khan, and Themrise Khan. "Land Tenure, Rural Livelihoods, and Institutional Innovation." Paper, Collective for Social Science Research, 2002.

Herring, Ronald J. "Zulfikar Ali Bhutto and the 'Eradication of Feudalism' in Pakistan." *Comparative Studies in Society and History* 21:4 (October 1979).

Hussein, Maliha, Abdul Razzaq Saleemi, Saira Malik, and Shazreh Hussain. "Bonded Labour in Agriculture: A Rapid Assessment in Sindh and Balochistan, Pakistan." Working Paper, International Labour Office, Geneva, March 2004.

Kayatekin, Serap. "Sharecropping and Class: A Preliminary Analysis." *Rethinking Marxism* 9:1 (Spring 1996).

Pakistan Institute of Labour Education and Research. "Unfree Labour in Pakistan: Work, Debt, and Bondage in Brick Kilns." International Labour Office, Geneva, March 2004.

Prakash, Gyan. *Bonded Histories: Genealogies of Labour Servitude in Colonial India.* Cambridge University Press, 1990.

Rashid, Harun-or. "The Ayub Regime and the Alienation of East Bengal." *Indo-British Review* 17:1–2 (1989).

Saleem, Ahmad. "A Rapid Assessment of Bonded Labour in Pakistan's Mining Sector." Working Paper, International Labour Office, Geneva, January 2004.

Social Policy and Development Centre Karachi. *Social Development in Pakistan Annual Review 2000: Towards Poverty Reduction.* Karachi: Oxford University Press, 2000.

Talbot, Ian. *Pakistan, a Modern History.* New York: Palgrave, 2005.

Tariq, Farooq. "Pakistan: $23.8 Billion Corruption from Privatization under Musharraf." Action in Solidarity with Asia and the Pacific. 2008. http://www.asia-pacific-action.org/node/69 (accessed 10 December 2009).

World Bank. *Pakistan: An Evaluation of the World Bank's Assistance.* Washington, D.C.: World Bank, 2006.

Zaidi, Akbar. "Land Reforms." *Daily Dawn,* 5 March 2008.

The Generals' Labyrinth
Pakistan and Its Military

AYESHA SIDDIQA

IN 2008, A POPULAR PERCEPTION was that Pakistan's political military's name was tarnished due to Army Chief Pervez Musharraf's ten years of rule. Indeed, the 2008 elections brought a civilian government to power. Many saw a major shift in Pakistan's civil–military relations. Analysts concluded that the military would never risk interfering in politics. By the end of 2010, however, the perception had begun to change. The role played by the military in combating terrorism in certain parts of the country, its standing up to American strategic ambitions in South Asia, particularly Afghanistan, and its providing assistance to people during the 2005 earthquake and later during the 2010 floods are some of the activities that seem to have improved the organization's image. The military even managed to deflect blame for the unilateral raid conducted on Pakistani territory by the U.S. to kill Osama bin Laden. Though the top brass presented itself before Parliament in the aftermath of the raid—a rare occurrence—the military's notorious spy agency, the Inter-Services Intelligence (ISI) and its army chiefs seem to have blackmailed the government and society into giving their organizations a clean bill of health. By mobilizing their various propaganda mechanisms, Pakistan's military managed to redirect responsibility for the OBL fiasco to the civilian government.

In fact, the military's ability to maintain a positive image in comparison to the civilian government has been key to sustaining and legitimizing its dominance in the country's power politics. While political parties and politicians have failed to establish a strong counternarrative, the military has successfully marketed itself and its national security narrative. In fact, the military's control of national politics depends on its ability to constantly reproduce its image as an alternative institution. This goes hand in hand with seeking multiple partners in society across the sociopolitical spectrum. Therefore, the Pakistani army's partners belong to all segments of the societal, political, and economic groups and class. This also means that it is very difficult to push the military back into the proverbial barracks. The military is here to stay in a dominant role. It has all the means and power to recreate itself and remain dominant in Pakistan's power politics and national psyche.

An Intervening Military

Pakistan's military remains the most powerful institution of the state. Its influence is historical and directly linked to the significance of the state's national security narrative. The first India–Pakistan war fought in 1947 set the basis for the primacy of national security, which, in Pakistan's context, is understood as military security. After the first war of 1947–48 the government set its priority by allocating about 70 percent of the estimated federal budget for defense.[1] As the military's primacy in the imagination of the state and society increased it was able to gain greater importance. The culmination of this dynamic was the army's resort to governance, with the first martial law administration of army chief General Ayub Khan in 1958. Ayub Khan remained in power till 1969, first as a military ruler, and later as a military-turned-civilian ruler. General Yahya Khan replaced Ayub Khan in 1969 and governed till 1971.

The 1970s saw the first uninterrupted civilian rule of Zulfiqar Ali Bhutto (1971–77). The return to democracy was shortlived as Bhutto's government was removed by military's intervention in July 1977. General Zia-ul-Haq remained in power until his death in 1988. A democratic interlude in the 1990s was followed, yet again, by a decade of military rule (1999– 2008).

Pakistan has emerged as an unstable democracy where the military intervenes periodically and has a strong interest in politics and statecraft. More than half of Pakistan's years have been spent under military rule. A popular perception about military in politics in Pakistan is that every army chief has a plan to take over the reins of the government provided he can find a suitable opportunity and a way to legitimize direct intervention.

"Every country has a military but Pakistan's military has a country" is a popular adage in Pakistan. After six decades of existence, people have, in one form or another, compromised with the tremendous power of the armed forces. Opinion ranges from positive to negative. While some believe that the military is the only capable institution, others think of it as the most powerful institution, which is now hard to challenge. In terms of civil–military relations I consider Pakistan's army as the "parent-guardian" type, which means that it is an organization that never truly leaves power even if it has, officially speaking, gone back to the barracks. It creates legal, constitutional, and political provisions to maintain its influence over other institutions and stakeholders.[2]

Pakistan, in fact, is under a military hegemony in which the organization exercises great economic and political power and dominates the public sphere and the social imaginary by controlling the sources and forms of communication and public interaction. In this way, the military controls the national narrative.

The Politics of the Military

The military has ruled the country directly and indirectly for about half of Pakistan's existence (see Table 1). However, that alone does not describe the extent of the military's political power. Having evolved as a political animal, the organization has developed partnerships within the political system. These linkages are built across the ideological and political spectrum—ranging from the political right and the center to the left. Besides periodically intervening in politics, there are three other ways through which the military strengthens its political prowess.

Direct involvement in the political process. Retired military officers join political parties. They can be found in Parliament as delegates of

Table 1. Patterns of Rule in Pakistan

Type	Duration (years)	Period
1. Direct military rule	17	1958–1962, 1969–1971, 1977–1985, 1999–2002
2. Elected government under a military president	15	1962–1969, 1985–1988, 2002–2007
3. Elected government under a civilian president "Rule of Troika"	11	1988–1999
4. Supremacy of the nonparliamentary forces under formal parliamentary rule	11	1947–1959
5. Civilian supremacy	6	1971–1977

Source: Mohammad Waseem, "Civil–Military Relations in Pakistan," *Pakistan in Regional and Global Politics,* ed. Rajshree Jetlee (New Delhi: Routledge, 2009), 185.

every political party. In the 2008 Parliament, for instance, there are twelve former military personnel in a three hundred sixty–member house. In the 12th National Assembly four former military officers sat in the house.[3] This may not be an impressive number but it indicates a trend. More important, these former military personnel in the Parliament play a critical role in special parliamentary committees, such as those on defense and national security. They watch out for the military's interests and their primary allegiance is to their former paymasters rather than the political parties they are part of. Interestingly, it is either former military officers or military friendly politicians who chair the parliamentary committees on defense or are its members. In any case, there is no history of any substantive discussion in the Parliament on defense issues. The military has built a strong fraternity glued together by organizational interests intertwined with personal interests. There is no other organization that takes care of its "own" in Pakistan like the armed forces. Although the membership of former military personnel in political parties happens by default rather than design, these people watch out for the interests of the armed forces. Since the military operates as a fraternity, the primary allegiance of a large majority of armed forces personnel including retired officers is to the organization rather than any other political or social entity. Moreover, over the years the military fraternity has developed a sense of superiority that they do not want to see challenged. For instance, Nawaz Sharif's act of forcing the army chief, Jahangir Karamat, to resign in 1999 upset even the junior officers in the navy, a service considered akin to a distant cousin of the army. Numerous young officers (of the rank of Lt. Commanders) were upset at the fact that a civilian politician humiliated an army general.

Direct intervention in the political process. Senior commanders make their own parties or provide direct patronage to political parties. The most salient three examples are General Mohammad Ayub Khan (1958–69), who extended patronage to the Pakistan Muslim League— Functional Faction (PML-F), which helped in his election as president, and Generals Mirza Aslam Beg and Pervez Musharraf, both of whom formed their own parties after retirement from service. (Given the desire of senior generals to appear professional, the military top brass does not engage in political parties during active service, as has been the case in numerous Latin American states.)

Manipulation of the political party system. The army is known for subverting elections, making new parties and political coalitions, or simply forming secret partnerships with individuals in the political parties. For instance, the military's prime intelligence agency, the ISI, was involved in rigging the 1990s elections.[4] Political commentators are suspicious of other elections as well. The army was also involved in forming a coalition of nine parties called Islami Jamhoori Itihad (Islamic Democratic Alliance) that contested elections in 1988.[5] Pervez Musharraf's government (1999–2008) was also involved in assisting with the formation of another right-wing coalition called Mutahida Majlis-e-Amal (MMA), which is the coalition of all Islamist political parties. The army then manipulated the 2002 election in MMA's favor to give the coalition control over the provincial governments in Baluchistan and Khyber Pakhtunkhwa (KPK).[6] The objective was to keep the two main national parties, the Pakistan People's Party (PPP) and Pakistan Muslim League—Nawaz Faction (PML-N), out of power. In any case, the religious right is one of the most significant constituencies of the army. The intelligence agencies are known to have mastered the art of what is called "pre-poll rigging" and of manipulating election results. Pre-poll rigging is done through managing election campaigns in a manner that would benefit a particular individual or party versus others. The country's establishment, which is dominated by the military, uses the state machinery and its influence on the media (including private media) to create a positive image of its favored candidate. The positive image building is used to send a signal to the society regarding which of the top political competitors has the support of the establishment. Unless there is a major crisis, in which case voting patterns follow the emotional instinct of the people, such signals have an impact on how people vote. The military's long involvement in politics has allowed it to make inroads into every single party. There are always some members in every party who are perceived as being closer to the "deep state" than to their own party leadership. These members watch over the party leadership and the party from inside and are known to intervene strategically at critical moments to save the interest of the establishment (to be read here as the military). This intense system of building partnerships at multiple levels is what gives the Pakistani scholar Akbar Zaidi the impression that Pakistan lacks a democratic sensibility.[7] In any case, he rightly says that Pakistan is a "praetorian democracy."[8] Political leaders are known to have collaborated with the military or to engage them in a political discussion at various times in the country's history. The most recent episode relates to the national reconciliation ordinance (NRO) that was signed between the PPP, Benazir Bhutto, and General Pervez Musharraf. This agreement was meant to allow Bhutto back from exile. According to the agreement, the Musharraf-led Pakistani state would withdraw cases of corruption against Bhutto, her spouse Asif Zardari, and numerous other politicians in return for their support of the general. Subsequently, the NRO was declared unlawful by the Supreme Court.

There are two explanations for why the civilian government and politicians engage the army in this manner. First, the military has grown so strong politically that it does not allow any political rival. The military today has become the main source of any internal political change. So, in Benazir Bhutto's estimation, as with leaders before her, it is better to build bridges with the army, return to power, and then attempt to bring change from within. However, that strategy has failed time and again because the political elite—whether the feudal landowners, the indigenous bourgeoisie, or the metropolitan capitalists—remains closely connected to the military through a host of strategic alliances.[9] This elite also prefers authoritarian politics, making it a natural ally of the army. In addition to these elites, the military itself has evolved into an independent class that protects its interests and keeps an eye on politics and political outcomes.[10] As a separate class the military has strengthened its links in all segments of the civil society, especially the business and industrial class, which, in any case, owes its establishment to the first military government of General Ayub Khan. The army chief had helped create institutional mechanisms to create an entrepreneurial class.[11] After six decades, major entrepreneurs continue to depend on official patronage for their growth and development. For instance, all major business groups owe their growth and size to state patronage. The careers of entrepreneurs such as Mian Mansha (a banking giant) and Malik Riaz (a real estate tycoon) illustrate how state patronage benefits certain individuals and their businesses. Under these circumstances, distribution of opportunities follows a kleptocratic cycle in which the military tends to benefit immensely due to the significance of key political players.

The Economic Giant

The military's political power is connected to its economic strength. It is a cyclic relationship: military's political power increasing its ability to gain economic dividends, which, in turn, give the military's echelons reason to enhance their political might. Consequently, the armed forces have built huge stakes in the economy. This is both direct and indirect. The former relates to the military's share in the central government expenditure. Officially, the defense budget is about 23 percent of the central government expenditure. However, the number rises to over 30 percent if one were to add all expenses left out of the budget. For instance, under Musharraf, the government stopped including military pensions in the defense budget, which, even without these pensions, stood at seventy-five billion rupees in 2009–10. The expense incurred on military personnel working in civilian departments or special projects is also not included in the defense budget.[12]

Beyond issues surrounding the slippery calculations in the budget, a more salient problem remains. Pakistan's military has penetrated the overall economy by developing its own corporate interests. The armed forces operate in the formal, informal, and illegal economy in all the main sectors, including agriculture, manufacturing, and the service industry. In agriculture, the military operates dairy and stud farms, and also distributes agricultural land to its personnel. In the service industry, it operates in several areas such as education, oil and gas, private security, banking, insurance, and airlines. In the manufacturing sector, the military owns companies that manufacture commodities such as fertilizers, cement, and cereals. The military has an organizational presence in corporate ventures through its subsidiaries as well as individual members of the military fraternity, whether serving or retired. The net worth of the military's business empire, thus, runs into billions of dollars.[13]

Control of the Narrative

What has strengthened the defense establishment's control over the state and society is its increasing penetration in sectors such as the media and academia. These are critical sectors in terms of establishing hegemony. As far as the media is concerned the military operates at three levels:

- Directly buying off journalists.
- Injecting retired military personnel or diplomats as columnists to present a pro–armed forces perspective.
- Penetrating newsrooms of television channels and newspapers with its own agents.

Over the years, the army command and its intelligence network have created institutional and extra-institutional mechanisms to engage civil society. The Inter-Services Intelligence (ISI), the Inter-Service Public Relations (ISPR), the Strategic Plans Division (SPD), and the office of the army chief are some of the institutional mechanisms for engagement with the media and the academia. A resource-rich military can offer journalists and academics a substantial boost to their careers. Leaking information to select journalists, co-opting academics to present the military's perspective, setting up think tanks or infesting these with "collaborators" are some of the tools of the military. The military penetrates public sector universities, especially social sciences departments, and controls them indirectly. The ISI is even reputed to invest money in national and foreign universities. It is known to have invested money and planted its agent in at least one well-known British university.[14] Organizations like the Strategic Plans Division (SPD) of the armed forces invest in building infrastructure in public sector universities and building links to individual faculty. One of the examples pertains to the social science departments such as the Defense and Strategic Studies and International Relations departments at Quaid-e-Azam University in Islamabad, where the SPD built rooms and other facilities for faculty members and also contributed toward scholarships and fellowships of some faculty members. This helps build a cooperative network that comes in handy as far as finding partners to present a pro-military stance to the public.

The army chiefs Pervez Musharraf and Ashfaq Pervez Kiyani are also known to actively engage with prominent media figures and present them with select information that supports the army's perspective.[15] The co-option is done both nationally and internationally. Over the past decade the ISI is known to actively engage with foreign journalists and academics. These people are hosted by the agency and presented with facts favorable to the army and the ISI.

Through such direct and indirect means, the army intervenes forcefully in the national narrative and promotes itself as the defender of the country's ideology. That ideology, of course, is of its own making. Over the years, it has built linkages with all kinds of groups across the ideological divide. The liberal-secular elite and intelligentsia are as much connected to the military as the religious right and the militants. While the secular-liberal views the military as the only bulwark against religious extremism and terrorism,[16] the religious right treats the military as a precious partner for furthering the objective of reestablishing an Islamic empire. Thus, the armed forces have developed this great capacity to break bread with the U.S. during the day and sleep with the Taliban at night. Domestically, this means that the army will engage with various forms of militants both positively and negatively. While it will fight some elements, it will protect others. Such ideological diversity helps in establishing control across varied sections of society. The link with the religious right is necessary because of its military strategic benefits, namely the jihad in Afghanistan and Kashmir, and for building a constituency among the conservative middle class, especially the trader-merchants, who are nationalists and connected with the military's conservative right-wing leaning perspective. These middle-class trader-merchants supported the anti-Bhutto movement sponsored by General Zia-ul-Haq's army.[17]

These diverse connections allow the military to present itself as the only alternative institution of the state and impress its western patrons into doling out rent for its services. In fact, the military's multilayered narrative connects it to a series of foreign benefactors. While the nationalist and anti-India agenda helps to bolster a relationship with the Chinese, the image of an anti-Communist and moderate Islamic state brings the organization closer to the U.S. and its allies. Yet another strand represents the connection with Islamic forces and orthodox religious states like Saudi Arabia that find partnering with Pakistan's army extremely beneficial to create a protective net in the region and at home against Shiite Iran and its influences. Saudi Arabia and some of the Gulf states have been involved in providing funds to various militant organizations in Pakistan. Such foreign partnerships, or client–patron relations, are aimed at the empowerment of the defense establishment versus other institutions. The weapons and military technology provided by the U.S. and by China are vital for making the military appear more robust. The links with Saudi Arabia and the Gulf states, on the other hand, are critical for political, ideological, and monetary reasons.

Taken together, these avenues build a narrative that imagines the army as the only credible organization in Pakistan. Notwithstanding the inefficiency and problems of the political leadership, the agencies whip up a vicious propaganda to undermine political parties and politicians in general. This helps the military stay afloat and remain relevant to ordinary people. Today, the military is politically a potent force with extremely sharp teeth. There is no other institution that has the capacity to challenge its might. The subtle but sharp confrontation between the Pakistan People's Party, led by Asif Ali Zardari, and the army, led by General Ashfaq Kiyani, may be just one opportunity for civilian institutions to define themselves and regain some of their lost power. However, given the lack of visionary leadership, the problematic character of the civilian political elite, and the immense capacity of the armed forces to sustain control, the empowerment of political institutions seems improbable at the current juncture. For Pakistan, the military is the state.

Notes

1. Abdurrahman Siddiqi, *The Military in Pakistan, Image and Reality* (Lahore: Vanguard Books, 1996), 70.

2. Ayesha Siddiqa, *Military Inc.: Inside Pakistan's Military Economy* (London: Pluto Press, 2007), 51–57.

3. Data compiled by the Pakistan Institute for Legislative Development and Transparency (PILDAT).

4. *Herald* (Karachi), April 1994, 25–32.

5. The former head of ISI, Lt. General Hammed Gul, confessed to being involved in creating the IJI to oppose Benazir Bhutto's PPP. He also hinted at providing support to the MQM during the mid-1980s to counter the PPP in Sindh. Personal interview, Rawalpindi, 15 May 1994.

6. Interview with the head of the Pakistan Liberal Form, Zafarullah Khan, September 2003). Khan's organization monitors elections. His view was that available evidence clearly points toward the army's support to the MMA during the 2002 elections.

7. S. Akbar Zaidi, *Military, Civil Society, and Democratization in Pakistan* (Lahore: Vanguard Books, 2011), 25–44.

8. Ibid., 26–27.

9. Hamza Alavi, "The Structure of Peripheral Capitalism," in Hamza Alavi and Teaedor Shanin, eds., *Sociology of Developing Societies* (New York: Monthly Review Press, 1982), 172–91.

10. Siddiqa, *Military Inc.,* 83–111.

11. Saeed Shafqat, *Civil–Military Relations* (Boulder, Colo.: Westview Press, 1997), 45–57.

12. Interview with officers of the Military Accountant General, Islamabad, 12 November 2010.

13. Siddiqa, *Military Inc.*

14. Discussion with various academics, including the head of the Peace Studies Program at the University of Bradford, England.

15. Discussion with Qatrina Hussain, Islamabad, 1 December 2010. Claims of meeting the army chief, Ashfaq Kiyani, were also made by other journalists, such as Imtiaz Gul.

16. This conclusion was drawn from discussion with various liberal political activists, including the renowned physicist and educator Dr. Pervez Hoodhbhoy.

17. Zaidi, *Military, Civil Society, and Democratization in Pakistan,* 40.

The Desperate U.S.–Pakistan Alliance

JUNAID RANA

IT IS BY NOW A FAMILIAR SCRIPT for anyone following Pakistani politics on a regular basis. First, the customary gambit: Pakistan needs to maintain its sovereign rights as an independent nation-state. After all, that was the raison d'être for Pakistan's formation and the partition of the subcontinent. Then, the rhetorical strategy turns to external interference from India, the United States, or foreign militants such as those hailing from Afghanistan. All the while there is the political give and take of an up and coming client state at the behest of foreign aid. At stake in this game of crying wolf is a patronage system that defines Pakistan's political hierarchy. In other words, as long as there is a threat to the idea of Pakistan, the status quo of Pakistani politics continues.

Take the events surrounding a recent flare-up. In the spring of 2009 the Obama administration was busy preparing an attractive aid package for Pakistan under the Kerry–Lugar bill. Working closely with the Pakistani government, the bill subtly changed the terms of the long-term relationship between the two countries. Setting a new standard for civilian aid projects, the bill proposed a vetting process channeled directly through the U.S. State Department and designed in response to claims of misallocation of funds by the Pakistani government. That such a policy was in the offing was met with outrage throughout various quarters in Pakistan. In a reliably knee-jerk response, mainstream journalism in Pakistan held that this was the latest episode in an arrogant and impudent attitude of the U.S. government. In the blogosphere such sentiments ran rampant without discussing the actual drafted policy of the Obama administration. The long-held sentiment in Pakistan of an unequal relationship was once again rearing its head. The debate became even hotter as Pakistani politicians took the opportunity to grandstand about the abuse of the U.S. government and the involvement of Pakistan in the War on Terror. Many argued that such foreign aid was a ploy to manipulate Pakistan's sovereign right to its airspace with drone attacks targeting Islamic militants and civilians—of course without acknowledging that this is the outcome of a clear agreement between the U.S. military and the Pakistani government.

In this example the notion of American imperialism, although it is without a doubt a fact, is a rhetorical smokescreen that glosses over two main rationales. First, it covers over the advantage this new policy gave to multinational contractors, often led by Americans. The second obvious elision is the fact that many of these politicos had their own ties to Pakistani companies that would be forced into restraint under this arrangement. The language of the bill itself clearly acknowledged the need for transparency in Pakistan's vetting process to curb corruption and control the particular knack of foreign aid ending up in the coffers of elected officials. Never mind the bureaucratic enormity of such oversight and the impossibility of measuring corporate competitors, the result in Pakistan was a fanning of the anti-American flame. Popular suspicions by Pakistanis of the U.S. government are old and deep. In the end, though, this was a major piece of legislation pushed through by Secretary of State Hillary Clinton and others who supported it. The bill signed by President Obama on October 15, 2009, was hailed as a victory for market reform and global competition. Within the larger scheme of the U.S.–Pakistan alliance, this was no more than business as usual. And certainly the important role Pakistan played in the frontlines of the war in Afghanistan and the larger War on Terror is nothing less than the renewal of the height of U.S.–Pakistan relations in the 1980s during the struggle to defeat the Soviets. It was an arrangement that could not come too soon.

And then the floods came.

Neoliberal economic policy quickly shifted to consideration of the disaster economy and the work of relief and recovery. The unprecedented floods of 2010 dramatically weakened an already suffering economy. Recorded as the worst natural disaster in Pakistan's history, a large portion of the country was decimated. Over a fifth of the country's land mass was suddenly underwater in the regions contiguous with the Indus river basin. Uprooting over 20 million lives, the untold story of the floods was the slow and steady death of those without access to clean drinking water and with shortages of food. The already poor and economically distressed regions of the country faced an environmental apocalypse. That the unprecedented monsoons might be the result of global warming and human intervention through a misguided system of water engineering was rarely part of the conversation, although some reports make a successful argument for the clear failure of the dam structure to control such catastrophic flooding.[1]

In many ways, this natural disaster highlighted how Pakistan is consistently dependent on the rescue of U.S. aid. When international donors failed to meet the bare requirements of relief, the U.S. government initially diverted funds from the Kerry–Lugar Act in lieu of formal disaster relief. The consequences were soon clear. Either by design or in an accelerated fashion brought on by the floods, the disaster relief became part and parcel of a civilian and military aid package that bolstered the American military presence in Pakistan and Afghanistan.

Although grumblings in the Pakistani military have persisted in opposition to this mandate of the War on Terror, the Obama administration has countered by periodically leaking assessments that Pakistan is failing in its agreements. The threat of reducing U.S. aid has kept the reins fairly tight on the Pakistani government until the recent killings associated with American spy Raymond Davis. Politicians in Pakistan have jumped at the opportunity once again to lambast the operation of American intelligence agencies and contractors. With the assassination of Osama bin Laden, many in Washington think the military role of the U.S. in Afghanistan and Pakistan is finished. Several prominent analysts have argued as much by proposing that aid to Pakistan should be greatly reduced because much of it is supposedly channeled into the border security with India and not fighting the War on Terror. Of course, these same analysts play down the well-documented strategic role of U.S. intelligence in training militants who have ended up in Afghanistan, Kashmir, and parts of central Asia for the past thirty years.[2] Such arguments complete the circle in which fiery politicians in Pakistan, with a barely masked agenda and despite their collusion, appear to be right all along: the U.S. wants its spies and military contractors to have their way in Afpak; Pakistan remains on a short leash as a client state; and the Pakistani political class legitimates itself through blustery anti-American rhetoric, while hatching plans to grab more dollars.

Running the Neoliberal War on Terror

In the broader scheme, the threat of U.S. contractors and the expansion of American-style neoliberal capitalism is more than the fear of competition and the realities of profiteering on both sides of this bi-national relationship. Long-held suspicions by Pakistanis of American covert activity and secret intelligence gathering are now out in the open. The presence of U.S. contractors in Pakistan barely disguises the thinly laid subterfuge of American intelligence agents taking on the nitty-gritty of the War on Terror. And in many ways this is the real plan of the U.S. government. The case of Raymond A. Davis that came to light in early 2011 makes this altogether too clear. As the story emerged it was first told as a robbery gone wrong. This story was put out mainly at the behest of the Obama administration that imposed a U.S. media ban on the initial details. Now it is clear that Davis worked as a reconnaissance scout sent to gather information on the militant group Lashkar-e-Taiba. After carrying out a mission close to the busy commercial area of Mozang Chowk in Lahore, Davis engaged in a gunfight that ended in several Pakistanis dead in broad daylight. Those murdered included two men apparently shot in the back, and a motorcyclist run over by a U.S. consulate driver who rushed to the scene to rescue Davis.

Reports state that Davis was observed taking photographs of the Pakistanis after shooting them, perhaps to add them to the files of secret intelligence. After months of diplomatic negotiations, Davis was freed by the payment of blood money by the CIA to the families of the slain Pakistanis, a buy-out option permitted by Pakistani law. The mysterious list of Davis's employers most certainly include Hyperion Protective Consultants and the U.S. consulate in Lahore, completing a picture of American spying agencies infiltrating Pakistan under the ruse of independent contracting. Davis's role will certainly be rewritten after the military killing of Osama bin Laden in Abbottabad. Lashkar-e-Taiba is one of the militant organizations thought to have been harboring Bin Laden possibly in cahoots with elements within the Pakistani military that might be now connected to the intelligence obtained by Davis. Regardless of the facts, secret intelligence and military contracting is being touted as an effective strategy in the U.S. War on Terror, while the Pakistan government is seen as soft on Islamic militants and a failure from the perspective of American interests.

Beyond the reality of clandestine activities as part of the strategy of economic and military aid to Pakistan, the turn toward spying must also be seen in the context of a failed commitment toward academic scholarship on the region. In the past few decades U.S.-based funding resources for scholars of Pakistan studies are continually uneven and irregular, even after 9/11 when the void of basic research in the social and humanistic sciences in places such as Pakistan and Afghanistan made obvious the need to know so much more. As the domestic situation deteriorates in Pakistan, so do the opportunities for funding cleared by the U.S. State Department based on travel warnings and prohibitions. Without academic knowledge the dependence on media experts and policy wonks leads to a skewed perception of the conditions and priorities in Pakistan. For the U.S. government, then, the clear strategy has turned in recent times to a dependence on brute force on the ground through covert operations and contracted espionage. The aim is simplistic if not naïve. Get rid of the bad guys in the short term without addressing the issues and problems of everyday life. Such an approach relies on bolstering the military in Pakistan. That then must have a continuous list of bogeymen to keep such aid flowing.

Undoubtedly, the tie between the U.S. and Pakistan is a messy one. Built on a relationship of necessity, Pakistan depends heavily on U.S.

aid that garners a number of lobbies in Washington and throughout the U.S. generally. The resentment that has surfaced into what is often labeled anti-American is a more generalized response. It is not so much that America or the American way is simply hated; rather, this relationship of necessity created a Pakistan that many Pakistanis have come to despise. Long gone are the heights of nationalist self-belief of a modern and progressive Pakistan for those who came of age in the 1950s and 1960s. And although recently glimpses of resistance have emerged as beacons of hope from the peasant rebellion in Okara and throughout the southern Punjab that began in 2000 to the lawyer's movement of 2007, the push for grassroots reform in the past decade or so consistently trips on a political system full of self-interested politicians and a military–civilian state structure. The tie of dependency for Pakistan to foreign aid is centered on a program of debt accrual and market reform that acts as a form of relief for this destructive political system. As funds from international loans are further drawn to an ever-expanding external debt, the politics of graft is given another lift out of what can only end in massive turmoil at the national level. Yet the necessity of dependence on foreign aid is far more entrenched in the Pakistani economy than will allow for a severing of this relationship.

In terms of how such a policy is crafted on the U.S. side the work of lobby organizations are at the heart of this relationship. The main lobbies are the result of efforts by the Pakistani embassy to maintain domestic and military aid, and the work of Pakistani Americans to influence changes in policies concerning Pakistan. Through a process of repackaging a tainted image, the Pakistan lobby in Washington has had a history of mixed success that in the current period is at an all-time high in terms of aid. The reliance on the Pakistan lobby in Washington is twofold. First it continues the process of image making and shifting that is a standard practice of lobby firms, and second it works to maximize the amount of aid packages for Pakistan. The unwieldy relationship between the U.S. and Pakistan is played out through this world of political spin and interest that often results in the pragmatism of a mutually beneficial need. Nonetheless, such realpolitik defines much of how policies are made and unmade by focusing on aid packages through specific notions of security and humanitarian concerns.

After the floods of 2010, humanitarian initiatives by Pakistani and Muslim Americans also proliferated. Although such a response came out of the necessity of alleviating human suffering and pain after the historic floods, the relative condition of poverty remains a structural problem. This stark reality also led to renewed calls of debt cancellation for Pakistan. Immediately after the breadth of the disaster was realized Pakistani activists began calling on international donor institutions to cancel the over $55 billion in external debt. The logic of such an argument would in some senses have the potential to shift the debate away from political leadership and patronage toward the conditions that maintain structural poverty.

Cleaning Up a Dirty Image

Pakistan has long had an image problem on the world stage. Terror, militancy, and patriarchal Islam are the conceits of a U.S. public obsessed with reducing a complex country into overdrawn stereotypes. Politicians in Washington are just as guilty. Few will actually take the time to conduct extensive research and do background readings, and thus must rely on lobbies for vital summaries of regions and countries to inform their policy decisions. Well aware of this situation, the government of Pakistan has maintained a tenuous relationship with Congress through a slew of firms that manage and attempt to recast this troubled reputation.

Pakistan's former ambassador to the U.S., Husain Haqqani, is a master of this public relations game. With an advanced degree in international relations from the University of Karachi, Haqqani spent his early career as a journalist and then entered politics assisting the campaign of Nawaz Sharif and later served three different Prime Ministers. Since 2008, Haqqani has taken over the mantle of ambassador with a diplomatic approach that has focused on the stabilization of the U.S.–Pakistan relationship through increased aid. Key to this is a specialized approach that highlights Haqqani's experience in journalism and expertise with militant Islam. From the viewpoint of the American government, this makes Haqqani an important interpreter of the fears and hesitations of U.S. politicians in the War on Terror. Successful stints in the U.S. media circus, including a sobering yet jokey visit to Jon

Stewart's *Daily Show*, show his ability to engage with sound-bite styles in which he appears to critique and applaud the Pakistani government at the same time. Haqqani personifies a PR strategy that simultaneously includes the military and economic needs of Pakistan and the criticisms of doubtful U.S. politicians who function through pragmatic certainty. This line of attack is emblematic of this approach whose highest priority is maintaining the flow of dollars to Pakistan. To achieve this end Haqqani had led the Pakistani embassy in hiring firms that draw their personnel from a range of specialized political experience, including former officials in leading lobbyist and public relations companies.

With the resignation of Haqqani, the latest installation to this post, Sherry Rahman, will perhaps prove even more efficient in terms of relegating access to the resources on offer by the U.S. government. Far from being anti-establishment, Rahman's role in the media and her long-standing place as a central component of the liberal left-wing of the PPP signals the ongoing realignment of Pakistan's current political structure with Asif Ali Zardari at the helm. The contortions and subterfuge in the name of Pakistan's civilian government and army will surely continue.

As is well known, the world of lobby firms maintains close ties to the U.S. government through their personnel. Lobbyists and government officials are often interchangeable over time in the revolving door of influence. Haqqani's approach followed on developing the partnerships his predecessors established with lobby organizations in Washington in the past decade or so. The arrangement in the context of 9/11 and the War on Terror is the result of specific repackaging of Pakistan as a major frontline ally. By claiming an important role in the war in Afghanistan, Pakistan continues in a familiar role cultivated over the past several decades. The new twist is the spread of the War on Terror domestically throughout Pakistan to defeat the Islamic militants that grew after the withdrawal of U.S. aid in the 1990s. The recent upsurge in lobbyist activity on behalf of Pakistan is generally presented in this context in order to argue for a process of invigorating military aid alongside the need for well-distributed civilian aid projects.

Starting in 2005 the Pakistani government hired the services of Van Scoyoc Associates, a registered lobbying firm, for $575,000 over fifteen weeks in order to further enhance its relationship with the Bush administration. At that time, the team of experts at Van Scoyoc was led by Lee Rawls, a thirty-year veteran of Capitol Hill, where he worked as the Chief of Staff for Senate Majority Leader Bill Frist, the Republican from Tennessee, and former FBI head Robert S. Mueller III. Specializing in military defense procurement, Van Scoyoc was hired to fulfill interests beneficial to both Pakistan and the United States. As one of the largest and wealthiest lobby firms in Washington, Van Scoyoc landed a coveted contract with Pakistan, regarded as one of the linchpins in the U.S. military campaign in Pakistan and Afghanistan that has an endless bottom in terms of military need. This victory of landing the Pakistan contract was not only striking a deal for military aid in terms of the defense and security needs of Pakistan, but also laid the basis of a partnership in the War on Terror that provided Pakistani military bases to the U.S. military and the guarantee of Pakistani sovereign airspace for U.S. drone attacks. Shortly thereafter the contract with Van Scoyoc was renewed in 2007 with a retainer of $55,000 per week—an increase of over 40 percent.

In 2007, Pakistan inked a deal with another one of the largest lobby firms in Washington, Cassidy and Associates. The deal worth $1.2 million was supposed to bring in the former assistant secretary of state for South Asian Affairs Robin Raphel to head the global affairs and trade consultancy group. Cassidy withdrew from this contract supposedly because of the declaration of a state of emergency rule by the then Prime Minister Musharraf. This came in the context of a row following the challenge of election results by the Pakistani Supreme Court as to Musharraf's eligibility to run for reelection. Raphel's role in Cassidy was to be enormous because of her experience as a career diplomat with stints including posts as economic and financial advisor in the CIA, USAID, and the State Department. As an advisor for the Clinton administration she worked with the newly formed Taliban government in Afghanistan, and later was appointed to the Iraq reconstruction team under the Bush administration. Since leaving Cassidy, Raphel was appointed by the Obama administration as the coordinator for non-military assistance to Pakistan under the Kerry–Lugar Act—bringing the circle of associations from lobby to policy to a close in terms of the argument presented here. From the perspective of Pakistan this was an even better arrangement.

Since 2009 and the departure of Raphel, Cassidy was hired by an independent Pakistani American platform organization called the Council on Pakistan Relations. Working through a pro-business advocacy and lobbying agenda, the ironically named CPR has worked on legislation including humanitarian relief for the 2010 floods, trade, foreign aid, national security, education, and economic development. The connection of government lobbies to independent non-governmental organizations is not always as clear as in this case. Nonetheless the presence of Pakistani American organizations with a main interest often based in humanitarian concerns and policy has also significantly made inroads into the lobby networks of Washington.

Apart from the major lobby power of Van Scoyoc and Cassidy, the public relations firm Ogilvy Public Relations Worldwide was hired by the Pakistani embassy in 2008 to improve the overall image of Pakistan in the United States. For $45,000 a month, Ogilvy trained members of the Pakistani embassy in writing and addressing press material and reporter outreach. Currently, the Pakistani government under President Asif Ali Zardari has at least nine different lobbying firms in the United States—two of which serve the individual interests of Zardari and the Pakistan People's Party (PPP). Since May 2008 Locke Lord Strategies was hired as a key advocate for the Pakistan lobby in the U.S. legislative and executive branches. With a contract at over $100,000 a month, Locke Lord Strategies has been hired to specifically promote a positive image of the PPP and to forge a lasting relationship with the U.S. government as part of a clearly partisan lobby of the current ruling party in Pakistan. The PPP has also hired the well-known public relations firms Burson-Marsteller, BKSH & Associates, Penn Schoen, and Berland Associates to promote the PPP agenda in Washington. In addition, such specific relationships have also been developed for particular ministries of the Pakistani government. For example, the Pakistani Ministry of Commerce was represented by Dewey & LeBoeuf to extend the business and trade interests of Pakistan.

In addition to these official lobby organizations and public relations firms hired by the Pakistani government, a growing number of Pakistani

American organizations have taken on the promotion of Pakistani interests in tandem with the efforts of the Pakistani embassy. For example, PakPAC formed in 1989 is a registered U.S.-based lobbyist organization composed mainly of wealthy physicians and businessmen. Its agenda includes changing Washington's opinion of Pakistan. This lobby grew out of an initiative of the Association of Physicians of Pakistani Descent in North America (APPNA) that was founded in 1976 as a charitable organization and is known for its social conferences as well as medical relief programs mainly in Pakistan. Numerous other Pakistani American organizations exist that attempt to influence public policy. Some of the main ones include the Pakistani American Public Affairs Committee, Pakistani American Congress, Council of Pakistani American Affairs, and the National Association of Pakistani Americans. For the most part, many of these organizations pursue relationships with local and national politicians in the United States for specific community needs and to present an image of civic responsibility and incorporation. Efforts toward policy changes in regards to Pakistan are often part of these relationships that for some of these Pakistani American organizations are implemented in collaboration with the Pakistani embassy.

It is no surprise that the overwhelming approach of this lobby work is pro-business, and so favors the Pakistani elite. Although Pakistani American organizations work to address issues such as poverty and access to education and healthcare, the main agenda of the lobby in Washington is to procure economic and military aid to Pakistan. Such a goal ultimately serves the purpose of bankrolling the Pakistani government and its security and military apparatus. It is in this way that the Pakistan lobby in Washington assumes its role of maintaining the Pakistani government's pro-business agenda while the efforts to ameliorate conditions of poverty and humanitarian disasters become the responsibility of Pakistani Americans. Ayesha Siddiqa has made this argument from a different vantage point in terms of understanding the military–civilian state in Pakistan that maintains itself through an independent and often invisible military economy.[3] Despite this cleanup job by lobby and public relations firms, humanitarian aid for the 2010 floods in Pakistan fell short, leaving those in the poorest areas to fend for themselves. That such aid fell short is more than compassion fatigue following the disasters in Haiti and other parts of the world. It is the result of a dirty image after decades of limited knowledge, misinformation, and the increasing lack of sympathy for the Muslim world by the American public. Yet, despite this collective shunning, there is a pragmatic reality in which the U.S. remains responsible for Pakistan through a complex aid relationship that both countries crave.

U.S. Aid to Pakistan: A Short History of Desperation

In 1982 the economist Rashid Amjad famously dubbed Pakistan a foreign aid dependent regime. Industrial growth in Pakistan depended on the continuous inflow of foreign aid. With continuous aid coming in, economic growth mimicked patterns of an economic takeoff. Historically, the reduction of these flows, in the absence of other forms of finance capital, repeatedly resulted in a drastic reduction of growth indicators.[4] Hence, the growth of Pakistan's economy is misleading and dependent on foreign aid rather than foreign direct investment. Although Pakistan benefitted from abundant remittances from overseas Pakistanis throughout the past three decades, foreign portfolio investment is a much tougher ambition. The country's consistent political turmoil with half its history led by the military and the current War on Terror makes investors wary of the future and adds to investor fears and skepticism over the reliability of an unstable market. In this schema, the lesson that the history of U.S. aid to Pakistan has produced is based on a clear dependency. Whenever aid is abundantly sent to Pakistan to float the economy, economic indicators point to growth; in moments of an American squeeze, the Pakistani economy flounders and the domestic political situation seems to run amok. The exceptions have come from remittances from abroad that gave Pakistan a steady stream of foreign capital in the absence of anything else.

The story of U.S. aid to Pakistan can be fairly easily divided into a decade-by-decade breakdown, largely guided by the tethering of military aid to civilian packages with the modern promise of economic development and defense security. Neither package would be easily defined as success stories that simply lead to development and security. Rather, civilian aid more often than not faces the accusation of squandering and corruption; and military aid for Pakistan is, well, shall we say more than just for defensive purposes.

U.S. aid to Pakistan begins in the Cold War era, when $2.5 billion came to bolster the loyalty of the Ayub military dictatorship. Up until 1964, some $700 million in military aid also built up the defenses of the Pakistani army.[5] The India–Pakistan war in 1965 and the ensuing ambivalent partnership with the U.S. meant a curb in economic aid to Pakistan. For the next fourteen years the total economic aid totaled approximately $2.55 billion with over $30 million in military aid, a dramatically low period in comparison to the prior period of military aid. By the late 1970s, U.S. aid did not flag, even though President Carter was dubious of the military dictator Zia ul-Haq. With the Soviet invasion of Afghanistan, Pakistan became a frontline state in the 1980s in the fight against Communism. With the U.S. strategy of funneling funds through third party countries, Pakistan received over $5 billion in aid largely funneled to the military for the role the Pakistani military and intelligence services played in the proxy war in Afghanistan.

The turning point came in the 1990s after the retreat of the Soviets and the emergence of evidence of Pakistan's nuclear ambitions. For the next decade, economic aid fell to $429 million with $5.2 million in military assistance. More specifically the U.S. imposed economic and military sanctions in accordance with the Pressler Amendment that stipulated the President certify that no risk exists toward the development of nuclear arms in Pakistan. Although the Pressler Amendment was passed in 1985, it was not used toward sanctions against Pakistan until 1990 after the Soviets withdrew from Afghanistan. The double standard that this represented, as has been widely discussed, demonstrated the role of Pakistan as a military pawn in an American proxy war. It was in this recent period of the 1990s that the deterioration of Pakistan's internal political situation increased dramatically. Those who went to fight in Afghanistan found themselves without political support and monetary resources. It was in this context that they reorganized into Islamic militants bent on attacking the Pakistani state, which had abandoned them. Notably, in this same period Japan emerged as the major donor shoring up the missing flows vacated by unreliable U.S. aid. It should also be remembered that this decade also marked the massive transition to structural adjustment dictated by the Washington consensus and the increase in tied-loans and debt accrual.

After May 1998 and the first atomic tests in Pakistan that followed the nuclear tests in India, U.S. aid was shortly thereafter renewed to $77.8 million in 1999 and $101.4 million in 2000. Aid increased massively in 2001 following 9/11 to $776.5 million in mostly economic aid designed for civilian projects. In the decade following 9/11, the U.S. government provided Pakistan with $9 billion in military assistance and $3.6 billion in economic and diplomatic initiatives. The future of aid packages holds much of the same with a clear dependence of the U.S. war in Afghanistan on Pakistan's military and the need to maintain a stable economy. With the unprecedented flooding of 2010, the economic and military aid promised through the Kerry–Lugar Act, and another $230 million in relief funds by the Obama administration, Pakistan continues to be reliant on multilateral aid primarily from the U.S. government.

After the 2010 Floods: The Future of Dependency

The constant fear of state bankruptcy and the Pakistan government's inevitable default on IMF and World Bank loans have created an atmosphere of economic crisis and dependency that seems incurable. With the Obama administration now promising an aid package to Pakistan worth $3.1 billion for the year 2012, the irony is that the World Food Programme was forced to suspend emergency food distribution in flood afflicted areas as of February 2011 after facing a shortfall of $548 million in donations. The basic need to fight the affects of poverty and the slow death of hunger brought on by disaster is brushed aside while the fat of U.S. aid goes to the Pakistani military.

In the theatre of national politics, Pakistan continues to be torn asunder by the silencing and murder of politicians who call for modest gains in liberal attitudes of tolerance and religious pluralism. Despite these exigencies of a seriously desperate relationship, the U.S. and Pakistan are hardly in a position to alter this situation without a drastic change. Based in a military–industrial relationship for over the past half century and as a central partner in the U.S. War on Terror, Pakistan stands at the brink of nothing short of a long-term dependency on U.S. aid.

That there need to be alternatives to the dependence on U.S. economic aid for Pakistan goes without saying. But what are the viable alternatives to a relationship that seems inevitable and forced? After the floods of 2010 a small group of Pakistani activists began calling for debt forgiveness to resolve the dependence of foreign aid primarily from the United States. Pakistan's external debt reached over $54 billion with the largest multilateral creditors including the Asian Development Bank, International Monetary Fund, World Bank, and bilateral creditors including Germany, France, Japan, and the U.S. The possibility of a debt free future may seem a far-off situation, but without the certainty of an infinite flow of economic aid from the U.S., anything is possible. Relinquishing Pakistan's debt would be a step in the right direction that would allow the economy a chance to restart. Otherwise it will be politics as usual from Washington to Islamabad.

Notes

1. See, for example, the editorial "Disaster Strikes the Indus River Valley," Middle East Research and Information Project, 17 August 2010. http://merip.org/mero/mero081710.

2. One of the more prominent of these arguments is represented in Lawrence Wright, "The Double Game," *New Yorker,* 16 May 2011, 91.

3. Ayesha Siddiqa, *Military Inc.: Inside Pakistan's Military Economy* (London: Pluto Press, 2007).

4. Rashid Amjad, *Private Industrial Investment in Pakistan, 1960–1970*. (Cambridge University Press, 1982).

5. All of these monetary units are in historical dollars.

I'll Be Your Mirror
The Politics of Pakistan's Populism

MADIHA R. TAHIR

IN 1972, when Imran Khan was still playing cricket, a commission set up by the Pakistani government to inquire into the causes for the loss of Bangladesh (then, East Pakistan) issued its report. Its conclusions were damning. The report described the military dictator, General Yahya Khan, the successor to General Ayub Khan, as a drunkard and called for the court martial of senior military commanders. By the time the report was issued, the General had already handed power over to a young politician who had served as foreign minister under Ayub Khan's regime before resigning from the government in 1967 — Zulfikar Ali Bhutto.

The new president — who doubled as a civilian chief martial law administrator — was in a strong position to pursue the commission's recommendations. After his resignation, Bhutto had galvanized people with his fiery political speeches opposing Ayub Khan. He gave voice to the anger churning in the country, drawing leftists, peasants, and the working class toward his newly instituted party, the Pakistan People's Party (PPP). Willing to thunder at the United Nations and able to deliver rousing speeches at home, Bhutto was, in effect, Pakistan's first major populist politician. The hopes of the country were with him. Yet, when it came to the commission's report, rather than put his trust in

A version of this essay was published in *Caravan* magazine on January 1, 2012.

the people and movements who stood with him, Bhutto immediately suppressed it and refused to act on its recommendations.

It was a telling move: the populist was more interested in power over the people.

More actions would follow. As the separatist movement in Pakistan's largest and most resource rich province Balochistan grew into a full-fledged rebellion, Bhutto unleashed the Pakistan army on the Baloch. It was the second time in less than a decade that the army had set upon the Pakistani state's own civilian population.

In the rest of the country, even as the populist Prime Minister spoke the rhetoric of socialism, his party launched an attack on labor activists and leftists arresting and torturing them. Instead, Bhutto now cemented alliances with capitalists and Islamists. On behalf of the former, he kept his reforms limited. And, on behalf of the latter, he banned alcohol and declared a minority Muslim sect, the Ahmadis, non-Muslim, banning them from practicing Islam. Thus, Bhutto's populism derived its messianic zeal from the people, but in the final calculation it remained unaccountable to them as Bhutto maneuvered to keep the elite and the army on his side.

On July 5, 1977, General Zia-ul-Haq, Bhutto's Chief of Army Staff, seized power in a bloodless coup. Zia had gained the top position in the army after Bhutto had forced out several other generals because he mistrusted them and feared a coup.

Bhutto was hanged on April 4, 1979.

Three decades later, it is now Imran Khan who has become the populist, inspiring Pakistanis to gather in mass rallies of the like not seen in recent years. When I met with him for an interview, he told me he grasped the nature of the 1971 war during a trip to East Pakistan shortly before the war. The commission's report was declassified in 2000, and the lesson Khan says he has drawn from that episode is that people should have been held responsible.

It is a worthwhile lesson, but better still would be to learn to refuse the machinations of the army, that is, to refuse to court it as a political player. Khan, however, is close to General Hamid Gul, who helped give rise to the Afghan Taliban and continues to make statements that favor the military even as Osama bin Laden was discovered in a military garrison town. Thus, it appears *that* lesson has yet to sink in. And, it may be the only one really worth learning.

SEX, OR AT LEAST THE IDEA OF IT, is never far from Imran Khan. It reveals itself in the casual remark of an urbane twenty-something friend, a well-educated and usually sensible woman who turned to me and said that she would "do Imran." "You know," she further explained, "as a feather in my cap." It sometimes hangs in the air, almost visible, and as thick as the cloying perfume of the "aunties"—well-heeled middle-aged housewives clutching their fading youth as desperately as they do the last yard of cloth at designer lawn sales, who thrash and push and shove, banging lesser folk with their bulky handbags so they can rub shoulders with Imran, if only for a furtive moment.

Heterosexual boys also desire Imran in their own way. They queue up impatiently, jostling each other among coils of barbed wire, shouting their passions to Imran's security team from behind the protest stage where the Great Khan is seated—wanting to be let inside, to see him up close, to be near him.

It seems safe to say that Khan is the only major politician in Pakistan presently capable of exuding this kind of appeal: this was how one sociologist summed up to me why Imran's party, the Pakistan Tehrik-i-Insaaf (PTI), or Movement for Justice, might pose a serious threat to Nawaz Sharif's Pakistan Muslim League (PML-N) in the latter's traditional stronghold of Punjab. "I mean, he's Imran Khan—he's not *ganju*," she said, using the word for "bald" to refer to the rotund and balding Sharif. A report in the *Christian Science Monitor* echoed the point: "With his good looks and seeming willingness to speak plainly," wrote Issam Ahmed, "Khan is to Pakistan what Sarah Palin is to the U.S."

For his part, Khan would probably prefer to be Pakistan's second Zulfikar Ali Bhutto—the fiery populist founder of the Pakistan People's Party (PPP). And certainly some similarities exist, even if they are not perhaps the ones that Imran imagines. Both men charmed significant segments of the country by coupling an Oxbridge appeal with a strident populist nationalism, though the inflections of that ideology differ from one man to the other.

For a long time after he entered politics, there was little reason to believe Khan posed a threat to anything other than his own status as a national hero. But that's no longer the case: after uneven turnouts at PTI demonstrations for the better part of 2011, the party defied predictions by rallying roughly 200,000 supporters in a roaring gathering in Punjab's capital city, Lahore, on 30 October 2011. It's too soon to tell whether that turnout will translate into votes in the elections scheduled for 2013, but it may well mark the moment that PTI went from being ridiculous to respectable in the mainstream.

The turnout in Lahore was a dismaying signal for Khan's many critics, some of whom churlishly declared that the massive demonstration held by Benazir Bhutto in Lahore after her return from exile in 1986 had been many times larger. It's a plausible argument, but it overlooks one significant fact: nearly 70 percent of Pakistanis are now below age thirty. They are not likely to remember Benazir's homecoming rally—and even if they did, it's hardly self-evident that their passions would be stirred by the recollection.

For a politician so marginal that his party has only managed to win one seat so far—his own from Mianwali—Imran summons scathing, fierce, passionate criticism from his detractors, the most passionate of whom tend to be urban liberals. He has been called "dangerous" and "naïve" and described as a man whose supporters "feed his delusion of being the messiah that Pakistanis await." The influential *Friday Times* editor-in-chief Najam Sethi, during an appearance on Pakistan's largest private Urdu channel, Geo TV, put it this way: "Some people learn too much and go crazy; others learn nothing at all and go crazy. Imran is half in each camp, and that makes him half-baked." For some time now, *The Friday Times* has even published a parody column written in Khan's voice, which is credited to "Im the Dim."

The night before I met Khan at his hilltop farmhouse just outside Islamabad, I had dinner with Shane Brady, a jocular Irish aid worker who was wrapping up five years in Pakistan. When I told him that I was going to interview Imran the next day, Brady exclaimed that one of our mutual friends was "going to be so jealous." The friend in question had once heard a rumor that Khan enjoyed the occasional puff of marijuana; ever since, he had been determined to find some way to meet Khan so they could smoke a joint together. Everyone dreamt of Imran in his own way.

The next morning, I headed to Imran's home in Bani Gala, a bucolic hilly neighborhood on the outskirts of Islamabad. As I neared his estate, the regimented grid and broad avenues of Islamabad's suburbs gave way to a bumpy road, winding along pastoral vistas. Imran has lived here since 2005, but he's not the area's most notorious resident: Abdul Qadeer Khan, the controversial former head of Pakistan's nuclear program, also lives nearby.

As the car climbed higher, the late afternoon sunlight shattered into trembling beads across the surface of Rawal Lake, the main water source for Rawalpindi, which has been heavily polluted by runoff from the area's many poultry farms. Ochre-skinned young boys splashed playfully in the lake. Further on, a herd of white and brown speckled cows blocked the narrow road, halting car traffic till they had sauntered lazily on. Still higher, I passed an odd collection of objects and buildings, the result of a neighborhood that's quickly expanding: a diminutive plain white mosque, half-built mud and brick hovels, a row of grimy shops, a row of freshly painted shops, red bricks heaped on a truck, water pipes piled by the side of the road, an inexplicable tent in a green field, a phone tower, a donkey cart. Past all this, the road widened out and then came to an end in front of a set of imposing and fabulously fantastical wrought iron gates: the entrance to Khan's home, nestled in a lush expanse of manicured lawn and wilderness.

Inside, pink flowering vines creep along the pale walls of the courtyard. The house mimics Pashtun architecture, and doors on all sides of the courtyard lead to other rooms. A slim man appeared and directed me to an impressively oversized but tastefully furnished drawing room with cream-colored sofas offset by colorful cushions. I thought for a moment about a photograph I'd once seen of Khan's London home, which one visitor had described to his biographer as "a Sixties art gallery crossed with a Sultan's harem."

Just as I began to notice and become unsettled by the uncanny, impeccable symmetry of the room—each object in one half of the room was duplicated in the other, with the exception of a photograph of Imran bowling signed by someone "To Skipper"—a door I hadn't noticed in a corner of the room burst open.

"Why don't you come in here." It was Imran, and it was only grammatically a question.

He was holding the door handle, leaning into the room, taller than I had imagined, wearing a stark white collared *kameezshalwaar*. I followed him to a sitting area in his expansive bedroom. The floor-to-ceiling windows were pitch dark now, but I could hear his dog barking just outside. He collapsed onto a sofa looking tired and scruffy, bags under his eyes, his leonine mane appearing finger-riven.

"So," he said, finally turning to me, "what do you want to ask?"

THE ICONIC IMAGE of Imran Khan—the one everyone still remembers—is the photograph of him wearing a lime-green uniform and holding the 1992 World Cup trophy aloft, arms above his head and a wide grin on his face—the last and greatest triumph of a spectacular career. Over the years, he had proven himself as a disciplined, persistent athlete with a dogged work ethic. During his on-and-off tenure as Pakistan's captain, he was regarded as an honest leader, though according to some accounts, a dictatorial one as well. According to Christopher Sandford's biography of Khan, a former teammate had once described his leadership style by comparing him to Stalin. When I put this observation to Khan, he came back with a quick retort. "Whoever it is neither understood Stalin nor understands me," he quipped. "I mean he probably couldn't even spell Stalin if he described my style as him." He laughed. "He probably means Churchill not Stalin. He probably confused the two."

When Imran first stepped onto a pitch in Lahore in 1969 to launch his career in first-class cricket at the age of 16, his performance was erratic—out of line with the legend he was to become, but par for the course given the state of Pakistani cricket in that era. The country had made its international cricketing debut in 1952, the year Imran was born, and since then had led a mercurial, fraught existence. Broader national politics consistently overshadowed the game. Only a few weeks before Imran's trial for first-class cricket, a three-Test match series between England and Pakistan had to be abandoned when spectators demonstrating in support of a teachers' strike for better wages and working conditions spilled onto the field in Karachi en masse. It was the last year of military dictator General Ayub Khan's rule, and the country was restless, wracked by labor and student strikes. The tourists, still unbeaten, fled the country as quickly as they could. For Khan, it marked the beginning of a political education in a game that was itself political. In Pakistan, cricket belonged to the elite. As a youngster from a wealthy, urban Pashtun family, Imran represented the rule and not the exception among cricketers in his day. Like his cousin, Javed Burki, who had briefly held the captaincy in the early 1960s, Imran also attended Aitchison College, the uppercrust English medium school in Lahore skilled at teaching Pakistani boys how to mimic—and perhaps desire— white British manhood.

If cricket represented class politics at home, it was embroiled in race politics abroad, a fact that was not lost on Imran. Schooled at Aitchison and then Oxford, and trained in British morality and values, Khan recognized the limits of his educational capital against the grim reality of racism in Britain. "At no point in my life did I ever, ever think that I was not going to live in Pakistan. Never," he told me. And then added, emphatically in his booming voice: "Although, you know, England became a second home to me, but I never ever thought that it would be the place where I would live because I was always a second class citizen there. And that was against my self-esteem: to live as a second class citizen."

For a boy who grew up rich and educated in English schools, the cultural components of colonialism reverberated far more powerfully than the material exploitation. In his memoir, *Pakistan: A Personal History,* Khan writes, "In my opinion the greatest damage done to the people of the Indian subcontinent was in the humiliation of slavery and the consequent loss of self-esteem. The inferiority complex that is ingrained in a conquered nation results in its imitation of some of the worst aspects of the conquerors, while at the same time neglecting its own great traditions. It destroys originality as the occupied people strive only to imitate the occupiers."

In the arc of Khan's post-cricket public life, which has carried him into the thicket of Pakistan's cultural and religious politics—toward an embrace of Pashtun identity and Islamic piety—the signs of his search for that missing originality seem clear, visible as a yearning for something of the authentic.

"I never live in my past," Imran Khan told me when I asked him whether he missed his life in London. "The past is only to learn from. My life was always controlled by my passions," he continued, stressing the final word heavily. "I was quite rootless in that sense that, you know, my passion was cricket so it took me everywhere. Then it became the hospital, so I came here."

Among younger Pakistanis, Khan is arguably better known and loved for his hospital in Lahore—formally, the Shaukat Khanum Memorial Cancer Hospital and Research Centre—than for his cricket career. The red-bricked state-of-the-art medical center, which opened in December 1994, stands as an awe-inspiring testament to Khan's dogged persistence and, in a country shattered by cruel class divides, thrilling evidence of the possibility that slumbers within liberal Pakistan. The hospital, which provides cancer treatment irrespective of a patient's ability to pay, was built with World Cup earnings as well as private fundraising. In stories that have quickly passed into folklore, as Imran Khan ventured forth into Pakistan to fundraise for the hospital, his reputation for honesty was such that women tossed their gold bangles and other jewelry at him. But if the public was behind him, the Nawaz Sharif–led government was not, leading some newspaper columnists to wonder whether the government feared Imran's competence.

When Sharif's government created yet more obstacles for the new hospital, Imran Khan wrote a lengthy article in the *Frontier Post* voicing his criticism in religious terms. "For me," he wrote, "the greatest feeling of satisfaction was that despite the curse of the un-Islamic VIP culture in the country, our staff made no distinction between the paying and non-paying patients."

By then, Imran Khan had taken a distinctly pious turn. "I met a man who was a very spiritual man and had powers like Ibn Arabi, that great 13th-century mystic who saw with double vision." He paused and corrected himself, then started again. "It wasn't that. It was just the wisdom of the man." Imran began to read the Qur'an, and he told me that he now regards the Prophet Muhammad as his role model. "Leave alone that he was a prophet of God. Let's say he was an ordinary man. No man has achieved what he's achieved," Khan argued. "No man has created a civilization. No man has been a lawgiver. No man was a leader as a leader, just purely as a leader." He made an emphatic gesture with his hands. "No man has achieved what he's done. I mean, he created leaders. When he left this world, everyone around him became a leader. Even if you look on him as a leader, no one has achieved as much. The civilization he created was the greatest civilization for 700 years."

It was around this time that Khan published *Warrior Race: A Journey Through the Land of the Tribal Pathans,* a book-length depiction, in deeply romanticized terms, of Pashtun tribal culture. He started to speak publicly against what he described as a bankrupt Pakistani elite—whose corruption he attributed to a lack of morals and religion. In a challenge to Pakistan's secularists, who argued that religion was a private matter and responded squeamishly to public mentions of piety, Khan came to embrace the idea that Islam provided a political and moral framework for living—a complete order that embodied the essence of universal human rights and justice. He began to draw inspiration from Muhammad Iqbal, the early 20th-century poet and philosopher—and particularly from Iqbal's critique of western rationalism and his efforts to retool Islam as a comprehensive and modern moral and political philosophy. For Imran, Iqbal's thinking seemed to provide an answer to the question he believed plagued all former colonies: how to be simultaneously modern and authentic to one's own cultural traditions. It is a journey well known among elite populists across the former colonies; Imran Khan's turn to indigenous traditions is equal to that of Dr. Mahathir Mohamad in Malaysia.

In the wake of Imran's self-reinvention as a preacher of national pride—and his stated promise to marry a Pakistani girl—the announcement that he was to wed Jemima Goldsmith, the daughter of a British businessman and philanthropist who was 22 years his junior, met with a cold reaction in Pakistan.

One English-language newspaper ran a column titled "Imran Meri Jaan!" (Imran, My Love), which sarcastically weighed the possible shortcomings of Pakistani women in an attempt to determine why Khan might have chosen a foreign bride. A few columnists in the Urdu press argued sincerely that the marriage was to be applauded, because Imran Khan had saved Jemima from hell by converting her to Islam. *The Nation,* an English-language daily, ran a tongue-in-cheek column satirizing this argument, which read, "I have a hunch and a good one too that the great Khan has a deep strategy in his mind to serve Islam and arrest the expansion of Zionism. It has been revealed that that lady was of Jewish origin but now has been converted to our religion with conviction through the body-chemistry of our great cricketer. In one go, he has denied many children of Israel to be conceived and come to this world."

The marriage did not last. "Put it this way," Imran Khan told me. "Marriage and politics are very hard to sustain together. One would have to suffer." Jemima and Imran still remain close; indeed, she's the source of much of his continued circulation through the western press circuit.

Imran has pressed on with his model of politics, a brand that draws connections between the religious and the political. Indeed, that is how he explains his entrée into politics. "You have to ask two questions if you're a thinking person," he said. "Some people blissfully never ask themselves these questions: What is the purpose of existence? What will happen to us when we die? These two questions, and only religion can answer. No science can answer that question." Khan's answer to the first question provides his rationale for having entered politics. "The purpose of existence is so simple," he said, with the tone of his voice rising as if to stress that this was self-evident. "The more the Almighty gives us, the more responsibility on us what we need to do for others. That's it. No rocket science. It's being a good human being," he continued, and then moved to a more openly political interpretation of the question. "In our society, people like us, who have an option of not doing anything—do we sit on our backside and watch our country go down the drain or do we stand up to this corrupt mafia who, in the name of politics and democracy, are plundering the country. Is anyone going to stand up to them or not?"

But this is ultimately a moral issue—who will stand up to the bad guys?—rather than a political one: in a similar vein, Khan typically argues that the problem in Pakistani politics today has to do with the personal ethical failures of politicians rather than the system that encourages, nourishes, buttresses, and supports them, or the forms of capitalism that reproduce that system. Breaking down that system will require land reform, wealth redistribution, and other wholesale structural changes about which Imran speaks little, if at all. It is Imran's displacement of political questions onto a moral framework—and not merely his resistance to political favor-trading, as some have claimed—that turns his political vision into a kind of "anti-politics." And that vision, unlike Bhutto's, does not have a broad horizon.

When Bhutto emerged, the question of socialism and redistributive justice was firmly on the agenda. Bhutto spoke in the language of socialism because the political atmosphere of the time required that of him. By contrast, Imran effaces questions of land reform and structural changes due in no small part to the kinds of politicians he now courts—feudals and capitalists. Without that politics, Khan can only offer moralism and proceduralism: Islam and the rule of law.

Imran Khan's moral orientation can yield trenchant critiques of sociopolitical issues, but it also walks him into a narrow politics that is often questionable in its particulars. Take, for example, his reply to my question about the Hudood Ordinance—a set of draconian laws enacted by Zia-ul-Haq that enforce severe punishments for extramarital sex, including rape: "Had it been debated properly by a proper Parliament rather than a dictator, using Islam, had that not been done, this would've been a well-framed law, but as it happened, this was not debated."

And this is what he said when I asked him about the so-called "blasphemy law," whose abuses had been widely chronicled even before Punjab governor Salmaan Taseer was murdered for opposing it: "Blasphemy is the same thing. You see blasphemy, as I told you, was a British-made law, and it was to create harmony in the society." Pakistan's current law bears little resemblance to that intention, but Imran Khan continued. "So what you've seen in Pakistan is a breakdown of rule of law. There is no law in Pakistan!" I pressed him, asking whether he really thought the problem was simply the way the laws were applied, rather than the laws themselves. "If you did not have a blasphemy law in Pakistan," he said, "you will have bloodshed in villages and communities because when someone will say someone has said this about the Prophet, then you will see fanatics going and killing people." But that's happening right now, I insisted. "No," he countered. "What happens now is that they hand them over to the law. At least these people then have a law to protect them. You would have lynching crowds otherwise."

So, I asked him, would you say the law right now is fine?

"No, the law—if it is implemented properly—it gives plenty of time for someone. Only a mad person can abuse the Prophet. Only a mad person can do it. And so they will get a reprieve by the court anyway. It's implementation," he continued. "It is a law that is open to abuse like every other law. So, in my opinion the law you need to pass is for perjury, false witnesses, because there is no law against that. A false witness can get away. So if you had a law against false witnesses, which is perjury, then you would immediately see these cases decreasing because people who wrongfully accuse would be going to jail."

Arguments like these demonstrate why Khan has become a target for many urban, secular liberals, even though he has sometimes—as was the case after Salmaan Taseer's murder—demonstrated more willingness than ostensibly secular politicians to condemn religious extremism.

WHEN I WENT TO SEE MARVI SIRMED, one of Khan's most unyielding liberal critics and the author of more than a few acerbic columns about him, she described the beginnings of her suspicions about Imran Khan, dating back to the moment of his political reinvention. "I used to respect him for living the life he wants for himself and for living it openly," she said, referring to his younger days, when he was often linked romantically with various London socialites. Though he was a fixture on the social circuit, Khan claims he never smoke or drank; he did, however, father a child out of wedlock with the daughter of a wealthy British industrialist. (Khan only acknowledged his daughter after the mother won a paternity suit in 1997.) "He did not used to be secretive about these"—Sirmed paused, hunting for the right word—"these scars. They're considered scars in our society. I respected him for that. But, when he comes into politics, he just forgets everything. His life starts from the 1990s, when he started advocating *jirgas* and these Islamic Republic of Pakistan type of things."

Sirmed and I spoke in her capacious office in a manicured Islamabad suburb at the UNDP's Programme for Parliamentary Development.

She also moonlights as a columnist in the English language dailies and appears sporadically on Urdu talk-shows to go toe-to-toe with right-wing televangelists like Zaid Hamid. She's blunt and gutsy. Before we began talking, she made a point of noting that her comments were not a reflection of the UNDP. For Sirmed and many others, it is in part—though not exclusively—Khan's turn away from his socially liberal lifestyle that makes him worthy of suspicion. Perusing through the enormous quantity of biting opinion columns, blogs, and tweets produced by this particular demographic, one can distinctly sense a bitter hot anger, born of a sense of betrayal. The tone of these pieces tends to be more than merely critical; it is often emotionally wrought. The subject of these articles is varied—Imran's brand of politics, his stance on the drones, his alleged anti-Americanism—but at the core of these essays beats the pulse of the same question: et tu Brutus?

What seems to motivate this sense of betrayal is a phenomenon whose scope extends far beyond Pakistan: a kind of lifestyle politics that has taken hold among sections of the elite in almost every part of the world. This is a political worldview that eschews matters of class and economic justice in favor of a politics of individual expression: the right to eat, drink, dress, or socialize according to an ethics of one's choosing. In Pakistan, while lower-middle class urban women have been able to move into the public in greater numbers, aided in part by the hijab, the space for social liberals to express their lifestyles has shrunk. Many liberals ignore the first half of this equation, and blame the second half on the rise of a constellation of disparate phenomena associated with religion—from the rise in public religiosity to Islamist militancy— which are then all lumped under the opaque banner of "Talibanization."

This specter of creeping Talibanization, according to Sirmed, is what makes Imran Khan "dangerous." "He's a face who could give voice to the youth, which is huge in Pakistan," she said. "It's a huge segment, and he's actually radicalizing the youth, God forbid they become recruits for jihadi organizations." Those young people, Sirmed continued, will become frustrated when they are unable to find jobs due to a tanking economy. "When this happens, and they are in the lap of Imran Khan, and he's telling them that those sitting in North Waziristan are our friends actually. They're just playing with us and killing us because we are fighting with them. He is actually pushing this very dangerous idea that it's America that's the root problem."

When I put this argument to Imran Khan, he looked irritated. "Marvi, this woman," he began, pointedly, "she has no understanding about what's happening in Pakistan. These people, all their assessments are from reading articles, and these articles are written by journalists who don't know what is going on. These people seem to think there's some chance of 'Talibanization' in Pakistan. They don't know Pakistan." He cocked his head sideways and emphatically gestured with his hands out, fingers splayed as though he were carrying a large, invisible box.

"These militant groups were created to fight America's war. I mean, it was basically a cold war we got into for dollars, and these jihadi groups were not a threat to Pakistan. These groups were used by the intelligence agencies as assets and they did these sectarian bombings at mosques. That was child's play to what's going on now! Pakistan is fighting for its existence!" Imran had hit his stride now, and his words were flecked with exasperated notes while his booming voice rose in pitch. In his telling, the rise of bomb blasts and suicide attacks inside Pakistan was a direct consequence of the country's involvement in the American "war on terror." His frustration continued to mount. "So what is she talking about? I mean, which world is she living in! These people should not even be allowed to write because these people are not equipped to understand what's happening in Pakistan." He paused, and after a few moments I began to ask my next question, but he jumped back in before I got very far, thrusting forward to the next point in his argument. "There were no militant Taliban in Pakistan until 2006," he said. "It took two years of military operations to create the Taliban."

For Imran, the situation in Pakistan's tribal areas essentially resembles a rebellion against colonial occupation. "The same people fought the British," he said, "and won. They were all called 'fanatics' by the British." The Federally Administered Tribal Areas (FATA), the semiautonomous tribal region in Pakistan's northwest, does have a long history of occupation and resistance. In fact, the British also subjected FATA to sustained bombing campaigns starting in 1919 in a failed attempt to subdue the local populace. Sirmed, however, rejected that characterization. "Imran Khan's view that there are no Taliban and that these are indigenous groups is simply"—she stopped, almost at a loss for words. "I cannot even call it moronic because even morons have some sense. This is completely insane."

Khan has long been adamant that the Pashtuns are now being demonized simply for resisting, but in our interview he also drew a more contemporary parallel, to the plight of Bengalis in the former East Pakistan. He recalled that he had been on the last flight out of Dhaka before the Pakistani army's assault began: then only 18, he had gone there to play a cricket match. Until he visited, he told me, he had believed the Pakistani state propaganda of the time—which painted the rebellion as the work of a few Indian-backed militants. "That was the first time I realized that there was a separatist movement going on," he said. "We knew nothing about what was going on in East Pakistan."

"There was the same sort of demonization of Bengalis which I still remember," he continued. "These ears heard people saying, 'Small and dark. Kill them. Teach them a lesson.' I heard it with my own ears. It's exactly the same language which I hear this time." Today, it is Pashtuns, he said, who are ill-treated. "In Pindi, in Lahore, in Karachi, they've been picked up and thrown into jail because they are Pashtun. This is a sad legacy." For Imran, the events of 1971 provided another lesson about the rule of law. "Had people been punished, we would not be going through this again."

A few implications follow naturally from Imran Khan's account of the FATA conflict: he maintains there can be no military solution, and he supports the creation of a truth and reconciliation commission for the people of FATA—the sort of stances that earned him the nickname "Taliban Khan" among hardline secularists who claim that he supports the Taliban outright. He has also argued on occasion for negotiations with militant fighters. For many, his position seems like a facile response to a situation that calls for more nuance. After all, negotiation with fighters isn't entirely new: the Pakistan army has tried it repeatedly. In April 2004, it signed the Shakai Agreement with Waziristan militant leader Nek Muhammad Wazir, but that broke down almost immediately when the parties disagreed on the meaning of the terms. In February 2005, the army again signed the Sararogha peace accord, this time with Baitullah

Mehsud, followed by another agreement in 2006. Yet, at each turn, the conflict ballooned and by late 2007, local fighters had formed the Tehrik-i-Taliban Pakistan (TTP). Even as recently as last month [December 2011], the Haqqani network's ally, Hafiz Gul Bahadur, threatened to abandon his truce with the army.

While peace deals, ceasefires, and temporary truces have done little to improve the situation, neither have the ruthless military incursions by an army whose ostensible responsibility is the protection of its own citizens. In response to army attacks in 2004 that killed scores, some tribes turned to local rebels for help and formed strategic alliances with them. "The actual hardcore terrorists that we need to deal with are basically five to six percent of this whole," Imran said. But Khan's version of the tribal conflict also involves rhetorically minimizing the army's continued support for elements of the militancy—and embracing a narrative in which the U.S. is the sole culprit. "What is the difference between what is happening in FATA and what is happening in Afghanistan? Hamid Karzai is calling, today, the Americans an occupation force. An American puppet is calling the Americans an occupation force!" Imran exclaimed. "And what is happening in FATA? Our army is acting as an occupation force. They went in on the behest of the Americans. I mean they get monthly salaries from the Americans."

This is as close as Imran Khan comes to criticizing the Pakistani establishment, that opaque and unaccountable nexus between the military and the Inter-Services Intelligence (ISI), which remains the ultimate arbiter of Pakistani politics. Imran's reticence on this front represents yet another bright red flag for his critics: a few insist that he and his party are secretly funded by the establishment; others simply contend that his political career has been propped up by the forces running the country, whether Khan knows it or not. Certainly, Imran Khan has been uncomfortably close to various military figures. General Zia called him out of his retirement from cricket. It was General Hamid Gul, the former ISI chief often dubbed the "father of the Taliban," and Mohammad Ali Durrani, then the head of the Jamaat-e-Islami youth wing, who encouraged Khan to enter politics and assisted him. When General Pervez Musharraf took power in a coup, Imran Khan supported him—although many of Imran Khan's critics did so as well. And when the U.S. launched a raid to assassinate Osama bin Laden, Imran Khan blasted the civilian government and demanded Zardari's resignation—rather than asking what might seem a more pertinent question, about how Bin Laden managed to take refuge in an army garrison town to begin with.

Among Khan's urban and middle-class base—historically, the recruiting ground for the army's officer cadre—his proximity, real or alleged, to powerful military figures is hardly cause for concern. Imbued with a strong nationalist sentiment, this class opposes the army's involvement in the American-led war, particularly inside Pakistan's own territory. Pakistani secular liberals, meanwhile, motivated by the fear of what they call "Talibanization," criticize the army's engagement with militants but support its collaboration with the Americans. Thus, secular liberals as well as Khan and his supporters are unable to break fully with the army's considerable ideological and institutional authority. They may not even want to. And those conditions will permeate Khan's populism.

FOR THE BETTER PART OF 2011, Imran Khan was touring Pakistan—darting into Peshawar, Faisalabad, Karachi, Gujranwala, and Islamabad to mine the country's discontent and breathe scorn on his political rivals. In Peshawar, he told the political workers of opposition parties they should either straighten out their leaders or correct themselves and join his party. In Karachi, he has fought with the Muttahida Qaumi Movement (MQM), which owns that city. In Islamabad, he wryly noted that the PML-N was worried about the gains his party was making, and then told PML-N workers they had more to fear from Nawaz Sharif's corruption than from the PTI.

The dharnas—for dharnas they were supposed to be, though as far as I know, the only that could properly be called that was the one in Peshawar—had an air of jubilant male revelry. True, there were women there, girls even, and a sizable portion too, but they remained wherever they had been cornered. The boys, however—they roamed. They made jokes. They exchanged verbal spars. They slapped each other's backs. They sang to the music bubbling up into the evening from oversized speakers set on either side of the stage. And when they were not singing, they bloated the air with the bombastic notes of young boys engaged in all the bluster and the swagger that is the pageantry of boyhood.

These rallies were not exercises in cultish discipline, as one sees with the MQM; they did not have the tired, stale stench of PPP demonstrations, which invariably dissolve, by the end of the night, into squabbles between party members over swag. And you were less likely to run across the paid-for dazed protestors who are ubiquitous at gatherings of every other major political party. PTI rallies feel more like a disorganized all-night bash, the kind where your favorite rock star might pop in and where the guest of honor, Imran, can show up fashionably late and deliver an hour-long toast. Shehzad Roy showed up at one. Ali Azmat sang at another. For the critical rally at Minar-e-Pakistan in Lahore, the locally famous DJ Butt came to spin and the band Strings performed.

"It was a lot of fun! We ran into families. With kids!" exclaimed Sheikh Muhammad Ahmad, a young Lahore University of Management Sciences (LUMS) IT graduate. "That doesn't happen a lot at political rallies. I even saw aunties. That's a strange sight." The PML-N attempted to constrict the demonstration, blocking off major roads, but droves of people simply came on foot instead. Ahmad doesn't support Imran Khan—he wants a candidate who supports separation of religion and state—but he said he understood why others did. "He's become a beacon of hope for a lot of people." Not too long ago, supporting Imran's party was considered a vaguely embarrassing condition symptomatic of hopeless idealism and naïveté. It was uncool. "Now, he's in fashion," Ahmad said. "He's the new stereotype candidate for the educated. Being a PTI supporter now means being rational and being a good person."

Imran's anti-corruption message, coupled with a nationalist sensibility that takes the sovereignty of the country seriously, resonates deeply among his young, urban middle-class base: college students, young engineers, accountants, media and IT workers. Among them, there's definitely a sense that Imran is the last man standing. "He's the only one who can give us justice," a college student told me as his friends milled around him at a PTI rally. "Without him, the country is useless. No one can save the country except him. The others come and fill their own stomachs. There's just one leader, Imran Khan, who can save the country."

"We're the only party that is now going to take Pakistan out of this, clear the mess that Pakistan is in," Imran Khan said when I asked him why he believed the PTI would fare better in office than its rivals. "There's no other party that can get Pakistan out of the mess," he argued, because it is the only one that isn't corrupt. "All the major political party heads have their money stashed abroad, in bank accounts which aren't declared, their properties abroad. They're in no position to fight corruption, and none of them give taxes so, therefore, the need of the hour is to have clean politics in Pakistan and raise revenue and fight corruption." This was the very same message that Imran delivered to packed press conferences in Lahore when he launched the party in 1996: "Today marks the beginning of a battle against corruption and injustice." He lashed out at government corruption to immediate effect: newspapers quickly followed suit with extensive reporting of government greed, from land-grabbing politicians to the exorbitant perks that parliamentarians were given.

It was a platform that initially attracted urban professionals like Nasim Zehra, now a respected Urdu prime-time anchor. The world-renowned environmental lawyer, Parvez Hassan, who has an entire wing at Punjab University named after him, also joined the party, as did Abdul Mateen, vice chancellor of Peshawar University. But, back then, the party wasn't garnering votes. By 1999, PTI had made little headway and Imran Khan, like a significant segment of Pakistanis, supported General Pervez Musharraf's coup.

In key respects, Imran Khan's message remains the same—for better and for worse. "He's only talking about corruption in politics. He's not talking about corruption per se," observed Muhammad Waseem, a political science professor at LUMS and the author of several books on electoral reform and democratization in Pakistan. "For example, he's not talking about the one million people who are agents of the state, top bureaucracy down to clerks." Nor is he talking about the army. Under civilian government in the 1990s, a public accounting committee was set up to inquire into army accounts. It found that roughly thirty-one billion rupees had been mislaid: some of it was simply unaccounted for while other money had been spent beyond the legal limit. "One doesn't even talk about it," Waseem said, because the army is considered "something sacred."

Nevertheless, Imran's anti-corruption rhetoric is attracting supporters—people like Zain ul Abedin, who works at an American communications company in Islamabad, and whose family switched over to the PTI after serving in the ranks of the PPP as politicians and bureaucrats for decades. Abedin said that his family had left the PPP after an incident at his former workplace, another telecommunications company. A high-ranking PPP official called Abedin demanding to have his phone number—which had been blocked for nonpayment—reinstated. After Abedin refused, the official began to abuse him, and when Abedin ended their phone call, it cost him his job. "Then the very next day, I gathered up all the documents, I went to Bilawal House," Abedin explained, referring to Benazir Bhutto's former residence in Karachi. He had hoped, considering his family's history with the party, that the PPP might help him find another job. "I said I have a masters and four to five years experience with a multinational. Even in the government, give me an 18 or 20 grade job, any small thing. That guy threw my file and said lots of people like you come here."

Abedin is in some respects the quintessential PTI supporter, angered by corruption and yet simultaneously willing to deploy his family and party connections to secure a job. Indeed, for the middle class, this is how the system works. "In Pakistan's case—and of course in India—it's the middle class which talks about corruption more than other classes," Muhammad Waseem said. But the majority of this class doesn't vote, he continued, "especially middle class women. You'll never see them making queues outside the polling stations. The middle class gets its interests articulated through other means, for example, through the bureaucracy, through the army, through those who are very well represented in the power structure." Its interests belong, in other words, outside the domain of electoral politics.

Imran Khan distinguishes the PTI from other parties by the caliber of its candidates. "Look at these people," he says, referring to his rivals. "They are all professional politicians." That's code for corrupt.

"Look down the line, and you will see that they've all minted money after entering politics and holding power. Most of the politicians are nothing without power." There's more than a touch of elitism to what comes next: "In Tehrik-i-Insaaf, all the top leadership have made their names outside. They don't need politics." This is Imran Khan's vision of politics: an elite, educated vanguard to lead Pakistan.

But many of the luminaries from his early days, like Nasim Zehra and Dr. Parvez Hassan, have since left the party. In their place are people like Shireen Mazari, a political scientist and newspaper editor best known for her unsubstantiated public attacks on foreign journalists. The influx of politicians to the PTI has swelled the party's ranks and included a few high-profile public figures: the former foreign minister of Pakistan, Shah Mahmood Qureshi; the renowned squash player Qamar Zaman; Walid Iqbal, the poet's grandson; and Saleem Jan Khan, whose grandfather was the famous resistance leader Abdul Ghaffar Khan.

But the bulk of the people now entering Imran's party are career politicians, a far cry from the urban professionals he has so long touted as his strength. To use Khan's terms, these are exactly the sort of people who need politics: second and third-generation politicians carrying on the family business, or careerists and opportunists who flit from party to party seeking advancement, and who seem to regard the PTI as a strategic opportunity to revitalize their flagging political fortunes.

A new recruit, Khwaja Khan Hoti, for example, is a career politician from KPK who served terms as federal minister and provincial minister with the PPP; at other times in his career, he served in senior position within the ranks of the secular, Pashtun Awami National Party (ANP). As with so many others, politics is a family business for the Hotis: Hoti's son, Omar Farooq, preceded his father's entry into the PTI. The younger Hoti is expected to get the ticket from Mardan.

Another politician whose addition to PTI has caused a stir is Sardar Faiz Tamman, from Punjab. Tamman, a careerist who appears to care for little else than ascending the political ladder, has drifted from one party to another throughout his time in politics. He shifted from the PPP to join a PPP split group, the PPP-Patriot, earlier in his career, but was elected to the National Assembly in 2002 as an Independent. Then, he was admitted to Musharraf's PML-Q but resigned in 2008, later joining the PML-N. In 2010, Tamman had to resign from his seat when it turned out that he had faked his college degrees.

Mian Mohammad Azhar, who has been active in Lahore's politics for nearly three decades, is yet another dubious figure. During Zia ul-Haq's era, Mian Azhar served as mayor of Lahore under Nawaz Sharif's governorship. In 1988, after Zia—quite literally—exploded, Azhar's closeness to the Sharifs earned him a ticket from Gujranwala in Punjab, and by 1990, he had become governor of the province. He left the office in 1992 reportedly over differences with the Sharifs. He was back by 1997, this time as an elected member of the National Assembly. He moved on from the PML-N, however, going on to become head of Musharraf's PML-Q. He has the dubious recognition of being a politician who lost his seat in the 2002 elections, even though it's widely alleged that there was massive rigging electorally that year in favor of the PML-Q. Clearly as with Tamman, Mian Azhar, too, views the PTI strategically as a chance to revitalize his political fortunes.

The most significant addition to date is Shah Mahmood Qureshi, the former foreign minister of Pakistan who lost his post during the current PPP-led government after taking a stand on the Raymond Davis affair. Qureshi maintained that Davis's documents did not show that the contractor who murdered two people in the streets of Lahore—a third was also killed after he was mowed down by a consular vehicle rushing to Davis's rescue—held any diplomatic immunity. After being courted by the PTI as well as the PML-N, Qureshi joined Imran's party in late November. He received the position of Senior Vice Chairman within the party.

Whatever the intentions of the leadership, the changes are causing unease within the party. Qureshi's immediate ascension to senior ranks, for instance, created murmurs of dissension within PTI's ranks among longtime loyal members who felt shafted. According to a local analyst in Swat, PTI's members are deeply unhappy with the new additions. A columnist for the Urdu daily *Aaj* reported that PTI's chairman for the party's local district coordination council, Fazal Rabbi, had suspended the local cabinet in early December saying that the party's leadership was responsible for creating discord in the ranks.

Dr. Mazari, too, is now considering quitting the party. She's reportedly upset that Imran may be softening his stance on drones and the

United States. The influx of new politicians who have checkered political careers may be another reason. A press release by the party denied the reports, maintaining that PTI's position on drones and the "war on terror" remains the same. The press release also said that PTI's central committee will vet applicants for election tickets to protect the party from "the opportunist remnants of the Musharraf era and Zardari regime now scrambling to enter the PTI fold." (Interestingly, that entire phrase was left out of the Urdu version of the release.) The swelling crowds at party rallies and the growing volume of politicians switching sides to join the PTI have contributed to the widespread perception that Imran is experiencing a sudden and meteoric political ascent, no matter what happens in the next elections. Many commentators, in fact, have begun to sketch comparisons to the mass movement that accompanied Zulfikar Ali Bhutto's rise to power. But the gap between this moment and that one is far more revealing than any similarities: Bhutto rode the tide of a broad outrage at the dictatorships of Ayub Khan and Yahya Khan, which crossed demographic lines and stood in opposition to the bureaucracy, the army, the Islamist parties, and even feudal landlords. And because of that, whether he liked it or not, Bhutto was forced to nod toward radical politics even if he failed to realize them.

For reasons that are both complex and unrelated to any comparison between Imran and Bhutto, it seems impossible to imagine a similarly broad movement today, one that could unite broad segments of Pakistani society behind an agenda of social and economic justice. The political worldview of the middle and upper classes—whether it's the politics of personal expression and individual rights, moral outrage against corruption, or the outspoken embrace of tradition and piety—has almost no point of overlap with the needs and desires of millions of Pakistanis who are too poor to exercise meaningful choice in such matters. Against this backdrop, the measure of Khan's significance looks to be less about what he does—in terms of attracting supporters and votes—and more about what his exploding popularity says about those who flock to him.

AT THE LAST PTI RALLY I attended—a big rally in Islamabad on Pakistan's Independence Day that was likely the largest PTI event prior to the October rally in Lahore—an enormous shipping container served as the stage, and I had managed to secure a spot standing at the back of this improvised dais, with Khan seated almost directly in front of me, right next to Hamid Gul. The party had granted me permission to watch from the stage, but it wasn't easy to make my way past the sweaty young men crammed on the steel stairs, wrestling with the security staff so they could be closer to their idol.

After I had made it onto the stage, a young man broke free from the stairs and lunged toward Imran. A stocky PTI guard yanked him back by his shirt, shouting "Khuda ki kasam!" and struggling to restrain the man who was flushed, shaking his head, almost senseless. "Is this how you show your love for Khan! You're wrecking it!" More security quickly appeared and pushed him back down the stairs into the heaving mass.

When I saw Khan later, he said he was surprised to learn I had managed to make it onstage. As far as I could remember, he hadn't actually turned around to look at the crush of people clamoring to get up the staircase and be near him—but he knew. He basked in their fervor—*junoon,* even—and in return, he mirrored back to them their best idea of themselves.

He can do that for many people.

The last time I saw Khan was in the autumn of 2011 in New York. He'd been invited, for the third time, to deliver a talk at Columbia University. Dressed in a dark suit, Khan appeared to be in his natural métier, responding to questions and effusive comments from a mostly expatriate South Asian audience, many of whom appeared to be Indian. In response to a question about whether he would uphold Pakistan as a secular state, Imran Khan responded bluntly. "I've been all over Pakistan," he said. "Never have I ever heard this from the ordinary Pakistani, about Pakistan being secular or Islamist." Certainly, there's some truth here: most Pakistanis, consumed by their daily lives, are much more concerned about rolling blackouts and the price of sugar. Khan continued: "This has never been the issue from the common people. They want rule of law. They want education. I have only heard this at dinner table conversations in Islamabad." The audience clapped wildly even before he was fully finished speaking.

Khan offered more. "Religion is—if it is a true religion—it should make you compassionate. All religion makes you compassionate."

"This is a theme that runs in every religion, so when Iqbal talked about religion or Jinnah talked about religion or Gandhi talked about religion, they meant the compassion that comes with religion as opposed to materialism, because what is a threat to humankind does not come from religion. It comes from naked materialism. It comes from greed, getting richer and richer and plundering other people's resources." Having delinked religion from violence, he went on to question secular violence. "Just because people kill in name of religion doesn't mean anything is wrong with religion. People are killing in the name of communism, democracy, freedom." The audience was quiet. "The whole of colonialism was in the name of educating the native—you know, the white man's burden."

This is Imran Khan at his strongest: delivering a trenchant critique of the often self-satisfied assumptions that underpin secular liberalism. Even as he fails to use that critique to articulate a broad politics, the force of his argument is not lost on significant segments of the diaspora—particularly Muslims—who have become attuned to the realities of lingering racism in a country where right-wing groups are still holding public rallies to condemn the construction of new mosques. For other Pakistanis, who have become accustomed to being embarrassed by the tragicomic coterie of politicians who currently rule Pakistan, Khan offers a welcome respite: urbane, charming, an Oxford-educated icon. For others still—particularly Indians who see Pakistan as a tinderbox of religious fanaticism on the brink of exploding into flames (a vision they share with secularist elites inside Pakistan)—Imran may appear to be the kind of conservative yet reasonable politician with whom dialogue is possible. Everyone dreams of Imran in her own way.

Even Marvi Sirmed, it turns out. I asked her what she thought of him when she was growing up. "I wanted to marry him," she laughed. "He had won a game, and we were in Qaddafi Stadium, and I was with my parents, and people were garlanding him. He was looking cute, and the media had projected him as a big-time hero. We all wanted to marry him, actually."

Feminism and "Fundamentalism" in Pakistan

AMINA JAMAL

IN PAKISTAN, the "Islamic" movements seem to be more successful in mobilizing women of different classes than the mainstream women's movement ever was.[1] These Islamic movements have enabled modest but noteworthy social transformations. For example, women of the middle and lower middle classes are becoming visible as factory workers, shop clerks, immigration officers, television program presenters, municipal representatives, and so on, while many elite women have become evidently conscious of their Muslim identity. This concerns Pakistani feminists.

Some Pakistani feminist scholars advocate a reassertion of the strict separation of religion and politics in public life (Zia 2009). Others want to counter religious conservatism with liberal readings of Islamic scripture and traditions (Shaheed 1998). Despite the differences, these two positions attribute the success of religiously driven women's activism to their effective manipulation of religious symbols. Based on a study of the Jamaat-e-Islami (founded in 1941), it seems that the religiously driven women's movement claims not only religious authority but is also able to pragmatically harness the benefits of modern life to the needs of lower middle class women. Jamaat women challenge the ability of the feminist women's movement to define Muslim women's social and economic priorities; on the other hand, they offer an alternative vision of women's personal rights and economic survival through Islamic NGOs, advocacy and support groups, and informal education and awareness raising efforts. A "feminism-versus-fundamentalism" framework fails to understand the social basis of these women's actions. It is certainly true that there is much to critique in their ideology (the rejection of women's leadership, their exclusion of religious minorities from full citizenship, the rejection of queer sexuality). However, an effective counterstrategy demands a full engagement with the lives of these women.

Jamaat Women in the Feminist Imaginary

A women's rights constituency emerged within the Pakistani upper middle class and elite from the 1960s fights around the Muslim Family Laws. They consolidated in the struggles against the Hudood Ordinances of the 1980s and the attempt to ratify the Convention on the Elimination of All Forms of Discrimination Against Women (CEDAW) in the 1990s. This bloc has had a significant role in contemporary Pakistan, where it continues in the ongoing struggles for women's human rights.

During the past few decades, a fracture has emerged in this bloc, as many women have been drawn to those women's movements that are dedicated to transforming Muslim women through ideological and behavioral changes in Muslim women's lives (Ahmad 2008, Mahmood 2005, Gole 1996, Deeb 2006). Saba Mahmood (2005) calls these movements for "piety," and Sadaf Ahmad (2008) shows that the most prominent of these groups is Al Huda, a serious contender for the loyalties of middle class and elite women in Pakistan. The new scholarship on these cultural and piety groups demonstrates the Muslim feminists' concern for the loss of their traditional constituency of middle and elite women, who were historically considered to be the main subjects and agents of projects for women's rights and feminism (Mushtaq 2008, Ahmad 2008, Mumtaz 1994).

Women of the middle class, lower middle class, and working class have traditionally been seen as the beneficiaries of, rather than participants in, such movements. Women from non-elite classes are involved in a different kind of politics at the local, provincial, and national levels. They are culturally active in the newly emerging gendered civil society comprised of NGOs and women's advocacy and support groups. Women of the Jamaat occupy this new arena, straddling formal politics and individual piety. It is also from this space that these women seek to challenge the claims of the mainstream women's movement in the formal arena of national politics and women's cultural identity.

In 2001, President Pervez Musharraf's military government, seeking international favor, reserved 33 percent of seats in national assembly and 50 percent in the municipal councils for women. This act induced the Jamaat-e-Islami and other religious parties to set aside their long-standing reservation to women's participation in public politics and to nominate women for electoral positions. A significant number of burqa-clad women as representatives of the Muttahida Majlis-e Amal (a coalition that included the Jamaat) entered municipal, provincial, and national assemblies and senate through the 2000–02 elections. These women, who were mostly elected to seats reserved for women as part of Pakistan's CEDAW obligations, have become vociferous critics and interlocutors of feminist activists in political bodies, civil society forums, and national mass media.

Assuming responsibilities as city councilors and parliamentarians, these women actively participated in political training, capacity building, and other programs to boost women's political participation that were conducted by government and nongovernment bodies, often with funding from international and national donor agencies (as told to me by a Jamaat city councilor in Karachi, Musfira Jamal). The significant position of women in politico-religious parties and in national politics was also recognized by the proliferating independent television channels that followed the deregulation of media as part of the government's compliance with international globalization imperatives. Independent television in Pakistan has become an important forum for burqa-clad Islamist women to publicly challenge unveiled feminists and to render normal discussions about religion, politics, and gender within the very minutiae of daily life. Although the religious parties including the Jamaat-e-Islami suffered a crushing defeat in the 2008 general elections in Pakistan, Jamaat women continue to remain publicly active as political and civil society actors and as media personalities.

Since the decision to support female candidates in formal politics at the local and national levels overturns a long-standing principle of the Jamaat-e-Islami, it is instructive to recall the history of the movement to understand the import of this change.

Jamaat-e-Islami

Maulana Au Ala Maududi founded the Jamaat in British India not to reject colonial culture but to bring Islam into a new relationship with colonial (European) modernity. No longer is it useful to see the Jamaat as a party of religious traditionalists opposed to secular modernizers (Smith 1957, Nasr 1994, Voll 1994). Maududi was not concerned about Muslims' adoption of modernity. Rather he encouraged them to abandon traditional knowledge of the ulema and Islamic scholars and adopt modern and rational modes of thinking, including scientific knowledge. Indeed, Maududi sought to reframe Islam in South Asia from its emphasis on faith and belief into a system of practices that linked religious energy to Muslim politics. This process has been described as a deviation from traditional Islam and especially from the devotional forms of Islamic thought that have flourished in South Asia from at least the 13th century (Nasr 1994 and 1996, Robinson 2000). "Muslim," for Islamist modernists like Maududi, was not simply a religious and moral category but also a social and political one.

With the end of British rule in 1947 and the partition of India into two states, Maududi took his struggle for an Islamic state to Pakistan, where he confronted the secular modernizing elites who had inherited political, social, and economic power from the British. However, despite its ideological influence, the Jamaat's incursion into formal politics remained minimal until it was enabled to penetrate key institutions of government during the military regime of General Zia ul Haq from 1977–1989. This period also coincided with the escalation in the cold war between the Soviet Union and the United States. A crucial event was the Afghan war during the late 1970s and 1980s and the enlistment of General Zia's military government as the frontline ally of the United States in its support for the Afghan forces fighting Soviet troops. The politico-religious parties such as Jamaat-e-Islami were key players in providing ideological support for government policy by legitimizing the Soviet–Afghan war as a jihad. Their position was boosted in multiple ways by massive funding from the United States and Saudi Arabia, which was dedicated to developing Islam as an ideological bulwark against communism (Rashid 2001).

We now know quite a bit about the insidious effects of such "Islamization" in Pakistani society, especially the production of an intolerant social climate in which questions of what is deemed to be Islamic and un-Islamic have started affecting the lives of ordinary Pakistanis more than ever before (Zafar 1991, Shaheed and Mumtaz 1992, Shakir 1997, Weiss 1986). Islamization did not have a singular impression on the Pakistan citizen. It is a gendered discourse of citizenship that facilitated the emergence of a particular type of society in a manner that institutionalized the existing inequalities of gender, class, and religion.

Central to Islamization was the formation of the idea of the modern Muslim woman. Even as women's legal and social status was systematically reduced and moral regulation of women and girls intensified, this was achieved through new ideas about the middle class Muslim family, which resonated with many men and women of the rising sections of the middle class. It is General Zia's blend of Islam and modernity that appears to resonate with the experiences of the present Jamaat-e-Islami women activists in Karachi and Lahore. They invoke and rework their ideological reliance on founding texts such as the writings of Maulana Maududi and his well-known disciple Maryam Jameelah. Indeed General Zia's socioeconomic and cultural policies may be considered a key moment in shaping the subjectivities of middle class women in Pakistan. Women supporters and members of the Jamaat-e-Islami were enlisted in promoting the image of chaddar-clad women in Pakistan's public spaces, and some occupied positions in Zia's nominated parliament, the Majlis-e-Shoora (Shaukat Ali 1997). Thus the appropriation of the modern universal public sphere as the necessary condition for securing the Islamization project has expedited, and been hastened by, the engendering of Islamist politics in Pakistan.

While it would be presumptuous to offer a causal relationship between General Zia's policies and the changed positioning of women within the politico-religious movement, these conditions certainly overlap and coincide for the Jamaat-e-Islami. Women, family, and gender relations have always figured as key concerns for the leaders and thinkers of the Jamaat-e-Islami. Maududi advocated not only veiling but also the seclusion and sequestering of Muslim women as part of his strategy to prevent the encroachment of both Western modernist ideas and Indian (Hindu and Muslim) nationalist projects into the cultural or so-called private spaces of Muslim society (Maududi 1939). Indeed for Maududi purdah, comprising veiling and sequestering of women, was the pillar on which rested the entire "superstructure of the social system of Islam" (218). This did not exclude women from the party since the Jamaat-e-Islami, even in its founding days, had women supporters; however, even when the party established a women's wing and an affiliated women students' party, it was clear that these women's groups were not to represent the party in formal political arenas. Thus a strict division of a primary/public male and a supplementary/private female political arena was maintained until the late 1990s.

Over the years the movement has changed its strictly religious reformist identity and transformed into a political party (Nasr 1994, Grare 2001). It abandoned its initial reluctance to engage in mainstream nationalist politics and embraced the compromises necessarily entailed by electoral politics. Therefore according to Nasr, "ideological zeal gave way to greater pragmatism and transformed the movement from holy community to political party" (Nasr 1994, Grare 2001). In this process membership in the party also altered such that political activism for both men and women is now not seen as additional to but as necessary to Islamic identity in the contemporary era. Thus the role of women within the party has developed from an emphasis on philanthropic, educational, and political activism in the private sphere to more public and political activism. This distinguishes Jamaat women's activism from women in many other Islamist movements. In contrast to women of the so-called "piety movements," Jamaat women are not simply interested in the cultivation of a moral self that emphasizes self-transcendence instead of self-fulfillment (Mahmood 2005). Nor are they akin to those groups of women in Iran that have been termed "Islamic Feminists," since Jamaat women do not engage in scriptural and textual reinterpretation in a feminist mode.[2] Jamaat women explicitly and unmistakably declare the political-as-public/communal, and not simply the personal/private, as the focus of their struggle.[3] They frame their project as the complete transformation of social relations and it is this focus on rights, selfhood, and autonomy that positions them against projects of feminism in Pakistan.

The public political participation of Jamaat women, however, has not led them to abandon their cultural project of Islamic revival and transformation of Muslim women's identity. On the contrary there is an enhanced awareness within the main movement of the important cultural–political role of women, and this is reflected in a proliferation of women's groups affiliated with the Jamaat. Women members of the party and others related to the Jamaat-e-Islami have formed numerous "nonpolitical" groups in Pakistan's urban centers offering education in the Quran and Sunnah, providing counseling and support for female victims of violence, developing working women's rights, and organizing literacy classes, legal aid, and support for marriage expenses. Among the most notable of these is the recent establishment of the Women's Commission, a nationwide advocacy and policy group dedicated to socio-economic, political, and cultural issues affecting women. This group has started social research in some of the same areas pinpointed by feminist NGOs—violence, employment, education, reproductive rights, and health—using similar social sciences methodologies. It has generated a substantial literature on women's rights and status from an "Islamic" perspective to counter the representational claims of feminist groups.

The purportedly Islamic NGOs, like their mainstream counterparts, have developed from the institutionalization of women's activities that were previously informal, voluntary, and philanthropic. What distinguishes the contemporary Jamaat women's NGOs from their predecessors in the party is a new consciousness among Jamaat women of their own role as not only engaged in philanthropic activities but also geared toward the public interest and national development. Jamaat women's new self-awareness as agents of national social development is no doubt connected to, among other things, their identities as university-educated, professional, and publicly active women. For, as in many other territorially decolonized states, it is the women of the middle and lower middle classes who have gained most from the postcolonial state's modernization project of higher education in Pakistan (since many elite women were always able to access modern, Western education in their own societies but also through universities abroad). During the 1980s, the period of the U.S.–Soviet proxy war in Afghanistan, an influx of funding for infrastructure development enabled the development of universities and thus increased opportunities for record numbers of women and men from the middle classes in Pakistan's urban centers. Many Jamaat women related to me their experiences in state universities where they became acquainted with the female and male student affiliates of the party during the 1980s and 1990s.

Local, National, and Transnational Conditions

Both in the arenas of formal national and local politics and in the newly emerging "nonpolitical" space of the citizen sector, Jamaat women claim to enjoy a moral and cultural advantage over the feminist women's movement in Pakistan. They suggest that they are ideally situated as educated middle class professional women and believers to offer a "balanced" solution to what appears to be an underlying dilemma of gender and development in Pakistan, i.e., to build a modern nation without undermining the cultural/religious identity with which the majority of citizens are likely to identify. It is in response to this dilemma that Jamaat-e-Islami women appear to construct their project. They seek to distance themselves from both "extremist" forms of Islamic ideology (such as those preached by the Pakistani Taliban in some parts of the country), which would deny women access to education, health, and employment. But they also reject the feminist demands for women's rights and autonomy; they believe that this would expose Pakistani women to unrestrained modernizing processes and thus destroy "the Muslim family." The Jamaat women's argument is not simply a rhetorical strategy. It is also a mode of occupying a political cultural space that has been opened by a number of changes at the local, national, and international levels that are related to processes of capital globalization, economic neoliberalism, and transnational feminism.

Among the conditions that facilitated the emergence of Jamaat women as public actors was the cultural political space that opened in Pakistani society in the past three decades due to the development of the NGO movement and the mainstream feminist women's movement. While seemingly contradictory to Jamaat women's interests, these movements have over the past three decades substantially expanded and transformed the public space for discussions about women's rights and issues of gender. The gynocentric focus of the global women's movement and its impact on the policies of international organizations such as the United Nations and the World Bank came to the attention of the politico-religious parties following the emergence within Pakistani national politics of a vocal and activist lobby for women's rights and human rights that comprises feminist scholars and activists, women's rights groups, and NGOs. These groups first came into prominence during the 1980s due to their highly publicized opposition to the Hudood Ordinances, and since then have been attempting to renegotiate Muslim women's relationship to family, tribe, and nation-state with the help of the transnational human rights activism of the contemporary era (Jamal 2005). While the success of these forces in bringing about legal and social change has been limited, there is no doubt that they have opened up a space in national politics for discussions of women's rights and women's social-political status, thus presenting a challenge for parties such as the Jamaat-e-Islami.

Many Jamaat women reported that while their political and cultural project preceded the mainstream women's movement, it was the visibility of the latter that motivated them into developing new strategies for publicizing their mission to counter the activism of the feminist women's movement (Nisar 2003). Furthermore, the NGOization of women's work in Islamic groups such as the Jamaat may be tied to new global development discourses that since the 1970s and 1980s prioritize women as key actors in the development and nation-building process. The articulation of Women-in-Development (WID) programs financed mostly by international agencies and Western donors with the state project of Islamization in Pakistan has had contradictory results for women. For example, the state under General Zia deferred to international pressure by creating a Women's Division in the government in 1979 at almost the same moment as systematic measures were enacted to reduce women's social and legal status.

As with many other economically beleaguered countries, in the past three decades Pakistan has fully embraced the philosophies of global deregulation, economic liberalism, and denationalization promoted by international agencies and organizations. The incorporation of the Jamaat-e-Islami into mainstream politics coincided with the prioritizing of new development policies of the World Bank and international donors that deemphasized the state sector and began to channel grants and aid to economically vulnerable groups through nongovernmental organizations. This privatization of social and economic development appeals to ordinary citizens in Pakistan due to their long experience of poorly funded and corrupt public institutions (Hasan and Junejo 1999). As a result the number of NGOs in Pakistan increased from a few hundred in the 1970s to nearly 30,000 in 1999 (Hasan and Junejo 1999). Even though politico-religious parties such as the Jamaat-e-Islami are the most vociferous opponents of the NGOs committed to women's rights, they are not opposed to the self-help ideology of the NGO movement since it resonates well with their own projects of charity and religious education. Thus they have countered the mainstream NGOs movement with their own community-based groups aimed at improving education and health within an Islamic framework.

Returning the Feminist Gaze

The mainstream feminist women's movement criticizes Jamaat women for their acquiescence to male dominance, their opposition to women's full citizenship rights, and their dogmatic interpretations of Islamic scriptures. Jamaat women, in turn, consider the mainstream feminists to be members of the elite Westernized classes. Just as Pakistani feminists deride Jamaat women for conceding to the patriarchal agendas of mullas and male party leaders, Jamaat women challenge secular feminists to disavow their traditional cultural and class loyalties. For example, one important criticism of the mainstream women's movement is their unwavering support for national political parties that espoused modernist ideas even though these were parties led by traditional patriarchal and feudal groups. Jamaat women repeatedly argued that in its zeal to pursue modernist agendas and to circumvent the rise of religious parties, the women's movement was unwilling or unable to see the complicity of so-called secular political parties in sustaining oppressive class and gender structures. This was evident in my interview with Atiya Nisar, convenor of the Jamaat Women's Commission, an organization set up to focus on issues of women's rights. Nisar argued that the Jamaat was better poised to represent Pakistani women than the feminist women's movement and feminist NGOs because she suspected that the latter's commitment to women's rights was seriously compromised by their loyalties to those parties that were led by feudal elites. Nisar argued:

> Many of the women who are presenting themselves as champions of women's rights also support political parties that are associated with the feudal class and upper class. The truth is that many women's problems are due to the feudal system and it is this feudal system that you favour when you support the Pakistan People's Party or the Muslim League. (Nisar 2003)

Nisar also criticized Pakistani feminists for supporting female representatives of the feudal system such as Benazir Bhutto, arguing that the feudal system was oppressive to both women and men of working and peasant classes. She related her own experience of working with peasant women in Sind, who, when asked how they felt about being deprived of their rights as women, answered, "Get my husband his rights and I will get mine too" (Nisar 2003). Nisar went on:

> Now you tell me, her husband is beaten up everyday and he beats her when he comes home. However it is repeatedly declared [by feminists] that "the peasant woman is being beaten up" but there is no awareness of the oppression of the man who experiences the boot of the landlord on his back and who has to witness the defiling of his women everyday . . .

Nisar argued that when feminists focus on women's oppression they tend to "compartmentalize" women's experiences and thus fail to understand the issues of poor women. She added that she was not denying the oppression of women but points out that "all the problems must be considered together" (Nisar 2003). In her recommendations for women's economic rights, Nisar has suggested that not individual women but their families and the state should bear responsibility of provision for women and their children. Nisar argued that this was in line with the desires and needs of Pakistani women as reflected in a survey conducted by the Jamaat among women from different classes. Nisar said the Women's Commission was working not for women's economic independence but their economic protection or *kifalat*. In questioning feminist strategies for women's economic autonomy, Jamaat women situate Pakistani feminist leaders in a different social class and cultural location from themselves and the mass of Pakistani society, and therefore consider them incapable of seriously engaging with the problems of non-elite women in society. Nisar argued that due to their socioeconomic and cultural distance from the majority of women in Pakistan, feminists from Western-educated elite backgrounds are suffering from "confusion" and lack of understanding about the real problems of women in Pakistan that cannot be solved by economic or political independence.

While Pakistan's feminist women's movement comprises and represents women from middle and lower middle classes, its leadership is undeniably in the hands of upper middle class (though not necessarily elite) women who have acquired Western education, are usually proficient in English, and are professionally trained. For Jamaat women, this opens the feminist project to charges of inauthenticity and disloyalty to the nation. In our interactions, many Jamaat women appeared to believe that the feminist project in Pakistan was ideologically flawed and therefore incapable of attaining the rights of not only the vast majority of women but middle class feminists themselves. Women often told me, as did Tasneem Durrani, a women's rights lawyer helping at a women's legal aid center, that despite decades of women's struggle, the majority of women including elite Pakistani women had been unable to attain "even the rights granted to them by Islam, therefore, how can these women be expected to grant other women their rights?" (Durrani 2003).

Faced with charges of being "Westernized" or "inauthentic," Pakistani feminist activists counter by pointing to the middle class lifestyles and economic prosperity of many leaders of the Islamic movement. Quite early in the women's movement in Pakistan, Said Khan (1994) attempted to put to rest the allegations of elitism against Pakistani feminists by arguing that the conflict of feminism-versus-fundamentalism was not a struggle of modernized elite women versus the masses of traditional men and women. Rather, she insisted, what was unproblematically referred to as a struggle of Islam and Modernity was in fact a contest between two groups of elite who were both equally removed from the daily existence of most of the people of Pakistan. Said Khan supported her arguments by pointing to the elite position of mullas who were exercising control over the masses by claiming a monopolistic control over religion and in the process erasing ordinary religious understandings and Islamic practices of peasants and poor citizens. She also observed, correctly, that Islamist groups such as the Jamaat-e-Islami include many economically and socially prosperous families and individuals who cannot be deemed to belong to "the masses" of Muslims.

Jamaat women, however, evince a different understanding of social and economic power. They base their construction of elite women not simply on economic factors but also in the colonial underpinnings of elite class construction in postcolonial contexts such as Pakistan. In this regard the description of certain ideas and modes of being as Westernized and elite situates individuals and groups in particular bodily-spatial-temporal locations. This reflects the ideas of the movement's leader Maulana Maududi whose main objective was to achieve the transformation of the middle class while expressing a disdain for those both at the top and bottom of the social collective of Muslims. Maududi dismissed both the English-speaking upper class as "Oriental Occidentals" and the vast majority of the illiterate population as incapable of forming an opinion. He therefore addressed his project to the middle class of Indian and Pakistani society, who were not incorporated in Western cultural projects, as the main agent of the Islamic revolution (Maududi 1939). His critique of the elite classes continues to resonate with contemporary Jamaat women and provides ammunition to these women in their contest against feminism. It is the leadership role of the cultural,

English speaking, and universally oriented upper classes that today's upwardly mobile Jamaat women challenge. The Jamaat women invoke a different kind of modernity for Pakistan than the one prescribed by the failed development policies of the Pakistani nation-state, World Bank dictates, superpower dominance, and the local elite cultural dominance. Thus almost all Jamaat women who participated in my study qualified their understanding of "being modern" as different from that of other women's groups in Pakistan and the West. Their position was clearly summed up by Rehana Afroze, a member of the Jamaat women's wing who had successfully been elected to the Karachi City Council:

There is a difference between being progressive and being Westernized. Our misfortune is that we have assumed all forms of progress to be Westernized. We have no development and no progress although our *din* [faith] itself is progressive.[4]

The majority of Jamaat women, regardless of their economic status, are divided from the majority of feminists in Pakistan by an intractable cultural barrier rooted in the histories of colonialism, class, and nation-state formation in Pakistan. Being holders of degrees and training in social sciences, technology, and natural sciences Jamaat women may be considered modern and similar to feminists in terms of education and skill and in many cases in economic and income levels. But they are divided in class terms, or more colloquially between the English-medium and the Urdu-medium. Not surprisingly the women I met preferred to converse in Urdu, even those who had been to "English medium" colleges such as Kinnaird, Lahore, or St. Joseph's, Karachi. Their sense of cultural marginalization is accentuated by their experiences of secular-elite dominated governments in Pakistan that have established a dismal record in achieving human rights and social and economic justice.[5] These women, therefore, challenge the claims of the modernizing elite women to cultural and social dominance. Their rejection of short hair, Western dress, and Western attitudes to the body were undoubtedly meant to signify the adoption of an Islamic self but it also indicated rejection of class-specific signifiers of modernity that are associated with the elite, upper class position in Pakistan. One must exercise caution in embracing the Jamaat women's critique of Pakistani feminist projects as inauthentic and alien. On the other hand it is imperative not to ignore the radically different experiences of the women who flow into the different political formations.

Conclusion

It is a mistake to see the struggle in civil society in Pakistan as a conflict of religious conservatism and secular modernity. The terrain of the secular-modern has become a major battleground in the cultural and political representation of Pakistani women. By seeking to shape the discourses of modernity in Pakistan, Jamaat women are attempting to overturn the terms of the debate through which were framed thus far the leadership claims of modernizing nationalist elite men and feminist activists. In such circumstances, feminist struggles must aim at much more than simply challenging religious patriarchies, for the desires of Muslim women of the middle and lower middle classes can no longer be translated into a struggle of "oppressive religion" versus "modern freedoms." Rather their options may now be constructed as religious liberation versus feminist emancipation. The task for feminism is to convince ordinary Muslim women why feminist modernity may offer more satisfying modes of being women than the modernist reworking of Muslim womanhood by Islamists.

Notes

1. I use the word Islamic in quotes not to question the claims of some groups or individuals to define themselves thus but to challenge the monopolistic use of Islamic by certain political groups and its denial to others.

2. For a discussion of Islamic Feminism, see Badran.

3. I prefer to use the term "Islamist" to refer to Jamaat-e-Islami women, drawing on the extant literature on Political Islam that theorizes it as the harnessing of religion with a political ideology that resonates with other political ideologies such as socialist, communist, fascist, and so on.

4. Interview with Rehana Afroze, councilor, Karachi City Government, 20 June 2003.

5. For comments on the failures of Pakistan's modernizing elites see Ahmad 2000 and Asghar Khan 1985.

Works Cited

Afshar, Haleh. *Islam and Feminisms: An Iranian Case Study*. London: Macmillan Press, 1998.

Ahmad, Aijaz. *In Theory: Classes, Nations, Literatures*. London: Verso, 1992.

Ahmad, Eqbal. *Confronting Empire—Interviews with David Barsamian*. London: Pluto Press, 2000.

Ahmad, Sadaf. "Identity Matters, Culture Wars: An Account of Al-Huda (Re)defining Identity and Reconfiguring Culture in Pakistan." *Culture and Religion* 9:1 (March 2008).

Ahmed, Leila. *Women and Gender in Islam: Historical Roots of a Modern Debate*. New Haven, Conn.: Yale University Press, 1992.

Alam, Muzaffar. *The Languages of Political Islam: India 1200–1800*. Chicago: University of Chicago Press, 2004.

Asghar Khan, Omar. "Political and Economic Aspects of Islamization," in Muhammad Asghar Khan, ed., *Islam, Politics, and the State: The Pakistan Experience*. London: Zed Books, 1985.

Badran, Margot. "Islamic Feminism: What's in a Name?" *Al-Ahram Weekly* (Cairo), 2002.

Baykan, Aysegul. "Politics, Women, and Postmodernity—Women between Fundamentalism and Modernity," in Bryan S. Turner, ed., *Theories of Modernity and Postmodernity*. London: Sage, 1990.

Deeb, Laura. *An Enchanted Modern: Gender and Public Piety in Shi'i Lebanon*. Princeton, N.J.: Princeton University Press, 2006.

Esposito, John L. "Introduction: Modernizing Islam and Re-Islamization in Global Perspective," in John L. Esposito and François Burgat, eds., *Modernizing Islam: Religion in the Public Sphere in Europe and the Middle East*. London: Hurst and Co., 2006.

Gole, Nilufer. *The Forbidden Modern: Civilization and Veiling*. Ann Arbor, Mich.: University of Michigan Press, 1996.

Grare, Frédéric. *Political Islam in the Indian Subcontinent: The Jamaat-e-Islami*. New Delhi: Manohar Publishers, 2001.

Haddad, Yvonne Yazbeck. "Islam and Gender: Dilemmas in the Changing Arab World," in Yvonne Yazbeck Haddad and John L. Esposito, eds., *Islam, Gender, and Social Change*. New York: Oxford University Press, 1998.

Jalal, Ayesha. "The Religious and Secular in Pre-Colonial South Asia," *Daily Times* (Pakistan), 21 April 2002.

Mack, Phyllis. "Religion, Feminism, and the Problem of Agency: Reflections on Eighteenth-Century Quakerism." *Signs: Journal of Women in Culture and Society* 29:1 (2003), 149–73.

Mahmood, Saba. *Politics of Piety: The Islamic Revival and the Feminist Subject.* Princeton, N.J.: Princeton University Press, 2005.

Maududi, Abul A'ala. *Purdah and the Status of Woman in Islam.* Lahore: Islamic Publications, 1939.

Mumtaz, Kahwar. "Identity Politics and Women: 'Fundamentalism' and Women in Pakistan," in Valentine M. Moghadam, ed., *Identity Politics and Women: Cultural Reassertions and Feminisms in International Perspective.* Boulder, Colo.: Westview Press, 1994.

Najmabadi, A. "Feminism in an Islamic Republic—'Years of Hardship, Years of Growth,'" in Yvonne Yazbeck Haddad and John L. Esposito, eds., *Islam, Gender, and Social Change.* New York: Oxford University Press, 1998.

Nasr, Seyyed Vali Reza. *The Vanguard of the Islamic Revolution: The Jama'at-i Islami of Pakistan.* Berkeley: University of California Press, 1994.

———. *Mawdudi and the Making of Islamic Revivalism.* New York: Oxford University Press, 1996.

Nisar, Atiya. Personal interview, Karachi, 2003.

Rashid, Ahmed. *Taliban: The Story of the Afghan Warlords.* London: Pan Books, 2001.

Robinson, Francis. *Islam and Muslim History in South Asia.* New Delhi: Oxford University Press, 2000.

Shaheed, Farida. "The Other Side of the Discourse: Women's Experiences of Identity, Religion, and Activism in Pakistan," in Patricia Jeffery and Amrita Basu, eds., *Appropriating Gender: Women's Activism and Politicized Religion in South Asia.* New York: Routledge, 1997.

Shaheed, Farida, and Khawar Mumtaz. "Islamisation and Women: The Experience of Pakistan," in *Fundamentalism and Secularism in South Asia.* Special Bulletin of Women Living Under Muslim Laws, 1992.

Shakir, B. "The State and the Minorities of Pakistan," in Neelam Hussein et al., ed., *Engendering the Nation-State.* Lahore: Simorgh Women's Resource and Publication Centre, 1997.

Shaukat Ali, Parveen. *Politics of Conviction: The Life and Times of Muhammed Zia ul Haq.* London: The London Centre for Pakistan Studies, 1997.

Weiss, Anita M. "The Historical Debate on Islam and the State in South Asia," in Anita M. Weiss, ed., *Islamic Reassertion in Pakistan: The Application of Islamic Laws in a Modern State.* Syracuse, N.Y.: Syracuse University Press, 1986.

———. "Implications of the Islamization Programme for Women." Ibid.

Zafar, Fareeha. *Finding Our Way: Readings on Women in Pakistan.* Lahore: ASR Publications, 1991.

Punjab in Play

HUMEIRA IQTIDAR

NARRATIVES OF AN OVERBEARING PUNJAB dominate discussions
about Pakistani politics. Yet Punjab today is quite easily the most paradoxical and divided province of Pakistan. It was not always so. The current dominance of Punjab in Pakistan's politics was not in evidence in
the early years of Pakistan's formation. Academic literature and public
debates in national newspapers from the time highlight various other
tensions, prominent among them the political dominance of the Urdu-
speaking Mohajir elite. From the leadership of the Muslim League to
the opposition parties, including both the Pakistan Communist Party
and the Jamaat-e-Islami, to prominent positions within the civil bureaucracy, the better-educated, relatively tightly networked Mohajirs dominated Pakistan's public life.[1]

However, today not only does Punjab direct the political trajectories of Pakistan but Punjabis associate most closely with the federation.
Indeed, other province and ethnic communities continuously point out
the precedence given to Punjabi interests. What explains, then, the current dominance of Punjab in Pakistani politics? Is it just a matter of size
and demographics as the Punjabi middle and upper classes are at pains
to point out? Or is there more to the situation than just the sheer number of Punjabis in Pakistan? And more critically, what does the reified
construction "Punjab" mean? Who forms this Punjab?

An Unexpected Beneficiary of Partition

Punjab is geographically the biggest province in Pakistan, and with a population of approximately seventy-three million it forms about fifty-six million of the total population of Pakistan. There can be little doubt that the sheer number of Punjabis has played a role in allowing them greater electoral strength at the federal level. But several other contributing factors have meant that today it is possible to argue that the biggest beneficiary of the Partition of India, at least on the Pakistani side, has been the Punjabi middle class. Notwithstanding the dreams of the Urdu-speaking salariat that Hamza Alavi had written about, or the ambitions of the bureaucrats of the princely states, the Punjabi middle class has filled the corridors of power in present-day Pakistan.

It was not the most easily predicted path to dominance, nor did the Punjabi middle class provide unequivocal support to the Partition of British India. It is an established norm of partition historiography that the provinces that were least supportive of partition initially bore the brunt of its materialization. Bengal and Punjab suffered the worst violence at the time of Partition. Both provinces were divided, and the massive movements of population across the newly demarcated, and only dimly understood, boundaries were accompanied by immense violence. Perhaps it was the uncertainty of the situation, the lack of a "clear narrative" as David Gilmartin (1998) has suggested, that triggered this violence, but the ultimate effect has been scars in the public psyche. Although there is little public discussion about it, I think it is fair to say that in the long term Pakistani Punjab has seen greater loss of religious and ethnic diversity than East Bengal or today's Bangladesh.

Lahore, the city of colleges, a one-time center of the Indian film industry, of poets and writers, of gardens and culinary delights, suffered a heavy setback with the exodus of Hindu and Sikh residents after Partition.[2] In fact, it took me much time to understand that the praises of Lahore that I came across in accounts of the city of the 1940s were not just hyperbolic, sentimental exaggerations.[3] For Punjabi Hindus and Sikhs, the loss of Lahore was traumatic, but Lahore, too, was not the same without them. Of course, part of the reason it took me so long to recognize their picture of Lahore is that the city that I grew up in during General Zia's regime and the Lahore of these accounts are two very different cities.

Lahore, today, is a predominantly Sunni Muslim, Punjabi city with a strongly provincial air. The vast majority of the city's 14 million inhabitants are recent immigrants from other cities of Punjab. The loss of diversity has, not surprisingly, also meant opportunities for many who would most probably not have been able to compete in a united India. At the time of Partition, Punjab was quite evenly divided between Muslims and other religious groups. More than in the other provinces of present-day Pakistan, the exodus of Hindu and Sikh bureaucrats, teachers, businessmen, politicians, shopkeepers, peasants, and landlords left a vacuum that was not easily filled by the refugees coming in from India. The emptying out of offices and universities, where Muslims of Punjab had historically been underrepresented, meant that many Punjabis were provided with opportunities to expand their businesses, gain promotions, manage projects, and take over lands.

The early years of Pakistan's formation saw much investment in educational institutions of which Punjab was a disproportionate beneficiary due to its existing infrastructure. It is a strange irony that the population of the very province where support for the idea of Pakistan was uncertain right up to the last few years before Partition should benefit so dramatically from the formation of Pakistan. The results of these expanded opportunities took several decades to play themselves out, but by the 1970s it was quite clear that Punjabi representation in the military, civil bureaucracy, industrial capital, and political elite was disproportionate to that of the other provinces.

But what has this meant for Punjabis, and not the somewhat abstract construction "Punjab"? Punjab today is riven by contradictions. It has been and continues to host the headquarters of many religious groups, from the pietist Tablighi Jamaat to the Islamist Jamaat-e-Islami and the militant Jamaat-ud-Dawa, as well as the sectarian groups like Lashkar-e-Jhangvi and Sipah Sihaba. While most academic commentators tend to focus on Khyber Pakhtunkhwa and Balochistan when talking about religious revivalism in Pakistan, it is in fact in Punjab that we find the greatest diversity of religiously inspired movements. At the same time, Punjab has been historically, and continues today to be, the hub of many left and liberal movements and groups. From Bhagat Singh and his revolutionary circle to the Okara peasants uprising, from the National Students' Front and Professors groups to the Lawyers' Movement, and from issue-based mobilizations that have erupted over the past decade, Punjab has acted as the forge of progressive groups and ideas.

Cities like Lahore, Faisalabad, Multan, Sialkot, Gujranwala, Gujrat, and Rawalpindi boast air-conditioned malls, international airports, and sleek hotels, but these only serve to highlight the contrast with other neighborhoods in these cities where the infrastructure seems to have deteriorated almost in direct proportion to the glitz of the malls. While international and national media remained fixated on the purported flogging of a woman in Swat in 2007 just before the Pakistani army invaded the region and as the U.S. continued to use the insurgency in Swat as an excuse for its continued failures in Afghanistan, the occurrence of similar atrocities in Southern Punjab—in the very constituencies of some of the same politicians who decried the Swat atrocities—remained unquestioned.[4]

Whose Punjab?

So whose Punjab do we talk about when we talk about the Punjab that identifies most closely with the federation? It is certainly not the Punjab of the villagers from Daira Deen Gaoon, one of the villages worst hit by the 2010 floods. The Indus River, a massive wall of water as high as eight feet, hit Daira village at 4 a.m. There had been no official notification, no warnings to move out of the village, no time to collect the animals and the grains that were the only savings most of the villagers had, and for close to two thousand people no time to save their lives. The villagers had been uneasy about reports that their village might be flooded to save the lands of Zulfiqar Khosa, an influential landlord of the area and a special adviser to the current provincial government. They had set up a rotation of men who would stay awake and look out for the flood. Yet, when the flood hit, there was little these men could do. The deaths from that village did not receive attention from the mainstream media in Pakistan. A young local activist, Zulfiqar (same name as the landlord, different life), had an unequivocal explanation for that. "Because they just won't," he said. "The deaths in Daira Din will never make it to national news." Officially counted in the province of Punjab, the area known as the Seraiki Belt, in which Daira village is located, has a distinctive cultural texture. Along with Sindh Province, Seraiki-speaking areas are home to some of the biggest feudal holdings in Pakistan. Feudalism, created under British colonial expansion, carries within it an exaggerated consolidation of political, religious, and economic power (Gilmartin 1988; Ali 1988; Ansari 1992). Precolonial structures of power were not as tightly coupled. Colonial grants of lands to prominent religious families, augmenting their previous landholdings, and their incorporation into the political structure of Punjab, a relatively late addition to the colonial enterprise, created a context where extreme brutality could coexist easily with claims to superior spirituality by virtue of descent. The creation of Pakistan did little to disturb the arrangements set up during colonial rule in this region.

A key threat to the large landholding *pir* families emerged during the rapid industrialization undertaken by the Ayub regime in the 1960s. The newly emerging industrial elite increasingly challenged the *pir* families' hold on political power. At the same time, leftist movements inspired by the success of the Maoist revolution in China provided some inspiration to local activists, although the thrust of left activism during this period remained within the larger urban areas. By the late 1960s, the demise of the Ayub Khan regime seemed imminent without any clear replacement in sight from within either the existing political parties or the military. Ayub's former Foreign Minister, Zulfiqar Ali Bhutto, provided a platform to, paradoxically, both the left activists and the sidelined landed elite. The meteoric rise of Bhutto and the emergence of his Pakistan People's Party (PPP) can be explained primarily through the rift in elite groups where some within the elite were willing to form an alliance with other social groups, including left activists (Tarrow 1998). His rhetoric and some genuinely progressive moves aside, Bhutto's party was soon the bastion of the very landlords who had feared marginalization under Ayub Khan's industrialization. PPP is a sentiment, not a structured party. As a sentiment it is democratic; as an institution it has degenerated to a monarchy.

The Seraiki Belt area continues to be a PPP stronghold, although local political families have diversified and hedged their political fortunes, often fielding candidates from opposing parties. The colonial arrangements of power have been augmented in contemporary times through the breakdown of the civil bureaucracy facilitated by World Bank-sponsored "devolution." A progressive-seeming idea at first blush (replacing Pakistan's colonial-type centralized bureaucratic structure with decentralized, local ones), devolution has actually allowed international agencies greater leeway in policy decisions. The decentralized structure, by design, limited the ability of local officers to shape policy through concentrated challenges to regional problems. These officers are also ill placed to resist the pressure that politicians exert over the general functioning of local infrastructure. The coming together of local political trajectories and international developmental experiments played itself out in a variety of ways during the floods in the area. Planned breaches in the embankment along the river were not maintained over the years, and even if they had been, at the time of the 2010 floods local influential groups or families did not allow breaches in their areas. As a result, either ill-planned, last-minute breaches were created by using private and government equipment, such as excavators, or the river forced its way out in a haphazard way when and where it could.

The consequences of these developments were in clear evidence in August 2010 at a medical camp in Kot Adu, located within the Seraiki Belt: children with scabies, boils, and skin rashes; women about to give birth at any moment suffering from gastrointestinal disorders; men with eye infections and more boils; the vast majority suffering from post-traumatic stress. Health problems caused by the flood were not in themselves fatal. In fact, when compared to the severed limbs, crushed spines, and gangrene-infected wounds of the people caught in the earthquake in Pakistan five years ago, these medical problems were minor. It is the fact that they were not treated quickly and competently that led, in some cases, to rapid escalation of severity and complexity. Coupled with inadequate diet, a continued lack of clean drinking water, and an ongoing uncertainty about the future, the displaced faced many challenges. And their anger and frustration may feed into the movements already developing in the region against the extreme imbalance in land holdings, the large "developmental" projects, and, in particular, against the expansion of old and the building of new dams and barrages on the Indus River.

Adding insult to injury were the Pakistani government's attempts at portraying the locals as hapless victims of this "unprecedented natural disaster"; the victims are, in these portrayals, incapable, dependent, and mute. The naturalness of the disaster is increasingly under question, and the managed mismanagement of the floods is being brought under scrutiny by Pakistani activists: Why did the floods go on for so long? After all, there had been no new water entering the river once it was past the Taunsa Barrage. Why were southern areas not prepared for the flood once its magnitude was clear in the north? Even more frustrating was the lack of acknowledgment not just of the warnings that local activists had raised about the dam projects but of the courage and initiative shown by the locals in combating the devastation caused by the floods. As in Haiti, and contrary to the proclamations in the international media, the most effective and immediate aid was provided by locals to one another. In each locality, households had taken in members of their extended family and their friends, and shared their food and their water supplies. In the dry areas around Kot Adu, locals had opened their homes even to complete strangers. They had been sharing their meager food reserves, living space, and other resources. We saw homes where the courtyards had been transformed into a maze of *charpoys* (beds made of a wooden frame and rope). Each of these *charpoys* held a family unit of sorts, often women and their children. One *charpoy* per family was clearly inadequate; yet, this should not obscure the absolute generosity of those who shared their scarce resources with others.

While these scenes of devastation and local generosity were repeated up and down the country in Noshera, Khyber Pakhtunkhwa, in the north to Sukkhur in Sindh in the south, the experiences in Southern Punjab and the Seraiki Belt are particularly useful to dislodge the notion of a unified Punjab. If the Seraiki Belt were excluded from Punjab, its explanation of dominance due to a demographic inevitability would be untenable. It is no doubt the case that political leaders from the Seraiki Belt exhibit a most opportunistic relationship to their Seraiki identity, taking on Punjabi positions at the national level, but the affective association of wide segments of population in these areas to a distinct language, culture, and social relations and higher levels of poverty in the region undermine quite effectively the notion of a homogenous, unified Punjab.

The ease with which leadership from Seraiki areas moves to a Punjabi identity highlights that the most glaring differences are not between the Punjabi and the Seraiki, nor so much between the urban and the rural, but between the inhabitants of distinct class universes. Perhaps it would be useful to explain why I think the urban–rural divide may not be as significant today as it used to be. In a reflective essay about the future of Indian political dynamics, Partha Chatterjee (2008) has argued that the peasant is no longer the same kind of peasant whose life he and others started exploring in the Subaltern Studies Collective under the leadership of Ranajit Guha. The peasant, in present-day India, is facing different kinds of pressures, not just from the capitalist push to create new labor but also from new desires and aspirations among the peasant youth. Coupled with a developmentalist statist framework that informs everyday life in rural areas and also allows some ways to redress the push to create new proletariats, Indian peasants today are facing a different set of challenges from twenty years ago, including the management of heightened levels of engagement with the state. In a similar vein, one can see that while Pakistani Punjab is still the biggest producer of agricultural products in Pakistan, it is no longer an agrarian economy or culture that pervades its towns and villages. It is no longer primarily rural, nor is the peasant "unchanged from centuries ago," as some influential commentators may suggest.

Not only has the balance of population shifted so that most of the population is now concentrated in cities and towns; in fact, the very nature of the "rural" has been transformed as villages and hinterlands have become much more closely integrated into urban life. With a continuous loop of migration, not just to cities within Pakistan but also to the Gulf, Africa, Europe, and the U.S., the circulation of goods, ideas, and practices is wider and much more deep than an initial look might lead one to suspect. Mobile phones and satellite television have transformed conceptions of the good life, foregrounding consumerism, even as they have made some aspects of everyday life easier for the lower and lower middle classes. Finally, the language of democracy, if not the practice of it, is widely understood and utilized mostly for issue-based concerns rather than ideological projects.

Jinay Lahore Nai Waikhya . . .[5]

Even as the distance between village and towns is steadily being eroded, a wide cultural gulf between other cities and the capital city is taking clear shape. If anything, it is the distance between the bigger cities that has grown wider even as that between the smaller cities and villages has shrunk. The current version of globalization, dependent much more than previous cycles of increased international trade and cultural exchange (Frank 1998) on technology and financial capital, has emphasized the emergence of a few global cities at the cost of many regional centers. At the turn of the past century, Multan, Sialkot, Jullandhar, Ambala, Bahawalpur, Sheikhupura, and Gujrat could all boast rich intellectual and communal lives. For instance, Iqbal and Faiz, two of Pakistan's most famous poets, could receive their early education in Sialkot and be nurtured through its local intellectual community to reach a regional and international audience. During the early years of Pakistan, many new migrants to Lahore from other cities of Punjab were able to keep links with their hometowns alive. Writers, poets, critics, and political activists from smaller cities found local and national audiences for their ideas due to shared cultural references and circulation channels.

Today, the cultural difference between Lahore and other Punjabi cities is much wider, in part because the elite in Lahore is no longer connected to a regional audience. While cinemas in Lahore show the latest Hollywood movies, the vast majority of cinemas in cities like Multan have shut down and a few subsist on Punjabi/Pakistani productions. While Lahore-based authors aim to publish in *Granta*, authors in Bahawalpur struggle to find bookshops that carry books and not just magazines and cards. The interlocutors for Lahore's cultural elite are other parts of the globalized elite of the rest of the world. The language divide that both creates and sharpens this distance is increasing at a rate faster than individual, privatized efforts to bridge it, often by attempts to enter the English-speaking world.[6] English is increasingly the language in which the youth of the elite in these global cities of Lahore, Karachi, and Islamabad talk, write, and think.

As the links with other parts of Punjab and Pakistan are severed, there has been an increased centralization of investment and infrastructure in

Lahore. This centralization of infrastructure includes the provision of governance. Small towns face a disproportionate number of dacoities, robberies, kidnappings for ransom, and rape (Siddique, unpublished paper). Sandwiched between the better organized Lahore and the more community oriented villages, smaller city and town dwellers are left to the mercy of their political patrons to gain access to services and rights. More important for middle class Punjabis, the difference in educational, healthcare, and cultural infrastructure is immense and increasing. This centralization has led to the huge influx of middle class migrants into the city.

Lahore, today, is a city of approximately fourteen million people and growing. The dramatic rise of middle class residential societies as well as upper class luxurious "farm houses" displacing local and poorer inhabitants all the way from Bedian village close to the border with India to Raiwind, the headquarters of the Tablighi Jamaat, is linked quite closely to a desire for upward mobility through better educational opportunities among immigrants from other cities of Punjab. However, life in Lahore is replete with new pressures to consume and new opportunities for expenditures often financed through debt. A survey by students of Lahore School of Economics showed that the move to the elite locality of Defense Housing Society resulted in increased consumption even for those moving from other elite areas of Lahore (Nasir 2009). Personal debt, a social taboo even a decade ago, has quite radically been transformed into a virtue by credit card, leasing, and consumer goods companies.[7] The implications of the rise of neoliberalism in the Pakistani and particularly Punjabi social imagination is an important yet hugely underresearched area.[8]

Often the lack of dialogue between the outwardly facing elite and the rest has been seen by the elite to imply a complete lack of reflexive thinking and debate among the rest. The intellectual life of the lower middle classes, in particular, is not easily apparent to the urban intelligentsia because much of it is not in text form, and, when it is, the magazines, journals, and other fora where the lower classes express themselves are in Urdu or vernacular languages and/or considered too low-brow to merit serious engagement.[9] For instance, in his reading of women's pulp fiction magazines or "digests," Kamran Asdar Ali (2004,

140) points out that upper-class feminists have tended to look down on these publications as regressive and betraying false consciousness especially in their reluctance to openly question certain norms. Yet, these stories of lower middle class or working class women allow us a window into their concerns and questions, and he suggests that the "construction of bourgeois individualism may be tempered by other visions of the self that co-exist with it . . . a self that may accept, contradict and even transgress the imposed construction of mythical but desired 'emancipated' autonomous individual." An important source, along with the left activism of the 1960s and 1970s, for supporting the growth of organic intellectuals in smaller towns as well as the lower middle classes of Lahore has been the Islamist party Jamaat-e-Islami. Many prominent Punjab-based thinkers and researchers of the past five decades, writing primarily in Urdu but also in some cases in English, such as Javed Ahmed Ghamidi, Maulana Israr Ahmed, Professor Khurshid Ahmed, Saleem Mansoor Khalid, have either been members or continue to be associated with the Jamaat. The Jamaat may be ill-equipped to produce an intellectual of the same stature as a Maududi now, but it certainly supports the generation of some research and debate on political, economic, and cultural aspects of everyday life in contemporary Pakistan. The interest in research, coupled with a structured presence in the smaller towns of Punjab, is a key asset for the Jamaat, which has yet to reap any electoral benefits from it because of the lack of a clear political vision on its part.

Mobilizing Punjab

The mythical Punjab of unified positions on a range of issues from Kalabagh Dam to drone attacks in Waziristan and a military response to the insurgency in Balochistan is the Punjab of the political leadership and upper middle class in Lahore. It is this Punjab that has the loudest voice and the easiest access to media channels. It is this Punjab that is confident of its homogeneity due to the social networks it has shared across schools, colleges, and clubs in Lahore. And this is the Punjab of the Generals whose residential colonies threaten to colonize half of Lahore, not of the soldiers from Jhelum who are weary of fighting an unwinnable war in their own country. Size and demographics have certainly played a role in giving Punjab an edge over other provinces. However, of greater help has been existing infrastructure and mechanisms for exploitation within the province and the country that have allowed upper middle class Punjab to expand as if organically. Punjab the administrative entity may be the most affluent in the federation, but Punjabis are not uniformly so.

A looming crisis for all in Punjab is the economic collapse that current policies of liberalization and unfettered privatization have engendered. The deindustrialization of Punjab in particular and Pakistan in general over the past decade has created severe challenges for the Punjabi middle class that had grown to expect a continuous rise in standards of living. So far, none of the political parties has formulated a response to this crisis. The Islamists, forced into a position of opposition against their former ally, the U.S., highlight the role of World Bank and IMF policies much more than other political parties but have not formulated any clear policy alternative. This has not been enough for the electorate in previous elections, but it remains to be seen whether it will be in the coming years.

The pressures of the "war on terror," an ongoing war in Afghanistan for over a decade, have for some years touched Punjab in the most profound manner. No longer isolated from the bombings in FATA and Waziristan, no longer able to pretend that Baluchistan is another country and that the war in Afghanistan will not impact their lives, Punjabis across the board are beginning to ask themselves hard questions about what kind of Pakistan they will be left with if they lose Baluchistan and Khyber Pakhtunkhwa to anarchy. A clearer sense of Punjabi identity may paradoxically be the result of some soul searching about what kind of Pakistan is possible in the near future.

Notes

Segments of this essay were published as "Why Do 'Natural' Disasters Impact Some Areas More Than Others? Structural Impoverishment and the Floods in Pakistan" by the SSRC. http://itemsandissues.ssrc.org/ pakistan.

1. Pakistan Communist Party's leadership in the immediately post-partition era was drawn from Muslim members of the Indian Communist Party. Jamaat-e-Islami's leadership, including Maulana Maududi, was drawn primarily from the

Urdu-speaking milieu of North India. See Iqtidar (2011) for evidence of some collaboration between the Pakistan Communist Party and the Jamaat-e-Islami in the years right after Pakistan's formation; Asdar Ali (2011) for debates within the progressive circles in the early post-partition years; and Daeschel (2009) for the Urdu-speaking milieu of North India.

2. Bombay had already started offering stiff competition to Lahore in the decade before partition, during the late 1930s and through the 1940s. However, many of the large studios continued to be based in Lahore. This in part also explains the significant presence of talent from Punjab and Khyber Pakhtunkhwa in the pre-partition Indian film industry.

3. See for instance Neville (1997).

4. Humeira Iqtidar, "Who Are the Taliban in Swat?" http:// www.opendemoc racy.net/article/email/who-are-the-taliban-in-swat.

5. A famous claim from pre-Partition Lahore that is still repeated in the city today, *jinay Lahore nai waikhya, au jamya nai:* one who hasn't seen Lahore has not really been born.

6. The rise of Berlitz and other language schools teaching English is one among many indicators of these individualized, privatized attempts.

7. A ubiquitous series of advertisements from 2008–09 for a bank's credit card emphasized the fulfillment of various social obligations, generally by the earning male head, enabled by the card. In one advertisement, a son is able to send his grateful mother to perform the Haj, a pilgrimage to Mecca. In another of the same series, a father adds to the happiness of his daughter by letting her buy a set of gold jewelry for her wedding. Yet another shows a proud husband surprising his wife with car keys.

8. For an initial attempt see Iqtidar (2011a).

9. Similarly, in the context of Chitral, Magnus Marsden (2007) has shown the interest in maintaining an intellectual life that rural Chitralis exhibit through music mahfils, debates, and discussions.

Works Cited

Ali, Imran. *The Punjab under Imperialism, 1885–1947*. Princeton, N.J.: Princeton University Press, 1988.

Ansari, Sarah. *Sufi Saints and State Power: The Pirs of Sind, 1843–1947*. Cambridge: Cambridge University Press, 1992.

Asdar Ali, Kamran. "Pulp Fictions: Reading Pakistani Domesticity." *Social Text* 78 (2004).

Frank, Andre Gunder. *ReOrient: Global Economy in the Asian Age*. Berkeley: University of California Press, 1998.

Gilmartin, David. *Empire and Islam: Punjab and the Making of Pakistan.* Berkeley: University of California Press, 1988.

———. "Partition, Pakistan, and South Asian History: In Search of a Narrative." *Journal of Asian Studies* 57:4 (November 1998).

Iqtidar, Humeira. "Secularism beyond the State: State and Market in Islamist Imagination." *Modern Asian Studies* 45:3 (May 2011).

———. *Secularizing Islamists? Jama'at-e-Islami and Jama'at-ud-d'awa in Urban Pakistan.* Chicago: University of Chicago Press, 2011.

Marsden, Magnus. *Living Islam: Muslim Religious Experience in Pakistan's North West Frontier.* Cambridge: Cambridge University Press, 2005.

Neville, Pran. *Lahore: A Sentimental Journey.* New Delhi: HarperCollins India, 1997.

Rizvi, Mubashir. *Masters Not Friends: An Ethnography of a Land Rights Movement in Pakistan.* Master's thesis, University of Texas, n.p., n.d.

Roy, Olivier. *The Failure of Political Islam.* Cambridge, Mass.: Harvard University Press, 1994.

Siddique, Osama. *Context Matters: Crime Perception, and Vulnerability across the Urban–Rural Spectrum in Punjab.* Paper, n.p., n.d.

Blood on the Path of Love
Faisalabad, Pakistan

QALANDAR BUX MEMON

AT ABOUT 3:00 IN THE MORNING on the day I left for Faisalabad in 2010, where I was to investigate a strike of 250,000 workers demanding a 17 percent wage increase, I picked up a poetry book from the side table in my bedroom and soon landed on a poem by the progressive writer Ali Sardar J'afri, "Robe of Sparks":

> Who is that
> standing in a robe of sparks?
> Body broken, blood spilling
> from his brains.
> Farhad and Qais passed away
> some times ago; who then is he
> whom people stone to death?
> There is no beautiful Shireen here,
> no Laila of spring seasons.
> In whose name, then, is this scarlet bed
> of wounds flavoring?
> It is some madman
> stubbornly upholding Truth,
> unbending to the winds of lies and cunning.

It is clear, his punishment must be
death by stoning!
[*Qais/Majnoon and Laila, Farhad/Kohkun and Shireen are personae in Urdu
poetry martyred on the path of love.*]

J'afri was born in 1912 in Uttar Pradesh and helped to found the Progressive Writers Movement (PWM) in the 1930s. The goals of PWM were clear, even dogmatic. The writers fought against British imperialism in India and argued against all imperialisms globally: J'afri himself faced jail for writing antiwar poetry during the Second World War. When the Progressives investigated British India and later postcolonial India and Pakistan, they found that the core problem lay in the power—and abuse of power—by the local bourgeois elite, who were supported by the international bourgeoisie.

Development and modernity, they argued, would not be possible unless the workers stood up and fought a class war—in today's liberal-speak, we can politely term this a "fight for rights." The role they assigned themselves as writers and poets was to champion the cause of the workers and create beauty in society, not just in escapist literature. Toward this end, J'afri joined the Communist Party of India and edited its literary magazines *Naya Adab* (New Literature) and *Indian Literature*. He went around the country supporting workers in their struggles and saw first-hand the brutality that bosses meted out to workers seeking sustenance.

Born of these experiences, his poetry abounds with celebratory references to the martyrs of working-class struggle. For J'afri, it is they who are the modern-day lovers; they are the modern-day Majnoons and Lailas, Farhads and Shireens. Their struggle isn't for an embrace of the beloved or the intoxication of individual pleasures. It is the struggle of a group that is disenfranchised; nay, severely exploited, a struggle of lovers for the right to live, for a chance to see their children eat healthy and full meals, to pack them off to school in the hope that these young ones may not be held to the sweating iron of machines as their parents have been. It is the struggle to humanize themselves and escape from the clutches of a system to which we are all too indifferent—and all too compromised.

Mian Qayyum, Bawa Lalif Ansari, and Muhammad Rana are three such lovers.

The Majnoon of Spring Seasons

It was early 2002, in the industrial city of Faisalabad, province of Punjab. Mian Qayyum, after taking his lunch break at the tea shop of his friend Malik Nazir, was walking back to his power loom station. Suddenly, he heard noises from the neighboring factory and hurried over. There, three policemen were beating up a middle-aged worker. The worker, already fallen to the ground, was taking fists and kicks from the three police officers. Enraged, Mian ran over, threw the police off the worker, and started fighting one of the policemen. Seeing this, other workers joined in. The police officers, outnumbered, ran off. Mian then returned to work.

Mian was then twenty-eight and had fathered four children. He recalled, "I was worried and sweating, thinking what is going to happen now? I was worried for my family. Will I have a job? Are they going to arrest me? My clothes were covered in sweat, and that night at home I did not sleep. I was worried; each knock or noise alarmed me. What will happen now?"

The next day came and brought nothing but the drudgery of a usual day. Soon, word got around that another Majnoon had awakened with the hunger for Laila's love. Workers began to seek out Mian Qayyum at his lunch break at the tea shop for help. He helped. Offering advice to some, negotiating with bosses for others, collecting donations for some, and settling disputes of yet others. His boss, frightened by Mian's growing reputation, laid him off, politely. "Take your salary but don't come to work," he told him.

Mian refused the money and embraced dignified unemployment. With more time, he had ever more demands on his hands from the factory workers of Faisalabad. He kept helping as best he could. Workers began to sit around the tea stall and analyze their situation. Why were they so poor, despite working in the heat for twelve hours a day? Why were the political parties not doing anything for them? And the religious parties—what use would it be if they followed them with their message of division and hatred—Sunni against Shi'a? Would this solve their basic problems of hunger, unemployment, bad working conditions, and low wages?

Mian, unable to find work at other power loom factories, began to sell biscuits, bread, and sweets house-to-house, riding a bicycle borrowed from Malik Nazir. He made about 400 rupees per day, and this kept his house going. But the tea stall meetings continued and the questions kept developing: What was the law there for? Why didn't they get their legal wages? Why would the bosses refuse to register them with the legal authorities so that they could get a pension? Why is it that the police always attack them and harm them at the behest of the owners? Weren't the police meant to protect them, too? How could they change things? And what must have been their original sin that they suffered so much misery, while a few zamindars (rich landowners) enjoyed the fruits of this bountiful land? What could they do to see the workers get legal rights and protection? How could they support each other?

While these questions rang in the ears of sixty or so workers who now gathered around the tea stall, Mian continued to ride his bicycle to make a living, support his family, and lobby for his fellow workers—until the answers started to arrive: we will fight as a collective for workers rights; we will unionize where we can; we will work with all those who want to help better the condition of the workers; we will support each other and stay away from religious parties that divide us on a superficial basis—worker against worker—or political parties that talk of the worker but wallow in riches looted from their sweat, from everybody's sweat; we will serve each other and unite; we will come together on the basis of what unites us, "that we are workers." Mian returned to the tea stall to find that he had been chosen to be the first full-time worker of the newly formed Labour Qaumi Movement (LQM). Sixty workers pooled together contributions to employ Mian, and the tea shop became their headquarters.

That was 2003. Today I arrive in Faisalabad on assignment, and I see that the tea shop has given way to numerous rented offices ranging from one-room shops to headquarters in a two-story building with about five rooms, a kitchen, and a toilet. The workers have established themselves in several areas in and around Faisalabad and have elected district leaders for each area. The main office stands next to Jattan Wala Chouck, Ghulam Mohammed Abad, Faisalabad. There is a small banner of the LQM on top of the entrance, and in the reception area—a ten-by-ten-foot room with a small television, a table, and a desk with newspapers lying around—I am introduced to Bawa Lalif Ansari.

Farhad Jhang

Bawa Lalif Ansari is famous among workers for his oratory and in particular for leading an energizing *tarana* (a call and response between leader and crowd). He is an entertainer and pedagogue, who hosts most of the workers' rallies for LQM. Bawa is of short and slim stature, with long black hair carefully combed backward and a small and trim jet-black beard—a look that made more sense to me as our conversation developed.

"I used to be part of Lashkar-e-Taiba. I joined them when I was young." LeT is a militant Islamist organization, suspected of involvement in the 2008 Mumbai attacks. It is banned in Pakistan but continues to operate openly in many areas. Sipah-e-Sahaba, another extremist organization, he tells me, was founded in the Jhang area, which neighbors Faisalabad and is where he has been working with the LQM. He explains:

> [The Lashkar] have a strong grip on the people and tell the poor to direct their frustration against the Shi'as. The local feudals and zamindars, who are extremely rich, are generally Shi'a, while the common bounded laborer is Sunni. The hate manifested over years of exploitation can easily be directed by these originations against all Shi'as. But many Shi'a are also laborers and workers, as are Christians. I came across Mian Qayyum and the LQM and their analysis made more sense. The religious parties wanted me to merely seethe with rage but didn't tell me how my material situation was going to change. What good does it do me to hate someone for being a Shi'a or a Sunni or a Christian? They too are poor people trying to work and feed their children. What good does it do a worker to fight a worker? I didn't agree with this.

Bawa believes in Islam, but for him it is a radical philosophy of liberation. A few hours later, at a workers' gathering, he said, "God is sovereign and God asks us to fight for justice. The bosses are nothing; we will not bow to them, these pharaohs. What we work we should be paid fairly for." Lashkar's loss has been the Labour Quami Movement's gain.

In July 2010, Bawa was instrumental in organizing the workers in Jhang around two demands. First, that all workers be issued social security cards and second, that they be given a raise of 17 percent, as recommended by the Minimum Wage Board, a government committee looking at labor issues. The social security cards give legal status to workers and allow them to get a government pension and access to government-run hospitals and medicines, among other benefits.

Farooq Tariq, spokesperson of the Labour Party of Pakistan, explained the background of workers' status in relation to social security cards:

> Only 2.1 million workers out of forty-five million Pakistanis in the labor force have secured social security cards. That is less than 4 percent of the total workforce. By law, every worker must be issued a social security card, however many bosses never register their workforce with the Social Security Department. Most factory owners pay for a few workers while the rest remain at their mercy. Why is this so? The answer is that bosses are required to pay at least 7 percent of each worker's total wages into the social security system.

Paying 7 percent of each worker's total wages would, of course, mean less profit for the bosses. That is, less money for those shopping trips abroad, less money to sustain those vulgar grand palaces in Lahore, Karachi, and Islamabad and the hordes of servants swimming around them (out of necessity, not desire), less money for the Rolex watch and the Chanel glasses — to be upgraded on a yearly basis. What of the government and this Social Security Department—why doesn't it register workers? Farooq answered, "The Labour Department, responsible for implementing the law, enjoys cordial relationship with the bosses. In fact, since 2003, the government in Punjab has banned factory inspections by the Labour Department, thus giving the owners a free hand."

That is, the government and the bosses go hand-in-hand; more often than not, the bosses *are* the government. Ayesha Siddiqa, among others, has explained that today's Pakistani elite are incestuously interconnected via family relations and marriages with a large patronage network of squabbling, but self-serving, interest groups. Their rationale is to keep the country and its resources for themselves: they negotiate among themselves and take the spoils from any sales to the international elite. In turn, if the international elite get a good deal, they turn a blind eye to anything and everything, as they did during the war against the Soviets in Afghanistan and as they have in this "War on Terror." Against these latter-day pharaohs stand the conscious and spirited workers.

Led by Bawa and the LQM, they organized twenty thousand workers on strike around these demands for social security cards and a raise. For seventeen days, workers struck, moving out from strike camps near main roads. Women, children, and male workers stayed together in the camps. Entertained by the *dhol,* poetry, and the skills of Bawa Lalif, they spent the nights and days hungry but determined. On the sixteenth day of the strike, they moved the camps around the office of the District Commissioning Officer (DCO). The DCO is the bureaucrat charged with local administration and is often the judge, jury, and executioner rolled into one. The strategy paid off, and after failed attempts by the police to raze the camps and pressure the leadership, the DCO gave in and informed the bosses that the workers had to be registered with the Social Security board and issued cards. Bawa smiled as he told me of this victory: "We had finally had our day."

Blood on the Path of Love

I—Whom People Stone to Death

Back at the LQM headquarters, Bawa points to a photograph taped to the wall. Three middle-aged men, all wearing white *shalwar kameez,* are shown, waist upward, smiling at the camera. Bawa points to the person to the far right in the photograph. This, he says, is Mustansar Randhawa, "our fallen hero."

Mustansar was a rising star of the LQM and had set up an office in a district of Faisalabad that had traditionally been the preserve of gangsters in the pay of local factory bosses. These gangsters ensured that the workers accepted low wages and their nonregistered labor status. Mustansar came from a neighboring village and set to work addressing the needs of local workers. He set up a small office on Sargodha Road, the main thoroughfare, and printed five thousand posters and thousands of leaflets urging workers to contact LQM and the National Trade Union Federation (of which he was the Faisalabad president) should they have any labor-related problems. Workers began to arrive in droves.

Maybe this was the reason for his death. At 1:00 in the afternoon, July 6, 2010, ten people burst into Mustansar's small office, where he was with his brother, listening to a worker who wanted help. One of the ten had a Kalashnikov rifle and started to fire. Naseer, Mustansar's younger brother, was shot dead. Mustansar managed to run into the second room and locked the door. It didn't help. The murderers broke in and shot him dead, too. His blood-soaked body sparked days of protests in the city. It also hastened a two hundred fifty thousand–strong workers' strike. But the police arrested no one for the murders.

I had heard of the murder of Mustansar before I had set off to visit Faisalabad, but now, on hearing Bawa's narration, I understand something of Pakistan that we ought not to forget: the violence of the Taliban is nothing compared to the systemic violence that the state and the elite have meted out in village after village, in police station after police station—for the poor, innocent, or guilty, they are torture stations—in city after city, and factory after factory.

II — Rana's Robe of Sparks

Leaving the reception area, I ask to be shown around the rest of the building, and Bawa leads me upstairs. At the top floor, I am invited into a rectangular room, about forty by twenty feet, with rectangular desks linked together and running through the middle of the room. Here, on the tables surrounded by standing and seated workers, lies straightened and in visible discomfort Rana Muhammad Tahir.

Rana raises himself to greet me. I sit down on a chair at his side and am asked if I would like a drink. Someone is promptly and quietly set out to procure tea. Workers arrive in twos and threes every few minutes, and upon entering greet Rana with respect and reverence. He tries to greet them, but it is clear he cannot move without incurring a great deal of pain. To break the atmosphere of quiet that a stranger's presence brings, I ask a direct and naïve question: "So what happened to you?" Rana smiles and answers:

It happened on the 20th of July, 2010. It was the eighth day of our strike. I was leading a procession of workers in my district, and the bosses had warned us not to lead the workers on this procession and that they would make an example of us. They organized thugs and amassed lathis and guns the night before—we didn't know this then. They also put stones on the roofs of the factories and houses on our path. Twenty thousand workers were in our peaceful procession. We were headed along fine, and then suddenly stones started to fall from above. Some people started running away and I turned to them to encourage them forward. It was then that thugs with lathis charged us from three directions—they sprang up from nowhere. They caught me and started hitting me. I was surrounded. The other workers had fallen back. I stood strong and continued to ask my fellows to move forward. Then they started firing guns from the roofs. More workers ran for cover. The thugs told me to run or they would kill me, some had pistols in hand. I told them that I had not come to run away—I was going nowhere. It was then that they lashed onto me with all their might. I don't remember much. I had blood pouring from my head, my clothes were drenched in blood and they just kept hitting me. I backed onto a wall and stood there taking the hits until I lost consciousness.

This continued for nearly ten minutes until Rana's fellows managed to avoid the bullets and beat away the thugs.

Rana showed me his bruised and blood-clotted head wounds, worn as a crown on the order of love, and then he moved up his shalwar to show me the bruises on his legs. Swollen and blue, purple and black—all over his body.

What of the police? Where were they? "They were there!" Rana grins. He continues, "And they started shelling us with tear gas from the other side [opposite the hired thugs]. Rather than protecting us, they too started attacking the workers, so we were caught with the police on one side and the thugs on the other, with stones falling from above and the bullets flying around." One can guess on whose orders the police acted.

Rana was put on a motorcycle, held up by a worker, and led away from the shelling, the lathis, and the stones. His spilled blood sparked the streets of Faisalabad.

For twelve hours the workers, embittered and fuming, fought the police shelling. Five workers were later arrested—no thugs or bosses. Rana explained the reason for the bosses' severity:

> They want to make us feel isolated and fatalistic, they want us to feel helpless, they want to scare us into believing they control our destiny and the world, so they shoot us when we demand justice, they beat us and plan elaborately so that we don't made demands. It's not going to work anymore. We stand together now, the workers know what their interest is, and together we are quite a force. We will change things. We will create better conditions for workers . . . for everyone.

My interview with Rana is interrupted every few minutes as workers, always in twos or threes, enter the room. They greet everyone, but in particular they are interested in the health of Rana, and he greets all of them warmly. One worker bids farewell and, in leaving, slides a hundred-rupee note into Rana's hand. After the worker leaves, Rana shows it to me and says, "It's the eighth day of our strike. He doesn't have much in his own house, but he is concerned and is aiding me with this—this is the workers' spirit today."

The money is to help Rana pay medical bills. The spirit is that of solidarity, a solidarity that pharaohs cannot break. Three days after the attack on Rana, seven thousand or so workers gathered outside his house. Workers showered his house with flowers, fruits, and other gifts. There was so much that Rana had to redistribute his bounty among his neighbors and family and the needy. "There was just so much of it. My house was full. I could have opened a fruit shop."

Rana is a loom worker. In his thirty-two years, he has found work, married, had two daughters and two sons. He started out in a soap factory where his aging father had worked all his life as a menial laborer. Rana's talent landed him a clerical position, but his politics got him fired. Alarmed by his questioning and will, the bosses ganged together and refused to employ him in a clerical position—these jobs, as we know, are best saved for the yes-persons. So Rana joined his father in menial labor, not at a soap factory but at a loom factory.

I ask him about the workers' pay and conditions and the reason for their strike. Suddenly, all the workers become alert and keen to answer, and Rana directs me to Nazir Ahmad, an elderly man who has been sitting quietly on a chair in front of me. He answers, "We get around 50–250 rupees per day. It depends on your position and work or if you are working night shifts or day shifts—night work pays more. We work twelve hours or thirteen hours and sometimes if, say, someone misses a shift, then even thirty-six hours." I ask him to explain, and he elaborates, "Well, you see, let's say I do my twelve hours, then the person who is to relieve me does not turn up for whatever reason, then I have to do his shift too and then it will be the turn of my shift again so I end up doing three shifts, which is thirty-six hours, all without rest." How do you manage that? "With lots of tea but not much food. If you eat too much, then you cannot work, you feel bloated." What about holiday pay? "Nothing," he replies. If you are injured at work? "Then it's the will of the boss what you get—normally a few thousand, and that depends on whether you get a good boss or not."

I have done plenty of surveys of workers to understand the logic: from the 50–250 rupees per day, you have to subtract the money workers need for food (packed lunch, in most cases), tea (10 rupees per cup; four cups would be necessary most days), and cigarettes. Then you have to subtract what they would spend on clothes they wear to work and the energy they need to regenerate themselves for this work when away from work (let's not forget that after twelve hours a worker is back at his machine for twelve hours, and after another twelve hours rest, he is back at his machine for twelve hours). Women often come as unwaged free labor with the male wage, as the task of regeneration is left to the wives, mothers, and others (generally women) around the house, who put effort into getting the male worker in condition to work the next day. The wage of the laborer then disappears as quickly as the Land Cruiser of the bosses on an empty Lahore road. It just passes by, like an illusion.

So that when the mother is ill and needs medicine—it isn't there. When the worker's hands get caught in the machine and the injury requires rest—this must be passed by. When, deep in pregnancy, a wife needs a Caesarean operation and the doctor demands fees—the money is already gone. When children need food—it's gone, and don't even bother thinking about school for the kids.

The conversation turns to suicide, as someone mentions the father who killed himself and his children in Lahore a few weeks before. He couldn't feed them and couldn't stand it anymore. Rana becomes irritated and raises himself: "We are not like those. We will not commit suicide. We will fight. We will suffer hunger but we will fight. Together, we will change things." All agree. This, then, is the choice the worker is left with: commit suicide or fight for justice and possibly face murder, beatings, and hunger. Some will choose suicide and the Lashkars, who make things more glamorous. Others will choose political struggle and its sacrifices.

More workers come in and greet everyone. One of them has a wad of cash in his hand and goes around the room, asking for contributions. I ask what the money is for, and they tell me it's for a truck they are hiring to go to a protest they have organized to support the five workers who were arrested a few days back.

I leave with Rana in a car—he won't be able to stand in the truck.

Madmen Stubbornly Upholding Truth

Workers have come to this demonstration mainly on foot and on bicycles, with a few on motorbikes, hired trucks, and one car. The rally is taking place in a school field. Police surround the perimeters. The stage is a few school tables pushed together and covered with carpet. On the microphone, Bawa is already busy. He announces Rana's arrival, and the five thousand or so who are already here stand up to clap and cheer him into the ground. They shout, "Mazdoor Ehtijaj Zindabad!" (Long live the workers' movement), and they applaud frantically. Bawa moves on to this *tarana*:

> BAWA: *Atta mehnga* (wheat is expensive)
> CROWD: *hay hay* (a verbal way of sighing)
> BAWA: *Bijli mehngi* (electricity is expensive)
> CROWD: *hay hay*

BAWA: *Roti mehngi* (roti is expensive)
CROWD: *hay hay*
BAWA: *Chini mehngi* (sugar is expensive)
CROWD: *hay hay*
BAWA: *Zara zor se bolo* (say it louder)
CROWD: *hay hay*
BAWA: *Siasatdan saray chor* (all politicians are corrupt)
CROWD: *hay hay*
BAWA: *Naqli degria'n* (with fake degrees)
CROWD: *hay hay*
BAWA: *Zara zor se bolo* (say it louder)
CROWD: *hay hay*
BAWA: *Atta mehnga*
CROWD: *hay hay*
BAWA: *Bijli mehngi*
CROWD: *hay hay*
BAWA: *Roti mehngi*
CROWD: *hay hay*
BAWA: *Zara ahista bolo* (say it softly)
CROWD: *hay hay*
BAWA: *Atta mehnga*
CROWD: *hay hay*
BAWA: *Bijli mehngi*
CROWD: *hay hay*
BAWA: *Roti mehngi*
CROWD: *hay hay*

Bawa and Rana are the main speakers. Bawa narrates the struggle of Jhang and encourages the workers to hold firm. This is the eighth day of their strike, and he tells them that victory is in sight—struggle, he says, will prevail. Rana is led up to the mike by two aides and supported throughout his short speech. The crowd tells him not to speak, as he is clearly in pain, but he carries on. We will not commit suicide as they did in Lahore, we will struggle. We are not made of that stuff. We know the workers' condition. We know the hardships we suffer. We know what it is like to go home and find empty boxes where there should be atta and sugar and rice. We know the look of our children as we put them to bed still bleeding with hunger. It's our situation, but we will not commit suicide. We will fight. The crowd, roused to tears and anger, launches into slogans and more clapping: "*Mazdoor ehtijaj zindabad!*" Rana continues, "We will fight, let them break our legs, let them rain stones on our hearts, let them shoot us, we will fight. We will fight as one, worker and worker. *Mazdoor ehtijaj zindabad.*" His last words ring all around as he leaves the stage. Frail, beaten up, stoned, but fighting.

Postscript

Two days after my trip, and on the tenth day of the Faisalabad workers' strike, I walked to Mall Road and the Canal from my house in Lahore and, in the bitter heat of the afternoon, got in a rickshaw to the Punjab Assembly. There, in front of the Assembly but outside its perimeters, I was to join workers and activists at a camp that had been set up to bring the Faisalabad strike to the attention of the political lords in Lahore.

I saw workers rejoicing as I approached. The bosses had given in, had to give in. The government had judged in the workers' favor and told the bosses to grant all two hundred fifty thousand workers a 17 percent raise. They had released the five arrested workers. I did the math: two hundred fifty thousand people each had a raise of 17 percent. If we assume they are each now getting at least the minimum wage of seven thousand rupees, then it would mean one thousand one hundred and ninety rupees per worker (per family) more per month. The average family in Pakistan is estimated to consist of around seven and a half persons. Given this, the workers' victory would positively affect nearly 1,875,000 people.

The statistics do not tell us of the spirit of that moment. That too is important. As I jumped into a rickshaw—enlivened by the victory in Faisalabad—and headed to Anarkali, I began to think of J'afri and his lifelong struggle in politics and his poetry.

I began reading J'afri in the monsoon of 2007 while lingering in Karachi, ill in bed. I had found his collected works at a local shop in Clifton, and over the next three days read this 300-page book front to back and back to front, and then once more front to back and back to front. Hard up for reading matter, I didn't really think much of his poems. One or two struck a chord, but compared to Faiz I thought him terse and dogmatic and, at the same time, overly dense with references and symbols. Since his rhymes were also lost in translation—Urdu to English—I thought maybe the translations let him down.

Now, a few years on, I understand him better. J'afri wrote for those struggling to create a more just society. Those who challenged the cruel status quo and who took pains to remove the granite block tossed on the neck of most Pakistanis by ruling elites and to carve into it some shape of justice. J'afri is better read with workers in the factories, among the struggles of working families in the fields, and above all with those lovers like Muhammad Rana, Mian Qayyum, Bawa Lalif, and the workers of Faisalabad, whose blood is on the path of love.

Balochistan Betrayed

MAHVISH AHMAD

ABDUL WAHAB BALOCH IS AFRAID TO TALK on the phone. In 2008, he was picked up by security agencies after leading a rally through Karachi protesting the tenth anniversary of Chagai-I—the notorious underground nuclear tests that polluted a Baloch district to serve Pakistan's national security interest. After a post-rally search for a friend[1] ended in a brutal three-day torture fest involving baggings, beatings, and injections, Wahab is convinced that Pakistan's Inter-Services Intelligence (ISI) is tapping his phone to keep an eye on his movements, carefully surveilling where he is, who he is with, and what he is saying. Another manifestation, says Wahab, of the oppressive state of Pakistan.

Wahab is among several hundreds of Baloch who have been kidnapped, tortured, and (at times) brutally killed by Pakistan's military and intelligence institutions. Their crime: political sympathies or activities furthering the cause for a more autonomous or outright independent Balochistan. Their fates have been met with a silent (or silenced) Pakistani media, where news of the atrocities only started trickling in during the summer of 2011.

According to Wahab, this spate of state-led pick-ups has not taken place in a vacuum. Rather, it is part of a "historical pattern of betrayal," where the Pakistani state has repeatedly broken specific agreements around the accession of Balochistan to Pakistan, the governing of the province and the sharing of Balochistan's natural resources.

It is easy to excuse Wahab's indictment of history as a separatist fantasy, one unsupported by facts or experience. He is, after all, the chairman of the Baloch Rights Council and a member of the Baloch National Front, a coalition of separatist political parties fighting for an independent Balochistan. Separatist to the core—a *sarmachar*[2] even, according to one bystander who observed our interview from afar. But Wahab and his companions are not alone with their memories of Pakistani betrayal. Baloch parties across the political divide share their sentiments, from the more pro-federation and pro-Pakistan Baloch National Party-Mengal (BNP-M) and National Party (NP), to the separatists of the Baloch National Movement (BNM) and the Baloch Republican Party (BRP). Diverging in their solutions, they unite in their memories. These memories have largely been silenced and, though difficult to reconstruct into an air-tight and unified narrative, they paint a picture of forced agreements, promises made and broken, of power brokered and unshared, and of deep poverty amid great wealth.

The First Betrayal: Annexation, Not Accession

> We are Muslims, but it is not necessary that by virtue of our being Muslims, we should lose our freedom and merge with others. If the mere fact that we are Muslims requires us to join Pakistan, then Afghanistan and Iran, both Muslim countries, should also amalgamate with Pakistan.
> —*Ghaus Bux Bizenjo, speech at Dar-ul-Awam, Dhadar, Balochistan, December 14, 1947*

Wahab Baloch has agreed to meet with me after a flurry of texts has been exchanged between my phone and his numerous mobiles. Tightly holding on to the microphone I've handed him, he speaks in a low voice, narrating a (hi)story that remains hidden to most Pakistanis outside Balochistan. Already in the first few words, he begins to part ways with the conventional narrative.

In March 1948 the Pakistani military forcibly annexed Balochistan. It is impossible to understand our demands if you do not understand this fact. You see, we never wanted to be a part of Pakistan. That is why we declared our independence on August 11, 1947 — three days before Pakistan. Our wishes were betrayed. By the British, and then, by Pakistan in March 1948 when their troops marched into Balochistan and forced us to sign an accession treaty.

The conventional narrative does not tend to the particularities of Balochistan's entry into Pakistan. Usually, it limits itself to the occurrence of accession in March 1948, followed by a swift move to the narration of parallel events around the country. But sometimes, Pakistani historians refer to a conference held in June 1947, two months before Pakistan's independence in August, where selected Baloch leaders called for Balochistan's accession to Pakistan.

Political activists like Wahab contest the idea that Balochistan voluntarily acceded to Pakistan. They point out that the June 1947 conference is misrepresented by Pakistani historians, who claim that it reflected the wishes of the Baloch. A closer look at the conference reveals that its participants were limited to British-appointed Sardars (tribal leaders) and municipal authorities from what was known as "British Balochistan," a northern strip of land ruled directly by the British and dominated by the ethnic Pashtuns. British Balochistan was separate from the much larger, southern Kalat State, dominated by the Baloch and governed by the British through a policy of indirect rule. Under this policy, the Khan of Kalat and a loose network of Sardars were paid a regular fee in exchange for leasing their territory to the British Empire and for promising their services and loyalty during the so-called "Great Game" with Tsarist Russia.[3]

Neither the Khan of Kalat nor the Sardars of Kalat State participated in the June 1947 conference. When the Khan signed the accession treaty in March 1948, people like Wahab argue, it was under duress.

The idea that the Khan signed the treaty under compulsion is contested by some scholars and by the Khan in his own autobiography. However, the Khan admits that he signed the document because he feared for the very existence of Pakistan, and he did not have the mandate to take the province into Pakistan in the first place.

The very existence of Pakistan was at stake. I realized that I must act now, and I must act quick. Therefore, without obtaining the formal sanction from the tribal Sardars, I signed the merger documents in my capacity as Khan-e-Azam on 30th March 1948. I confess I knew I was exceeding the scope of my mandate.[4]

The Khan-e-Kalat's autobiography served a political purpose, to disarm the new state's animosity toward the Khan. The Khan ignored the very instrument that he had created prior to the accession, the two-chamber Kalat Assembly, consisting of a lower Dar-ul-Awam (House of Commons) house and an upper Dar-ul-Umara (House of Lords) house.[5] The houses are still criticized as being unrepresentative—many members appointed by the Khan of Kalat himself—but since no other institution or referendum took place in Balochistan to represent the interests of the Baloch, it is typically considered the only reflection of Baloch interests at the time. Both houses declared that they did not want to join Pakistan, and it was as a member of the former that Ghaus Bux Bizenjo, at the age of only 29, spoke words that still reverberate among Baloch today. He argues that being Muslim does not equal being a nation, and that though he was prepared for an "honorable relationship," he did not want Balochistan to join Pakistan:

> I do not propose to create hurdles for the newly created state in matters of defense, external affairs, and communications. But we want an honorable relationship and not a humiliating one. We don't want to amalgamate with Pakistan.

Later, Ghaus Bux Bizenjo became a pro-federation man, serving in government and contesting elections within Pakistan. Today, he is the symbolic father of the pro-federation National Party and the father of Senator Hasil Khan Bizenjo. But despite his pro-Pakistan actions, he never disowned his speech, and even the most ardent pro-federation politicians today are hard-pressed to suppress the declarations of the only people's institution at the time: that Balochistan wanted independence.

The Second Betrayal: Pakistan's Broken Promises

One week after meeting Wahab Baloch, I meet with five students from Quetta, all members of the Baloch Students' Organization—Azaad (Freedom). Just like Wahab, they have been difficult to get a hold of. But after various phone calls from different borrowed cell phones, I manage to set up a meeting.

I meet them in their large and roomy homes. The boys sitting around me are no more than twenty-two years old, ardent supporters of an independent Balochistan. Knowing that there are a fair number of political parties and groups within Balochistan who prefer engaging with the Pakistani state, I ask whether working with rather than against the government makes sense. "Only a fool or a traitor would do that," they answer. "What's the point of negotiations with a state that never keeps its word? It's time to pick sides."

These young people are obviously in favor of an independent Balochistan, but they are not alone with their views. These are broadly shared, even by the likes of Jahanzaib Jamaldini, the acting president of the pro-cooperation Baloch National Party (Mengal). From him one hears the tales of Prince Abdul Karim Khan and Nawab Nouroze Khan Zarakzai, two Baloch heroes remembered as leaders of the First and Second Baloch Uprisings (1948 and 1958) and both betrayed by Pakistan.

Prince Abdul Karim Khan fled to Afghanistan after 1947 with seven hundred armed followers, arms, ammunition, and treasury funds. He had fled to gain Afghan support for a revolt in Balochistan, a move that was perhaps encouraged by his brother, the Khan-e-Kalat.[6] There is a dispute about what happened in Kabul: the dominant Pakistani narrative suggests that Karim's forces were substantially expanded by Afghan support, but most Baloch nationalist historians point out that Kabul refused to support Karim (Kabul wanted Balochistan to be part of a Pashtunistan state). Karim decided to return to Pakistan after the new government threatened reprisals against his brother, the Khan. Karim was offered "safe conduct and amnesty" by the Pakistan government, but when he crossed the border the state's forces attacked and arrested Karim and his followers. His arrest became the first broken promise of the Pakistan state in Baloch memory.[7]

The second broken promise followed ten years later, and is now celebrated as Martyr's Day every July 15. On October 6, 1958, one day before Ayub Khan established Pakistan's first military regime, the military arrested the Khan-e-Kalat, seized his treasury funds, beat his supporters, and "detained fifty of his retainers as well as an estimated 300 Baloch political leaders in other towns."[8] According to the dominant Pakistani narrative, the reason for these actions was that Abdul Karim and an uncle of the Khan were negotiating with Afghanistan for support. Scholars, such as Selig S. Harrison, dispute this. The only visit to Kabul around that time took place when the Khan's wife visited the Afghan city on holiday. Nevertheless, the Pakistani military's actions sparked a revolt, and it was the 750–1000 man guerrilla force of the then ninety-year-old Nawab Nouroze Khan Zarakzai, the chief of the Zehri tribe, that proved to be one of the most successful. For over a year the elderly Nouroze Khan fought for the return of the Khan and the abolition of the newly formed One Unit Plan. Observing that the fighting would have no end, the army and Nouroze Khan's guerrillas met in early 1960 to negotiate a peace deal. According to the dominant Pakistani narrative nothing came of the discussions. But Baloch historians say that the army promised an abolition of the One Unit Plan, a return of the Khan, and amnesty to the guerrillas. The safe return of the guerrillas was, according to popular stories in Balochistan, promised with one hand on the Qur'an. When the time came for Nouroze Khan to return with his guerrillas, however, they were arrested and "his son and five others were hanged on treason charges on July 15th, 1960."[9]

Selig Harrison describes the hanging and its place in Baloch memory:

Popular accounts relate that the condemned cried, "Long Live Balochistan!" as they went to the gallows. One of them reputedly tied a copy of the Koran around his neck, shouting that if he were hanged, the Koran must also be hanged, since the government had broken its holy oath. Nauroz Khan's sentence was commuted to life imprisonment, and he died in Kohlu prison in 1964, a martyr to the Baluch cause. Stories of his alleged torture by the army are still a staple commodity of Baluch magazines. On a visit to Quetta headquarters of the Baloch Students Organizations in 1978, I saw a montage, covering an entire wall, which showed Nauroz next to scenes of his son's hanging and other atrocities.[10]

The feeling of distrust toward the Pakistani state continued into the Third Baloch Uprising of 1962, among others, led by the Lion of Balochistan, Sher Muhammad Murree. To symbolize their distrust toward the Pakistani state, the (now more organized and strategic) guerrilla force under Murree called themselves *pararis,* someone whose concerns cannot be solved by talk.

The Third Betrayal: Trumping Self-Rule

Hasil Khan Bizenjo looks a lot like his father, the larger-than-life historical symbol of Balochistan, Ghaus Bux Bizenjo. Now the vice-president of the National Party, Hasil Khan serves as a Senator in the National Assembly.

Puffing on a cigarette in one of the parliamentary lodges in Islamabad, he makes his views crystal clear. He is a pro-federation man, through and through, just like his father, but one who still believes that provincial autonomy and self-rule have eluded his province for too long.

Whether separatist or pro-Pakistan, Baloch political activists agree that Balochistan has gotten a raw deal from the beginning. Like their neighboring Pashtun province, NWFP now Khyber-Pakhtunkhwa, they were livid at the One Unit Scheme, and both the Second and Third Baloch Uprisings were a response to this. They were also enraged with the aggressive military presence of the scheme, led by none other than General Tikka Khan. His leadership tactics earned him the title the Butcher of Balochistan, foreshadowing his future sobriquet, the Butcher of Bengal.

By the end of the 1960s and early 1970s, the Baloch resistance seemed to pay dividends. In 1969, General Yahya Khan ordered the withdrawal of the much-criticized One Unit Scheme. The next year, Zulfiqar Ali Bhutto allowed the Baloch to have their first provincial government, with local stalwarts like Ghaus Bux Bizenjo and Ataullah Mengal in charge under the auspices of the National Awami Party, a coalition of nationalist and left forces.

The hopeful mo(ve)ment was short-lived. When Bizenjo and Mengal wanted to replace Punjabi bureaucrats with local Baloch, the central government resisted arguing that such demands went against constitutional provisions. The continued involvement of the military further aggravated local rulers. Baloch remember a local government with limited authority to decide on its internal affairs.

The arrangement fell apart on February 12, 1973. Nawab Akbar Bugti told Bhutto about the London Plan, which was an alleged conspiracy hatched by the Baloch and the Pashtuns with Iraq and the Soviet Union to overthrow the Pakistan (and Iran) government. It is unclear if these accusations have any merit. Harrison argues that a split between Sher Muhammad Murree—who wanted a far more aggressive and armed approach to the Pakistani state—and Ghaus Bux Bizenjo—who was pro-negotiations—might have opened up the possibility of a conspiracy. The conspirators were arrested. The Hyderabad Trials were highly one-sided, giving credence to the Baloch view that the state sets up bogus institutions to give a veneer of legality to its illegal actions.

The Baloch feel a certain kinship with Pakistan's former eastern wing, Bengal. Bhutto's dismissal of the Baloch government came only two years after he rejected the outcome of national elections that gave the Bengali leader, Sheikh Mujibur Rehman, the prime ministership and Rehman's National Awami Party a majority in the National Assembly. For the Baloch, Bhutto's dismissal of their provincial government was a repetition of his historical mistake in Bengal.

Bhutto's subsequent legal charade did not prevent the Fourth Baloch Uprising of 1973–78. The government responded with 80,000 Pakistani troops and Irani pilots flying F-14 Fighter Jets and AH-1 Gun-ships (courtesy of the Shah of Iran). Bugti handed in his resignation on January 1, 1974, to protest the Pakistani assault.

Assaults against the Baloch mirrored the bloody civil war that Pakistan had just exited in Bengal. But a media blackout on the Bengal issue was followed by a similar blackout on the attacks in Balochistan. Pakistanis around the country knew little of the events that transpired.

A few years later, Zia's takeover temporarily relieved Baloch leaders. Zia released the leadership and declared a ceasefire. Self-rule was out of the question, as it was across the country, now in the grips of a military regime. Zia installed Lieutenant General Rahimuddin Khan, a Pashtun who did not support the idea of an independent Balochistan, and who successfully crushed all rebellions. Political parties were banned, and an iron fist was used against the revolt. Here Balochistan was a mirror to the rest of Pakistan. Zia told Harrison that he had no sympathy for the "Baloch problem":

> We want to build a strong country, a unified country. Why should we talk in these small-minded terms? We should talk in terms of one Pakistan, one united, Islamic Pakistan.

According to Harrison, Zia attempted to implement the "ontology of Islamic nationhood," supporting the establishment and flourishing of right-wing Islamist parties in the province in an indirect attempt to quench Baloch opposition.

Today, these parties are becoming increasingly powerful, especially in the Pashtun-dominated areas of northern Balochistan, including Quetta. A drive through Quetta reveals an overflow of Islamist slogans written by the likes of Lashkar-e-Jhangvi, an outfit known for its targeting of the city's Shiite Hazara minority, the same ethnic group that was a target of genocidal killings in neighboring Afghanistan during the Taliban regime. Quetta is also home to the pro-Baloch Pakhtunkhwa Milli Awami Party and the Hazara Democratic Party, but both operate without state sanction. Baloch parties, on the other hand, are targets of the Frontier Corps, the notorious paramilitary unit of the Pakistani armed forces.

In the 1990s, Balochistan's Sardars began to hold genuine power. Both Bugti and Mengal served as chief ministers and governors during this period, intermittently replaced by various central government loyalists. The inclusion of Baloch leaders and political sentiments of all stripes to head provincial governments reduced support for secession. But it did not give the Baloch a sense of achievement. The federal government continued to resist attempts by Baloch leaders to replace Punjabi and Mohajir[11] bureaucrats with local Baloch. As *Pakistan Today*'s Shahzada Zulfiqar put it:

> Look at the Saindak Gold and Copper Project that started in 1993. Bugti wanted to have a local Baloch head the project, but the federal government refused, insisting that someone from outside the province should take over its reins. Baloch looking back at that period see a very deliberate policy to

Mahvish Ahmad

maintain central government hegemony by ensuring that Mohajirs and Punjabis remain in administrative power—whether it was in the bureaucracy, the police, or the military.

Attempts at provincial autonomy were resisted by Islamabad. That had to wait until the passage of the 18th Amendment and the Aghaaze-Huqooq Package more than a decade later.

The Fourth Betrayal: "In the National Interest"

On a visit to Gwadar Port, water rights activist Sharif Shambazi met a *machera*—a fisherman. Living on the banks of the multimillion dollar warm-water, deep-sea port project, the *machera* spoke words that Shambazi found hard to forget:

> They enter our homes and turn us out, settling others from far away. If someone breaks into your home and throws you out, and you scream your powerless scream, can you be blamed? These people think we oppose megaprojects. We don't. But we're never consulted. None of this is built for us.

Built in 2007, Gwadar Port was one of the Musharraf era's notorious adventures into multimillion dollar investments for the Pakistani economy. Strategically located at the apex of the Arabian Sea and at the entrance of the Persian Gulf, the port has come to represent much of what the Baloch feel has gone wrong with Pakistan's adventures into megaprojects and other initiatives "in the national interest." The Gwadar Port itself has been accused of not employing local labor (preferring to import labor from other provinces) and selling the surrounding land at rock-bottom prices to influential politicians and brokering unfavorable deals with the Port Authority of Singapore (PSA), the contractor that now manages the port.[12] One NGO, the South Asian Partnership Pakistan, has said that the Port creates "a new power structure which places the local people at the lowest rung or . . . simply [. . . throws] them out."

Islamabad argues that Balochistan should share its resources. They argue that the province is sparsely populated but covers over 40 percent of the land constituting Pakistan. From a national planning perspective, Balochistan should share.

But Baloch of different political stripes disagree. According to them, Balochistan gets little benefit from Gwadar and other major investments. Pro-federation politician Jahanzaib Jamaldini points to the unfairness of Islamabad's development strategy:

> Would it be fair for me to ask Punjab to give me one of its rivers? No. In the same way, it is unfair of Punjab to constantly ask Balochistan to share of itself, especially when we get next to nothing in return.

The Port is not the first instance of the imbalance. The story begins in the 1950s with the Sui Gas Fields and is repeated in the 1990s with the Saindak Gold and Copper project. "If you go to the Sui Gas Fields in Dera Bugti," Jamaldini points out, "you'll see a cantonment protecting personnel, ensuring that they are supplied gas and electricity all day, everyday. But if you walk around outside the cantonment, you'll find Baloch living without access to gas. That too in an area that supplies gas to the entire country."

The megaprojects fall into two categories: *developmental* and *extractive*. The former include Gwadar Port, Mirani Dam, the *kacchi* irrigation canal, and a coastal highway linking Gwadar to Karachi, built primarily for transporting goods from the port to the country's closest commercial hub. Shambezi, who was visiting Lahore with his four-man team when I met him, has been actively campaigning against the Mirani Dam. Like the port, Mirani Dam has been accused of putting the interests of locals last. Built in 2001, local activists were concerned that the Mirani Dam construction team led by Descon Engineering Ltd. failed to take local knowledge of the Dasht River on which it was built into consideration, instead erecting manmade constructs ill suited to the river's natural flow and cycle.

"We were proved right," says Shambezi. In late June 2006, Cyclone Yemyin struck the area around Mirani Dam. The dam worsened the effect of the cyclone. Subsequent floods demolished 6,500 homes, displacing thousands of people. Five years later Shambezi, his team, and the thousands around Mirani Dam are still waiting for compensation.[13]

The other set of projects facing similar criticisms falls into the extractive category. Based on the lucrative Tethyan Belt that stretches into Waziristan and Afghanistan, Balochistan has extensive tapped and untapped resources (copper, gold, oil, gas, lead, and zinc). A cursory glance at a map reveals the Reko Diq and Saindak Copper and Gold mines in the eastern Chagai district, the oil and gas fields in the districts of Kohlu/Lorelai and Dera Bugti, home to the Bugti and Murree tribes, and the lead and zinc mines down south in district Lasbela. The projects tend to be criticized for furthering a state and elite-centered rather than people-centered paradigm.

According to Shambezi, Jamaldini, and others like them, mega-projects are problematic because of their *structure* and *output*. On the one hand, unfair ownership arrangements, exorbitant costs, inefficient processes, and unfavorable profit-sharing agreements between either the contractor or the federal government and the Balochistan government or the locals frustrate the Baloch. On the other hand, Musharraf and the formally democratic central government's promise of socio-economic development, employment, and poverty reduction has not been fulfilled. In the eyes of the Baloch, the lucrative outputs from the mega-projects in their province are pocketed by contractors from China to Chile and a federal government that does little to address its people's rampant poverty.

Project Structure: "Unfair"

Jamaldini is not alone in thinking that there "needs to be a proper investigation into these projects." Those down south face problems with Gwadar Port, and those a little further north—like Shambezi—are still dealing with Mirani Dam. Move a little west and witness the extraction projects in the Saindak and Reko Diq Copper and Gold Mining Projects. Operations for copper and gold mining in Saindak are currently leased out to the Metallurgical Corporation of China (MCC) by the federal government, which, according to a source within the mining department, leased the site from the provincial government in 1982 under the reign of Zia ul Haq (begging the question of whether the lease was voluntary). The same source argues that the Chinese are known for "over- and under-invoicing," and the *Asia Times Online* journalist Syed Fazl-e-Haider argues that the Chinese have been overproducing at

Saindak: "Such a high rate of production may end the life of the mine, previously estimated at 19 years, before the 10-year lease of the Chinese firm expires if excessive mining goes unchecked."[14] The federal government has increased the lease to the Chinese for another five years, seemingly leaving out the Balochistan government—and local residents—from its decisions.

The Reko Diq Gold and Copper Mining Project faces an even larger—and far more public—criticism. Twenty-six senators and other plaintiffs filed a petition to the Supreme Court demanding a cancellation of the Reko Diq contract with the Tethyan Copper Company (TCC—co-owned by Canadian Barrick Gold Corporation and Chilean Antofogasta). They protested what they perceived as project delays, demanding a larger share (at the moment the Balochistan government owns 25 percent of the project) and disagreeing with the US$3.3 billion cost estimate presented by the company (arguing that two-thirds of it was budgeted to build a pipeline from the mine to Gwadar Port, to ease exports of minerals for refining in Chile—something the Baloch have read as siphoning off minerals rather than building a refinery in Pakistan). Some observers say the province is to blame since its government agreed to the deal in the first place. But whether you believe one or the other, one thing remains true according to Maqbool Ahmed and Nasir Rahim in a *Herald* investigative report on Reko Diq ("Treasure Denied" in *Herald,* March 2010)—everyone has forgotten the people.

The Chamalang coal mines in Lorelai and Kohlu further east in Balochistan have moved from words and court paper protests to gunfights and army intervention. A few years ago, the Pashtun Looni tribe fought the Baloch Murree tribe over ownership rights of the mines. In an attempt to intervene and control the situation, the state has stationed the Frontier Corps in the area, at a time when the Pakistani armed forces face enormous criticism in the province for abductions and extrajudicial killings of Baloch activists—of which the Murree tribes with their history of rebellion are prime targets. Though the army portrays itself as a peacemaker, its current reputation across the province in general, and in that area particularly, betrays another story.

Project Output: "Putting the Baloch Last"

"We have the most impoverished population in Pakistan . . . But we're also naturally endowed with minerals, resources, and the longest coastline in this country. We could be self-sufficient, but we're not," Jamaldini says. "That in itself tells you a lot."

Officially the government, military, and various corporations are attempting to co-invest in social sector projects. At the moment, the TCC has invested in clean water and women's health in the Reko Diq area, and the Saindak project has some local labor requirements (some even claim 80 percent local labor currently operating there though the number cannot be verified). The army is currently building schools and making other social investments around the Chamalang coal mines.

According to Jamaldini and Shambezi, the rampant poverty around many of the megaprojects tells another story, and attempts by the military to invest in socioeconomic development is a white-wash—especially at a time when they are accused of a host of other atrocities. According to them, the Baloch are at the bottom of the rung, less important than company profiteering and national interests.

From Sui to Saindak, gas and gold leave the province. At the end of the past century, the Pakistani state is seen as having replaced these precious commodities with trash. At Chagai, in 1998, the state deposited atomic material into the province, devastating the health of nomads and cattle living in the region.

"And the Betrayal Continues . . ."

"Nothing has really changed over the past sixty years," Wahab says. "If anything it has gotten worse. Since July last year the Pakistanis have been kidnapping and killing our people."

People around us have started to look over their shoulders, whispering to each other and recognizing Wahab, "the sarmachar." About an hour ago, the waiter brought two cups of tea, but with the heat of the city and the conversation we haven't touched our chai. The thin film of *malai* on the tea and sweat on our brows seem to betray our less-than-innocent conversation to all those around us. A conversation that is finally reaching its end point, unfolding the betrayals of today.

In July 2011, Human Rights Watch unveiled a much-awaited report slamming the security agencies for extrajudicial kidnappings and killings in the province.[15] Earlier, the Human Rights Commission of Pakistan had produced a confirmed list of one hundred forty tortured bodies discovered on empty roads and desolate mountaintops across the province.[16] And according to a local organization, Baloch Voice for Missing Persons (BVMP), several hundreds more have died, and several thousands are still missing. Whether there is talk of a few hundred, or many thousands, there is little doubt that the security agencies are carrying out crimes against what the Pakistani state claims are its own people. In a continued attempt to push the state, media, and security institutions to do something about the atrocities committed against the Baloch, BVMP sets up a daily camp outside the Quetta Press Club. Of the four families and friends of missing persons that this writer met in Karachi and Quetta, at least half of the missing persons have been found dead.

To assuage Baloch frustrations, the state has attempted to recommend and implement various reforms. In 2004 the then Prime Minister Chaudhury Shujaat Hussein formed two parliamentary committees comprised of sixteen senators and twelve members of the National Assembly drawn from a wide range of Baloch political parties (not including, of course, the separatist ones). And on November 23, 2009, the Pakistani government introduced the Aghaaz-e-Huqooq package, meant to initiate a wide variety of political and socioeconomic reforms and initiatives to address some of the grievances in the province.

A cursory look at this latest agreement between the Pakistani state and Balochistan confirms that the central government has done little or nothing to implement most of the proposals in the package. The monitoring committee responsible for overseeing its implementation was originally headed by Senator Raza Rabbani, but, after little to no progress was made on the package, Rabbani resigned in protest. In his capacity as Interior Minister, Rehman Malik replaced Rabbani. Anyone who has visited Quetta or met Karachi's Baloch political activists knows that Rehman Malik is anything but popular. A thirty-eight-page progress report presented to parliament in March 2011 confirmed the ways in which the package has been stalled. Only a quarter of the proposals have been implemented in the past two years.[17] Some of these include proposals like the replacement of the army by the Frontier Corps. According to Malik Siraj Akbar, the editor of the Pakistan Telecom Authority–censored *Baloch Hal,* an online news magazine, the Baloch see no difference between the army and the Frontier Corps.[18] For them, both are arms of a central state that kidnaps and kills their people, and both are not to be trusted.

Rabbani took over the monitoring committee at the request of the Prime Minister, but Islamabad's package has not been implemented. Rabbani, as well as the provincial government, is a questionable representative of Baloch interests. Visit Balochistan and many will point out that a large range of political parties boycotted the provincial elections in 2008, resulting in more pro-central government parties in power. Furthermore, those political parties that represent separatists in the province have no place in the formal seats of power in the provincial government. The very idea of contesting elections would negate their agenda.

The interview is over and Wahab is ready to go home. The entire interview has been a murmur of a conversation, barely audible from where I sat across from him on the rickety plastic chair. He excuses himself but as soon as those around us can see he is finished, he is approached. Can he come speak about torture at a human rights seminar? Is he available for an interview? Wahab has more to say, recounting Balochistan's betrayals to all those who listen. The lament, however, is joined by a hope of changing the fate of his land and its people.

At the end of the interview Wahab reaches into his *shalwar kameez* pocket and pulls out a small, square piece of paper. He unfolds it, irons it out with his large hands, and gives it to me.

"Read these," he says. "They'll help you learn more."

On it he has written the names of authors and books, one of which — Martin Axmann's *Back to the Future* — brings me to Gul Khan Nasir, one of the most celebrated Baloch poets of his time. On one of the many websites dedicated to him, one of Nasir's poems seems to embody the long conversation I had with Wahab.

> If you can cross the carcasses then come listen to me!
> Our fates have been entwined, my freedom means you're free.

Notes

1. The friend was Ghulam Muhammad Baloch, the president of the Baloch National Movement (BNM), a coalition of separatist parties. Ghulam was later killed in what is known as the 2009 Turbat Killings alongside Lala Munir Baloch, vice president of the BNM, and Sher Mohammed Bugti, vice president of another separatist party, the Baloch Republican Party.

2. *Sarmachar* is Balochi for fighter, or freedom fighter, depending on one's perspective.

3. The Great Game refers to the almost century-long "secret war" between Imperial Britain and Tsarist Russia. The British feared a Russian invasion into their Indian Empire and used Afghanistan and the border regions of current-day Pakistan as buffer zones to protect their treasure.

4. Mir Ahmed Yar Khan Baluch, *Inside Baluchistan: Political Autobiography of Khan-e-Azam* (Karachi: Royal Book Company, 1975), 162.

5. Martin Axmann, *Back to the Future—The Khanate of Kalat and the Genesis of Baloch Nationalism* (Karachi: Oxford University Press, 2009), 226–32.

6. Selig S. Harrison explains, "K. B. Nizamani, one of the participants in this mini-revolt, recalled in a 1980 interview that Abdul Karim had the tacit approval of the Khan, who saw the move as a last-ditch means of pressuring Pakistan and regaining some of his princely prerogatives." *In Afghanistan's Shadow: Baluch Nationalism and Soviet Temptations* (Washington, D.C.: Carnegie Endowment, 1981), 26.

7. Ibid., 26–28.

8. Ibid., 27.

9. Ibid., 28.

10. Ibid., 28–29.

11. Punjabis constitute Pakistan's dominant ethnic group. Mohajirs refer to Muslims who migrated to current-day Pakistan from what today constitutes India. Many came from affluent backgrounds and have since sat in powerful positions within the state.

12. *Herald* investigative journalist Maqbool Ahmed has uncovered Gwadar Port's unfavorable deals with the Port Authority of Singapore (PSA) and the sale

of land to influential politicians. See Ahmed, "Sold in Haste," *Herald* (Karachi), February 2009, and "The Great Land Robbery," *Herald* (Karachi), June 2008.

13. On this particular visit to Lahore, Shambezi and his team met with the WAPDA chairman to address their concerns. This time WAPDA promised it would deliver, but time will tell whether they will come through.

14. Syed Fazl-e-Haider, "China Digs Pakistan into Hole," *Asia Times Online,* 5 October 2006.

15. Human Rights Watch Report 2011, *Pakistan Security Forces "Disappear" Opponents in Balochistan,* www.hrw.org/news/2011/07/28/pakistansecurity-forces-disappear-opponents-balochistan.

16. Human Rights Commission of Pakistan 2011, *Blinkered Slide into Chaos,* www.hrcp-web.org/pdf/balochistan_report_2011.pdf.

17. Zahid Gishkori, "Aghaz-e-Huqooq-e-Balochistan—Reform Package Stopped in Its Tracks," *Express Tribune,* 7 March 2011.

18. Malik Siraj Akbar, "A Lasting Solution for Balochistan," *Dawn News,* 25 April 2011.

A Tempest in My Harbor
Gwadar, Balochistan

HAFEEZ JAMALI

Life in the Dystopia of a City (to Be)

On first sight, Gwadar, a small coastal town in the southwestern Balochistan province, is a landscape of abandonment, a bit like a frame from a decaying movie reel that has suddenly wound to a halt and the objects have frozen in action. Skeletons of unfinished buildings, parks, stadium, hospital, and offices litter the landscape. Craters and potholes have developed in the middle of recently built wide-lined avenues and roads. In some places, the Shamal wind blowing from Iran has buried unused dual-carriage roads under big piles of sand that render them impassable. If one ventures outside the town, the windswept sandy plain is dotted by tiny whitewashed concrete cabins, the "site-offices" of incomplete residential schemes, with shiny names like Sun Silver City, Platinum City, Florida Heights, and Miami Villas. There is an occasional flurry of activity in the town when a large cargo ship, lured by promises of government-subsidized transportation, docks at the newly built seaport. But most of the time, the townsfolk seem to wait anxiously for a promised future whose arrival has been delayed or deferred, at least for now.

That promised future was the Pakistani government's ambitious plans for developing Gwadar into a Duty Free Port and megacity of international standards that would rival Dubai and Hong Kong in its splendor. It would attract commercial traffic from the busy waterways of the Persian Gulf and propel a stuttering and phut-phutting Pakistan onto the highway of hypermodernity. Since 2003, General (Retd.) Pervez Musharraf kept telling Pakistanis that Balochistan province would be the engine of growth for Pakistan's faltering economy. He followed up on his promise by inaugurating a series of large-scale development projects that included Gwadar Deep Water Port, Mirani Dam, Mekran Coastal Highway, and Saindak and Rekodek Copper-Gold Projects. Gwadar occupied the pride of place in this futuristic vision of Balochistan and Pakistan. It was to be the jewel in General Musharraf's crown, the El Dorado where middle-class Pakistanis' dreams of becoming "world class" citizens would come true.

Soon an army of bureaucrats, private entrepreneurs, industrialists, hoteliers, real estate agents, marketers, and builders—many of them Musharraf's cronies—descended on Gwadar. Aided by local middlemen and corrupt revenue officials, they poured in billions of rupees to buy land from local people and turn it into commercial and residential real estate. Television commercials, billboards, and newspaper ads showed urban Pakistani couples walking hand in hand on the golden beaches of Gwadar as the sun set behind them into the Arabian Sea. They invited onlookers in Karachi, Islamabad, Lahore, and even expatriate Pakistanis living in Europe and North America to buy land in Gwadar. It was touted as "a place where dust turns into gold" (*jahan mitti sona ban jaye*) and where one could enjoy "a forty-year tax holiday," that is, not having to pay taxes on goods and services until 2040.

Absent from this picture of capitalist development were the fishermen and ordinary Baloch people elsewhere in the province. Ethnic Baloch people form the majority of Balochistan's population but count as a small minority in Pakistan, which is dominated by civil and military elites from the majority Punjabi and Urdu speaking ethnic groups. Working in their small boats (*yakdars*) bobbing on the shimmering and gently heaving waters of the semicircular bay, Baloch fishermen were at once the background and provided the requisite element of oriental mystique. They were meant to be the blank slate or tablet on which General Musharraf would inscribe his saga of modernization. They were the silent wall against which metropolitan Pakistani dreams of modernity were being projected.

Except that they refused to be. The Baloch have maintained historical grievances against the Pakistani state since the country's inception in 1947, giving rise to four armed insurgencies in the past sixty years.[1] When General Musharraf announced his plans for developing Gwadar at the turn of the millennium, Balochistan was in the grip of a growing armed insurgency, or a war of national liberation as the Baloch call it.[2] The guerrillas were disillusioned by the failure of the parliamentary politics of the 1990s to win any significant measure of political autonomy for the Baloch to defend Baloch rights over their land and resources (sahel-o-wasail). The democratic interlude in Pakistan that followed the death of dictator General Zia-ul-Haq in 1988 turned out to be a failure for Baloch people, and for Pakistani masses generally, because the political leadership could not address the critical issue of the rights of marginalized ethnic groups in Pakistan. The guerrillas also wanted to stake a claim for Baloch people's recognition as an independent and sovereign party regarding the future of Balochistan's resources and its strategic coastline. They made this claim in the context of an evolving regional competition between Pakistan, Iran, India, and the United States over the energy resources of Central Asia and proposed plans for establishing transnational trade and energy corridors passing through Balochistan.[3]

Within this context, the exclusion of Balochi people from key decisions over the future of Gwadar Deep Water Port, the displacement of local fishermen from their ancestral lands and fishing waters, and the anxiety regarding the future influx of migrant Punjabi labor into Gwadar have increasingly fed into the ordinary people's disillusionment with the state's plans for initiating mega economic projects. These processes have deepened the Baloch sense of alienation and loss of faith in mainstream parliamentary politics and have become one of the driving forces behind the resurgence of Baloch identity and militant Baloch nationalism at the beginning of the twenty-first century. In an ironic twist, the Pakistani government's historic apologies to the Baloch people for past wrongdoings and promises according the province its due place on the national agenda have instead led to a violent confrontation between Baloch nationalist insurgents and Pakistan's military and political elite.

Hafeez Jamali

These developments raise important questions from the perspective of comparative political economy, identity politics, and the study of social movements. How do out of the way places like Gwadar come to occupy a central place in the imagination of state authorities and ordinary people and become objects of competing nationalist desires? Why and how are these places quickly abandoned when they become unsuitable or inhospitable? How do local people inhabiting these abandoned or in-between places live or survive? To what extent, and in what ways, do these developmental or globalizing processes make them rethink their ideas of self and place as well as their political identities? This essay throws light on these issues through an extended meditation on the developments in Gwadar as seen from the perspective of ordinary Baloch fishermen.

Port, Pipelines, and Pipe Dreams of Modernity

> The past is never dead. It is not even past.
>
> — *William Faulkner*

In frontier regions like Balochistan that mark the inside/outside of the state, strategic security concerns and economic interests fuse together in a complex knot that goes to the heart of how nation and territory are imagined in Pakistan. In order to ensure the integrity and longevity of the sovereign body of the nation (*mulki salmiat, baqa, aur khushali*), the state must imagine a different geography and vision of territory. Pakistani rulers not only need to reassure their anxious audiences about the security of the national territory but also compel them to understand that reorganization of places like Gwadar along neoliberal lines, and the accompanying dispossession of Baloch people, is critical for the long-term survival of the nation.

General Musharraf's vision involved leasing parts of national territory in Balochistan that were considered good investments in terms of their natural resources (oil, gas, iron ore, and copper–gold) or probable sites for setting of Export Processing Zones and Free Trade Zones to multinational companies (MNCs). Under this scheme, Gwadar was set up as a "hub port" that would become a conduit for north–south transfer of newly discovered oil and natural gas from the landlocked Central Asian Republics (CARs) as well as west–east transfer of existing oil resources from the Middle East.[4] In addition, it was expected to provide the CARs and the western parts of China such as Xinjiang access to the "warm waters" of the Arabian Sea through a network of roads, railroads, and pipelines.

While the idea of a strategic port at Gwadar was an old one dating back to the 1970s, its rebirth as a project with a regional and global reach was entirely new. Journalist Amir Mateen (2010) puts this vision of territory and accompanying Pakistani desires succinctly:

> The dream was that the sight of Gwadar's emerald green waters would make us shake our shoes off to stroll on its white sands. It was supposed to fulfill our longing for the beaches of Bahamas, the skyscrapers of Shanghai, and the lifestyle of Dubai. It was meant to be a strategic deep water port that would snatch away trans-shipping business from regional giants like Dubai and Muscat; outsmart Iran's upcoming Chahbahar port in unlocking the gateway to the central Asian markets; and in turn transport their oil and gas to the "warm waters" of the Persian Gulf. It was designed to be a tax-free trade and industrial hub that would link China's western regions to the outside world through the ancient silk route.

Accordingly, the Pakistani pedagogical project moved away from advocating the benefits of state-led development as in the 1970s and 80s to promoting export-oriented growth and wooing foreign investors in the 1990s and 2000s. In this reimagining of economy and territory, the Pakistani leadership invoked the colonial image of Balochistan as an empty land (*terra nullius*) inhabited by tribal (read "savage") peoples who must be either co-opted peacefully or "pacified" by military means in the larger national interest. To the strenuous complaints and objections of Baloch fishermen, boatmakers, and day laborers in Gwadar regarding their future, the metropolitan Pakistani replies with a shrug of his or her shoulders: "I am sorry, brother, but you are standing in the way of national prosperity!" For instance, on the occasion of inaugurating the Gwadar Port in 2007, General Musharraf exhorted the Baloch to accept the presence of MNCs and foreign investors in Gwadar for the good of the nation:

I am very glad to be standing at a place where five to six years back there was *nothing except for sand and dust,* no roads or buildings, etc. However, today we see progress—infrastructure is being built, there are roads, buildings, power supply, and a hotel has also been constructed that is equivalent to other hotels in Islamabad, Karachi, or Lahore. . . . Some elements here are reluctant and misguide that foreigners would confiscate the land from locals and pressure them. *My brothers and sisters, nations who are not afraid of outsiders succeed. But those who resist investors remain backward and poor.* [Emphasis added]

And for those who dared to ignore his fatherly advice and chose to resist, the General issued a stern warning:

There are two or three tribal chiefs and feudal lords behind what is going on in Balochistan. The past governments have made deals with them and indulged them. My government is determined to establish its writ. It will be a fight to the finish.

These tropes of "tribalism" and "backwardness" have been invoked since the time of the British Raj to launch aggression against the Baloch and to integrate them into the mainstream of colonial rule in India. Nevertheless, British authorities viewed them largely in favorable terms through the figure of the "noble savage" (*Encyclopedia Britannica* 1910, 194; Titus 1998) and adopted a relatively decentralized system of managing Baloch tribes through the institution of tribal *jirgas* or councils of elders (Bruce 1896). Accordingly, official policy in the late colonial period was geared toward maintaining the status quo in Balochistan by limiting intervention in Baloch social life and protecting the "tribes" from the "corrosive" influence of mainstream politics of anticolonial nationalism (Radaelli 1997). This was achieved through draconian curbs on political organization, press and publications, and movement in and out of Balochistan (Yousufzai 1997; Nasir 1979). Beginning in the 1960s, the postcolonial Pakistani state gradually tried to "rationalize"and centralize the administrative system in Balochistan. This effort was geared toward assimilating the Baloch people politically and culturally into the national body and establishing homogeneous authority of the state over its territory. In this reformulation of the state–population relationship in the postcolonial period, the Pakistani authorities introduced large-scale infrastructural projects in a bid to recast this older colonial relationship around the discourse of development.

While the slogan of development had some popular appeal for the masses in metropolitan centers like Lahore and Karachi, in the frontier territories of Balochistan both the rulers and the ruled were under no illusions as to what development really meant. Much like its colonial predecessor, the Pakistani state continued to intensify its penetration of territory and control over land in Balochistan by military means while justifying the appropriation of territory in the name of modernization and development. Accordingly, the promotion of Gwadar as a commercial hub was accompanied by intense militarization of the entire Mekran Coast. This includes the construction of the Jinnah Naval Base at Ormara, the allotment of seventy-three thousand acres of land to the Pakistan Air Force at Hingol National Park, and the allotment of six thousand acres of land to the Pakistan Navy in Dasht Valley. Within Gwadar itself, the provincial government allotted ten thousand acres of land to the military for building a Joint Defense Complex (JDC) while the Pakistan Navy controls six hundred acres of prime commercial land on Batel Mountain. When some observers pointed out this apparent contradiction between rhetoric and reality, it elicited quiet novel explanations from the military leadership. One claim put forward in favor of building military installations in Balochistan was that military cantonments actually foster the process of development!

Moreover, we need to abandon certain preconceptions in contemporary political economy in order to understand how an out of the way place such as Gwadar came to occupy a central place in the imagination of Pakistani policymakers and urban citizenry in Lahore, Karachi, and Islamabad. The unfinished story of infrastructure development in Gwadar suggests that global capital is not a "thing" that comes to inhabit certain parts of the national territory based on its needs and then stays or leaves, nor does this process take place in a "rational," uniform, and incremental or progressive manner. Instead, desires for consumption of global/cosmopolitan things colonize thought and imagination as a prelude toward the appropriation of territory. Pakistani leaders like General Musharraf try to emulate neoliberal utopias revealed by the gods of commerce to the detriment of local peoples. They enact elaborate, at times farcical, public rituals to please and entice these gods and create spectacular public displays to convince their publics that they have the capacity to bring prosperity to the nation. Their successors keep repeating the farce long after it becomes obvious that the gods have abandoned them and are not likely to return.

For instance, on the occasion of the Gwadar Port's inauguration in 2006, the port authorities failed to attract any commercial ship since importers were not interested in booking their cargo for Gwadar. To make up for this, the authorities duly rounded off two empty vessels anchored in Karachi Port for repairs, the *MV Yazdan* and *MV Sibbi,* and brought them to Gwadar to grace the inauguration ceremony. Four years later, the democratically elected Prime Minister, Yousuf Raza Gilani, decided to hold the National Finance Commission Award meeting aboard a ship in Gwadar to promote the port.[5] This ceremony cost Rs. 5 million at a time when the Pakistani government was celebrating "austerity week," besides disrupting daily life and causing hardship for Gwadar's residents. The National Highway Authority (NHA), the Provincial Buildings and Roads Department (B&R), and the Gwadar Development Authority (GDA) worked day and night to clear the sand dunes and debris covering the newly built roads and give the visiting dignitaries the impression that all is well (*sab achha hai*). The Balochistan Chief Minister, accompanied by the Chief Ministers of the other three provinces, fixed the inaugural plaques/ foundation stones for Punjab House, Sindh House, and Frontier House in a desolate location at the town's periphery, which nobody has since cared to visit.

Rude Awakenings on the Shores of Desire

> Go, watch the moon from your own house!
>
> —*Order by an anonymous soldier*

One community that answered General Musharraf's call toward progress was the small neighborhood of Mulla Band, which stood at the proposed site for the construction of Gwadar Port. The bargain was negotiated by the district administrator (DCO) and the mayor (**Zila Nazim**) in person. In return for voluntary relocation from their old houses with adobe walls and thatched roofs near the beach, each family from the community would get their plot of land in the planned New Town Housing Scheme and would also be given money to build their own cemented (*pukka*) house. The government also undertook to provide civic amenities such as sewerage, water, electricity, and social services such as schooling, healthcare, etc. The people of Mulla Band were resettled into a part of New Town Housing Schemes that was renamed New Mulla Band. Noor Bashk, a resident of Mulla Band, recalls vividly the heady mix of expectation and anxiety:

> When construction on the Port started near our neighborhood, people got worried. You could hear the giant cranes working day and night and digging up the beach. We were all afraid of losing our homes and risking our livelihoods. Many people said that the government could not be trusted. But we were also excited by the promise of a good future. We wanted pucca houses, wide streets, and steady income. Price of land was increasing by the day in Gwadar and we thought that having our own piece of land and house in New Town scheme will allow us to benefit from the opportunities in the future city. We dreamt that our children would study in an English medium school and grow up to be doctors and engineers, not poor fishermen like us.

Seven years on, the residents of New Mulla Band feel abandoned by the government. Although they are grateful that the government kept its promise and gave them a piece of land and money to build their own houses, there are no basic amenities or any school or hospital nearby. If a woman, child, or an elderly person becomes ill, people have to pay a huge sum to hire a taxi to take the patient to the local hospital because there is no public transportation. Most families in the neighborhood cannot afford to send their kids to school for the same reason. Those members of the community still engaged in fishing are suffering debilitating losses. They live far away from the beach on the periphery of the town and it costs a lot of money to travel back and forth. Several individuals who owned their boats have been compelled to sell them and are now forced to work as hired hands (*janshoo* or *khalasi*) on other folks' boats. For the past two years Noor Bashk and his colleagues have been running from pillar to post to get the title deeds for the land on which they built their houses, but without success. They met with the mayor, the district administration, and the parliamentarians from Gwadar but nobody seems to care about them anymore.

In contrast to the rest of Balochistan province, where people saw Gwadar as a symbol of occupation of their land by non-Baloch outsiders, the people of Mulla Band were resentful about being abandoned and left to fend for themselves. Their views suggest that the Pakistani government's propaganda regarding the local Baloch being "anti-development" (*taraqee mukhalif*), presumably on account of lack of schooling or tribalism, is a figment of the metropolitan imagination. As anthropologist Partha Chatterjee points out in his book *Politics of the Governed,* people living at the margins of the state want development but they want it on their own terms, not on the terms dictated by others.

The more experienced boat captains and young political activists, however, were much more strident in their criticism of the Port and what it did to the fishermen. Allah Bashk is an experienced Nakhuda and veteran seaman whose wizened face told of his long years at sea. He made fun of my light skin and warned me that if I kept hanging out with the fishermen, the salt and the sun would get under my skin and darken and wrinkle my face. His voice trembled with frustration and rage as he recounted the fishermen's growing disillusionment with developments in Gwadar:

> I am an old campaigner. I know of many countries and I have travelled to many places. I know what is going on with us and difficult circumstances surrounding us. We see that we are not getting any benefits from developments here in Gwadar. We just labor to feed and support our kids. We hear about the mega projects but these have only taken away our sea (without giving anything in return). Our circumstances have not changed. They have taken away our harbor and we don't have a place to protect our *yakdars* during a storm. This was both our jetty and our belly (food). You know several *yakdars* were broken into pieces during the recent storms. You saw it with your own eyes! You see how these things are making life a living hell (*azaab*) for the fishermen. Fishermen are from a weaker class of society and we don't have the wherewithal to suffer these kinds of losses.

The fishermen's sense of disillusionment and being pushed to the wall was deepened by the strangle-hold of federal security forces like Pakistan Coast Guards, Frontier Corps (FC), Pakistan Navy, and Maritime Security Agency (MSA) on Gwadar. Their presence is ubiquitous. When you enter the town, you are greeted by the FC personnel. The beaches on either side of the town are patrolled by soldiers from the Coast Guards, and taking a walk after sunset appears a hazardous enterprise. The Port area itself is a closed security zone and an innocent gesture like taking a picture of the port can lead to interrogation by the secret service. The fish-landing jetty and nearby waters are manned by Marine Security Agency personnel. The road leading to the top of Batel Mountain is dotted with Coast Guards and Navy checkpoints and the Navy controls much of the land there.

> My friend Barkat, a young social activist, observed that the commercialization and militarization of Gwadar had closed out places that people used to visit to spend their down time, or as part of their annual gatherings or to make offerings at sacred sites (*ziarat*). Barkat wistfully recalled the memories of old days before the building of the Port. When it rained, all the families in nearby neighborhoods would go to the top of Batel Mountain after the rain. Women took their soiled clothes with them. They sat around the water ponds (on the mountain), washed their clothes, and chatted among themselves. They would go out in the wee hours of morning, when it was still dark so they could not be seen by other men, and come back after sundown. He pointed out that there were several large holes on the other side of the mountain near the graveyard where the Frontier Corps checkpoint now stands. These holes would fill up with water after the rain and young people would come over there to bathe and women would wash their clothes some distance away. The women would cook their food and eat, smoke their hookah (*chilim*), and wash their clothes.

He then cited a personal encounter with Coast Guards personnel to illustrate his point. He and a friend were walking toward the beach where the Port and the Fish Harbor now stand. At that time the Port was still under construction. It was a full-moon night and they just wanted to hang out there and watch the sea. While they were sitting on the beach and watching the moon, a soldier from the Coast Guards, who was patrolling the area on foot, approached them. He rudely asked them what they were doing there. Barkat and his friend replied that they were watching the moon. The soldier tersely replied: "Go away from here and watch the moon from your own house!" (*Chand ko ghar say ja kar dekho!*).

The soldier's brusque intervention in what appears to be a poetic moment is a metaphor for the awkwardness of Baloch desires for modernity in Gwadar. It is a future that many desire privately even as they publicly contest it. The problem is that they can enjoy this future only if they accept their subordinate position within Pakistani society. The anonymous soldier, the most potent symbol of state power in Pakistan, rudely wakes them up from their dreaming.

Forging Identity: Fisherfolk's Movement and Baloch Nationalism

The encroachment of land and sea by private capital and state authorities seems to have engendered two kinds of responses among Baloch subjects in Gwadar. On the one hand, there has been a resurgence of ethnic Baloch nationalism and revival of Baloch identity all over Balochistan with its highly charged discourse of demanding independence from Pakistan. There has been a growing awareness among ordinary Baloch residents that both the Pakistani state and multinational companies and foreign powers are after their land and coastal belt because it is full of precious metals and other natural resources such as oil and gas. Baloch nationalists oppose Gwadar Deep Water Port and other mega development projects. They see these as colonial enterprises meant to impose Punjabi settler colonialism on them. They maintain that Balochistan's mineral resources and its strategic coastline (*sahel-o-wasail*) belong to the Baloch nation alone. Outsiders, namely the dominant Punjabi and Urdu speaking ethnic groups, have no right to steal their property (*maal-o-maddi*) and violate the sanctity of Baloch land (*Gul zamin*).

Alongside the pan-Balochistan struggle of ethnic nationalism, however, a local politics of fisherfolk's identity revolving around fisherfolk's rights to the sea and to the future city of Gwadar also evolved. While they were inspired by the words of Baloch nationalist leaders like Nawab

Akbar Khan Bugti, late Balach Marri, and Sardar Ataullah Mengal, their position as a subaltern class within Baloch society shaped their response to the nationalist movement. The fisherfolk of Gwadar were initially suspicious of the fiery rhetoric of Baloch nationalists in Mekran and elsewhere in Balochistan who came from more educated, prosperous, and powerful families. They were, therefore, initially reluctant to get involved with the revolutionary politics of Baloch national liberation. Instead, their response to the occupation of land and sea came in the form of mobilizing around the notion of fisherfolk's identity and rights. These two narratives of identity and resistance to the encroachment of Pakistani state and global capital in Gwadar emerged not so much in opposition but in tense coexistence with each other.

The Fisherfolk's Movement or **Med Ittehad** was initially a civil society organization or Anjuman that sought to bring together fisherfolk of the entire Mekran Coast under one umbrella to protest illegal fishing in the waters of the Arabian Sea. They successfully rallied fisherfolk against the use of nylon or plastic nets that destroyed fish egg and compromised the fisherfolk's livelihoods. Emboldened by their initial successes and propelled by the fisherfolk's resentment and anxieties about the ground slipping from under their feet, Med Ittehad became politicized. In particular, it staked a claim for representing the fishing community's interests at the local council level. Med Ittehad also raised its voice against the mistreatment of fisherfolk at the hands of the security forces. Fisherfolk were routinely mistreated by the personnel of the Maritime Security Agency and the Pakistan Navy when they tried to cast their nets in the waters close to site of Gwadar Port. At times, they were deliberately humiliated, slapped, and made *murgha* [sit in a crouched position, like a chicken] by the Maritime Security Agency personnel. Med Ittehad's championing of the fishing communities engendered faith among the fishers in their own collective power. They could now take pride in their identity as fisherfolk in a social milieu in which they were traditionally looked down on as menial laborers.

However, the nonviolent politics of Med Ittehad could not sustain itself in the face of the growing militarization of Gwadar. A series of violent encounters with the security forces exposed the limits of a peaceful social protest in the face of a state security apparatus that is armed to the teeth. The federal security forces in Gwadar were suspicious to the point of being paranoid about opposition to and criticism of the Pakistani government's development plans. Nakhuda Rahim Bashk recalls a time when a large group from the Gwadar fishing community was staging a sit-in or road-block against the security forces' behavior. The district authorities asked the fisherfolk leaders to sit down with them and negotiate for an amicable solution to avoid confrontation with the police. While the leadership was engaged in negotiations, a vehicle carrying soldiers from Maritime Security Agency (MSA) tried to pass through the crowd. On the activists' refusal to let the vehicle pass, the armed personnel opened fire and several fisherfolk were injured in the incident, some seriously. Rahim Bashk's eyes became misty as he recalled the scene to me:

> While our leaders were holding peaceful negotiations with the local administration and Port authorities, the MSA personnel opened fire on us. When the leaders came back to the scene of the bloodshed, people became angry. They asked what the point was in negotiating when we were being fired on?

The heavy-handed attitude of the security forces eventually pushed the townsfolk, especially the youth, over the edge. The peaceful struggle of the fishing community appears increasingly irrelevant in a political environment characterized by arrests, illegal disappearances, torture, and death of political activists. The community elders, although bitter, are still trying to hold on to their dreams of having a share in Gwadar's future and are reluctant to come out in favor of armed resistance. The younger generation, however, has cast its lot with the Baloch national movement. When I visited Gwadar in 2007-08, the slogans and graffiti on the walls were written mostly in black and asked the government to stop illegal fishing and provide basic amenities like water, electricity, and sewerage to people. By 2010 the writing on the wall had changed. Now the slogans were written in red ink and they demanded an independent Baloch homeland. The powerful Pakistani military and federal security forces have resorted to extreme measures such as throwing the tortured dead bodies of political activists, some as young as twelve years old, every week in a desperate bid to terrorize the people and stem the groundswell of nationalist feeling. However, each new incident of torture, disappearance, and death seems to fan the flames of discontent.

Conclusion

Gwadar is a microcosm of the abusive and violent relationship between the Pakistani state and its Baloch subjects. It is a relationship characterized by the state's refusal to recognize the legitimate aspirations of the Baloch people for economic and political autonomy and suppress them through the use of brute force. This policy has been followed elsewhere in Balochistan and has led to the deaths of hundreds of people and displacement of more than eighty-four thousand internally displaced people. Yet, obsessed by a narrow focus on the "war on terror," the Pakistani and international media have ignored the plight of the Baloch people despite the enormity of human rights violations in Balochistan. When anchorpersons and commentators do take up the issue of Baloch identity and the Baloch national question, the debate is always couched in terms of a primitive and tribal reaction to the advance of modernization and development, which tends to cloud the issue.

The interplay of development, identity, and place in Gwadar suggests that this view of nationalist politics in Balochistan is deeply flawed. Baloch identity and the Baloch national movement do not represent the resurgence of a primitive tribalism in the face of the modernizing mission of Pakistani state. Baloch fishermen and members of particular tribes are not mute and gullible people who blindly follow the diktats of their tribal chiefs and leaders. Instead, they are thoughtful and perceptive actors who forge their collective identities in particular moments through specific struggles against concrete circumstances threatening their economic and cultural well-being. People in Gwadar may be ethnically Baloch but yet they may emphasize their political identity as part of the fishing community until changing life experiences and their reading of those circumstances compel them to do otherwise.

Notes

1. See Harrison (1978, 1981); Salim (1993); Grare (2006).

2. Pakistani analysts and anchorpersons usually ascribe the rise of militant Baloch nationalism to the Pakistan army's decision to assassinate the veteran Baloch leader and the chief of Bugti tribe, Akbar Khan Bugti, in 2006. This is a mistaken belief since the insurgency predates Akbar Khan Bugti's death by a few years and its underlying causes lie elsewhere. Sporadic incidents of armed resistance had started as early as 1999, around the time General Musharraf overthrew the elected government of former prime minister, Nawaz Sharif. It is true that Akbar Khan Bugti's tragic death strengthened Baloch nationalist movements by compelling ordinary Baloch who were watching the armed struggle from the sidelines to join the ranks of the insurgents. Nevertheless, in this author's opinion, the resistance would have continued even if General Musharraf had reached some kind of a compromise with the Bugti chief.

3. See Rashid (2002); Wirsing (2008).

4. The concept of a hub port is based on the "Hub and Spoke system." This is a distribution system based on a "hub," i.e., Gwadar, moving cargo to and between several "spokes." Spokes can be smaller ports or land cargo distribution areas. A hub port collects numerous trades at a single concentrated point and distributes them efficiently (Hassan 2005).

5. The NFC Award or National Finance Commission Award is the formula for sharing of resources among the four provinces of Pakistan and the federal government. A number of taxes collected by the federal government are pooled together in the Federal Divisible Pool and then redistributed to the four provinces according to a weighted formula based primarily on the population but also includes such factors as relative poverty, natural resources, area, etc. The seventh NFC Award meeting was held in Gwadar, Balochistan, on December 31, 2009.

Works Cited

Baloch, S. "The Great Baloch Martyr." *Daily Times* (Lahore), 26 August 2010.

Bruce, R. I. *The Forward Policy and Its Results.* London: Longman, 1900.

Chatterjee, Partha. *The Politics of the Governed: Reflections on Popular Politics in Most of the World.* New York: Columbia University Press, 2004.

Chisholm, Hugh. "Baluchistan." *Encyclopedia Britannica, 11th Edition.* Cambridge: Cambridge University Press, 1910.

Dutta, S. *Imperial Mappings—in Savage Spaces: Balochistan and British India.* New Delhi: BR, 2002.

Grare, F. *Pakistan: The Resurgence of Baluch Nationalism.* Washington, D.C.: Carnegie Endowment for International Peace, 2006.

Harrison, Selig. *In Afghanistan's Shadow: Baluch Nationalism and Soviet Temptations*. Washington, D.C.: Carnegie Endowment for International Peace, 1981.

Hassan, A. *Pakistan's Gwadar Port: Prospects of Economic Revival*. Master's thesis, Naval Postgraduate School, Monterey, Calif., n.p., 2005.

Mateen, A. "The Agonizing Contrast of Gwadar Dream," Amir Mateen Dot Com, 2010. http://amirmateen.com/?p=307 (accessed 31 March 2011).

Nasir, Mir Gul Khan. *Tareekh-e-Balochistan* (History of Balochistan). Quetta, Pakistan: Balochi Academy, 1979.

Nicolini, B. "Baluch Role in the Persian Gulf during the Nineteenth and Twentieth Centuries." *Comparative Studies of South Asia, Africa, and the Middle East* 27:2 (2007).

———. "The Makran-Baluch-African Network in Zanzibar and East Africa during the Nineteenth Century." *African and Asian Studies* 5:3–4 (2006).

Rashid, Ahmed. *Taliban: Islam, Oil, and the New Great Game in Central Asia*. London: Tauris, 2002.

Redaelli, Riccardo. *The Farther's Bow: The Khanate of Kalat and British India (19th–20th Century)*. Frenze, Italy: Manent, 1997.

Salim, A. *Balocistân: Sòûbah, Markaz Taalluqât, 1947–77*. Balochistan: Province-Center Relations, 1947–77. Lahore: Frontier Post Publications, 1993.

Titus, P. "Honor the Baloch, Buy the Pushtun: Stereotypes, Social Organization, and History in Western Pakistan." *Modern Asian Studies* 32:3 (1998).

Wirsing, R. G. *Baloch Nationalism and the Geopolitics of Energy Resources: The Changing Context of Separatism in Pakistan*. Carlisle, Penn.: Strategic Studies Institute, U.S. Army War College, 2008.

Yousufzai, F. M. *Yaad'dashten* (Recollections). Quetta, Pakistan: Progressive Writers' Association, 1997.

Swat in Transition

SULTAN-I-ROME

SWAT LIES AT THE CROSSROADS of South Asia, Central Asia, and China.[1] Once the cradle of the great Gandhara civilization, Swat is now part of Pakistan's Provincially Administered Tribal Areas (PATA) of the Khyber Pukhtunkhwa province. The "Switzerland of the East," Swat attracted travelers and adventurers over the centuries.[2] In recent years, it has become famous for another kind of adventure: war. Since the 1990s, it has been home to the Tahrik Nifaz-e-Shariat-e-Muhammadi (TNSM), whose rebellion against the government resulted in armed clashes with the Pakistani military in 1994 and then again in 2007–09 (under the leadership of Fazlullah).

The entry of militancy into Swat is related to certain important historical factors, such as the manner in which Swat was incorporated into the state of Pakistan and the wars in Afghanistan. This essay lays out these elements in some detail. What is important to establish before we get to these details is that Swat society is remarkably independent. The Swatis were known to be instinctively restive and hence always at daggers drawn prior to the 1920s, defending their Pukhtun code (*Pukhtu* also called *Pukhtunwali*). Occupied by the Yusufzai Afghans in the sixteenth century, Swat nonetheless was ruled by the tribal welter, divided into two opposing blocks (*dalay*). As well, the people of Swat have had a long history of patronizing religious figures, the babas and mullas of the past such as Mian Noor, Akhund Abdul Ghafur (Saidu Baba), Sadullah Khan (Sartor Faqir), and Sandakai Baba.[3] Between 1879 and 1881, the Khan of Dir occupied the right bank of Swat. The combination of independence and the role of the babas pushed the people of Shamizi, Sebujni, and Nikpi Khel cantons to unite under the patronage of a religious figure, Sandakai Baba, in 1915. After various encounters, they defeated and expelled the Dir forces, formed a five-member council to manage the affairs of the liberated area, and installed as their king Sayyad Abdul Jabbar Shah on April 24, 1915. Two years later, in September 1917, he was made to relinquish power.[4]

In the place of Abdul Jabbar Shah, the people installed Miangul Abdul Wadud, the grandson of Saidu Baba. Abdul Wadud (Bacha Sahib) was dynamic and energetic. He expanded and consolidated the emergent Swat State. The drive, initiative, and policies of the new king made Swat a model of peace in the Pukhtun tribal areas. A sense of peace and respect for the authority of the state prevailed in an overwhelmingly illiterate tribal society. Under the term of an illiterate but enlightened person, Swat became "a unique State."[5]

In December 1949, Abdul Wadud abdicated in favor of his son, Miangul Abdul Haq Jahanzeb (Wali Sahib). The Wali Sahib put his energy into developmental work, such as in the education, communication, and health sectors. His modern education and outlook pushed the Wali Sahib to consider certain Western developments, which also included education and health policies as well as his secularization and modernization of the state institutions and the society. Both Miangul Abdul Wadud and Miangul Jahanzeb gradually altered the centuries-old social organization and introduced drastic changes. Although autocratic, they evolved governmental machinery that not only controlled but also served the people: they provided quick disposal of disputes and cases, standard civic amenities like education, health care, and communication systems, and ensured peace, security, and order. These changed the outlook, behavior, and temperament of the people and eroded the tribal ingredients of the society.

The emergence of Pakistan in 1947 did not affect the Swat State's independence. The Swati ruler signed the Instrument of Accession to join Pakistan, but he formally held most of the power to manage the Swat State.[6] Although the Wali Sahib surrendered more power to Pakistan by signing the Supplementary Instrument of Accession in 1954, matters remained as they had been. However, on July 28, 1969, the Chief Martial Law Administrator and President of Pakistan, General Yahya Khan, announced the merger of the State; and on August 15, 1969, the Wali lost his seat. The Malakand Division absorbed Swat and a Commissioner took charge. The Commissioner and Deputy Commissioner came to administer the Wali's former state as well as Kalam (the area the Wali Sahib administered on behalf of the Pakistan government).

The Pakistani state brought an alien administrative apparatus, characterized by federal and provincial centralization, and a bureaucratic mindset. Decisions regarding development policy and financing were made at the federal and provincial levels. The implementation of these policies was done through a bureaucratic hierarchy. Even though the constitutional status of Swat as a tribal area remained, the judicial system was changed. It was now characterized by technicalities, delay, and high costs.

Gradually, the number of educational and health care institutions increased. The chain of communications was extended into the remote parts of Swat by the 1980s. But the Pakistani authorities were not prepared to commit themselves to the full development of Swat. The first commissioner of the Malakand Division, Sayyad Munir Hussain, wrote a note that "further developmental works are no more needed in Swat. *These are more than sufficient* [my italics]. We should have only to maintain them."[7] Civic amenities faded away. Along with them went the quick disposal of cases. The new officers and bureaucrats were mainly concerned with how to pass their time rather than how to solve the people's problems. In April 1979, ten years after incorporation, the Wali Sahib compared his Swat State with that of the Pakistani government:

> The present administration functions very differently from mine. Cases must wait for years before they are decided; security has become poor, maintenance of public facilities is poor. Officers in charge come and go; they never have time to learn, or to see any project through. The different branches of Government do not coordinate. At the time of the State, one mind and one purpose controlled it all; we could coordinate all the efforts and pursue persistent and long-term policies.[8]

It is this condition that generates nostalgia for the past. But it also drives the people to seek positive change, especially in the judicial system. It is for that change that people sometimes feel sympathy for the idea of Islamic courts, and it is in this context that the Tahrik Nifaz-e-Shariat-e-Muhammadi (TNSM) makes its appearance in Swat in the early 1990s.

Pakistan's Swat

After the emergence of Swat State, the tribal social organization of Swat changed. Nevertheless, Swat remained formally a "tribal area" of Pakistan. It has a different constitutional status from the other parts of Pakistan, being part of the Provincially Administered Tribal Areas (PATA).

Even though Swat's ruler held power over the state between 1947 and 1969, he surrendered his authority over defense, external affairs, and communications. Additionally, the Wali executed the Supplementary Instrument of Accession, which surrendered his legislative authority to the Pakistani federal legislature in the Federal Subjects and also authorized it to legislate, if it so wish, in the Concurrent Subjects. The federal legislature could now enact laws for the Swat State in the same manner as it could make laws for the rest of Pakistan over Federal and Concurrent matters. The Pakistani State would then be able to exercise executive authority over these matters.[9]

Under the Establishment of the West Pakistan Act of 1955, the Pakistan Constituent Assembly declared that the North-West Frontier states (including Swat) be part of the Special Areas. These Special Areas were guaranteed a special relationship with the Pakistani State.[10] Swat retained its status as a "Special Area" under articles 104 and 218 of the *Constitution of the Islamic Republic of Pakistan, 1956.*[11] The special status was retained in all the subsequent constitutional documents, i.e., *Constitution of the Republic of Pakistan, 1962, The Interim Constitution of the Islamic Republic of Pakistan, 1972,* and the *Constitution of the Islamic Republic of Pakistan, 1973.*[12] Therefore, no law made or act passed by the central and provincial legislatures applies to the area, unless specially extended under the special and specific extra procedures. And the special status of the area as a tribal area can only be changed with the consent of the people, represented in a tribal *jarga*.

The special status of Swat has since allowed various actors to call for different ways to manage its affairs, separate from those sanctioned by the Pakistani legislature. Insurgencies in 1994 and 2007–09 called for the enforcement and implementation of Islamic laws also on the basis of this separate constitutional status.[13] This special status made it possible for the TNSM to call for Islamic courts rather than to campaign for the Pakistani judicial system to be made more effective.

The area's constitutional status created a diarchy: as a PATA, the region is under the control of the provincial government, which is responsible for law and order, and yet the provincial government has no authority to make or promulgate laws for the area. The law-making function rests with the governor of the province and the president of the country. They are not part of the provincial government, to which they do not need to be accountable. Neither the governor nor the president is accountable to the people either.

Law and Disorder

Swat State's judicial system was not based fully on Islamic law. Either the local *jargas* fixed the fines by their *dasturul amals* (codes of conduct) or the Wali set the rules.[14] For murder cases, for instance, political considerations and repercussions of the decisions were considered instead of the *shariat* (Islamic law). The judicial system and Swat's laws were a synthesis of the traditional codes and Islamic norms, compatible with these codes and the commands of the ruler. While the ruler was supreme and possessed final authority, the traditional codes held secondary status. Islamic laws were subservient to both of them. Final authority in all sorts of cases was vested in the hands of the ruler, who was not bound by the codes of conduct made by the local *jargas* or the *shariat*.[15]

The question that arises then is despite this, why do people view this period with such nostalgia? The reason is that the judicial system during this period was an effective one: the trials were quick and cheap; the judgments/verdicts were properly executed; and the cases were usually decided on the first or second hearing. Moreover, "some of the short-comings of the Western judicial system—technicality, delay, and high costs" did not exist.[16] Thus, before the merger of the state, whether just or unjust, decisions were quick and cheaper. The litigants were spared the trouble of bearing high expenses and prolonged procedures.

The situation changed with the merger. Regulation I of 1969 divested the ruler of his powers, and delegated these to a person, officer, or authority to be appointed or empowered by the provincial government. All old laws, including regulations, orders, rules, notifications, and customs, having the force of law, were kept enforced.[17] This situation created much confusion and uncertainty as there were no codified laws, rules, and regulations; it was left to the new administrative-cum-judicial officers to define and pronounce the *riwaj* (customary law/practice). Though the main domain of law, *riwaj*, was not codified, it continued to be enforced at the whim of the administrative–judicial officers.

The government gradually started to extend Pakistan's laws and created a Sessions Court for the entire Malakand Division, including Swat. In the 1970s, the government created administrative rulings commonly called the PATA Regulations. These Regulations (Regulations I and II of 1975, and Regulation IV of 1976) transferred the power to decide both criminal and civil cases from the judiciary to the executive branch.[18] The government, however, was not able to address the grievances of the people through its various regulations. The executive referred the cases to the *jargas* (under the PATA Regulations).[19] This did not always work well. There was no clear demarcation between civil and criminal matters, which were sometimes manipulated for ulterior motives. This is why the people's resentment and grievances increased. Moreover, the cases were not quickly decided, which generated resentment; instead of redressing the grievances and facilitating the people, the PATA Regulations made a bad situation worse.

Some litigants challenged the PATA Regulations before the Peshawar High Court in the 1980s. On February 24, 1990, the Division Bench of the High Court declared the Regulations null and void, as to the Bench the Regulations were in opposition to Articles 8 and 25 of the

1973 Pakistani Constitution. The provincial government filed appeals to the Supreme Court, but the court dismissed the case on February 12, 1994, with cost.[20]

Islamic Laws

In 1989, the Tahrik Nifaz-e-Shariat-e-Muhammadi (TNSM, Movement for the Enforcement of Islamic Law) was started in Dir District and Sufi Muhammad was made its head. TNSM wanted the Pakistani authorities to enforce Islamic law, particularly in the Malakand Division. The movement entered Swat soon after.[21] Longstanding grievances against the judicial system produced sympathy for the TNSM activists and their agenda. Even the executive was not opposed to the TNSM, because its unbounded power had been diluted. Therefore, the executive tacitly gave the TNSM free rein in Swat. The TNSM overcame the initial reluctance among the Swatis with its determination.

In May 1994, the TNSM organized a sit-in on the main road at Malakand. The road remained blocked for almost a week. To pacify the protestors, end the agitation, and open up the road, the provincial government agreed to TNSM's demands for the enforcement of Islamic laws and to make the judicial system an Islamic one.[22] The government had yet to implement these demands as it was still working out the modalities when the uprising of November 1994 took place in Swat, in the course of which Swat's government machinery was left paralyzed for three days and resulted in casualties on both sides.[23]

To fulfill their promise and meet the demands of the TNSM, the Provincially Administered Tribal Areas (Nifaz-e-Nizam-e-Shariah) Regulation, 1994 (NWFP Regulation II of 1994) was promulgated. Under this regulation, twenty-three Ordinances and Acts (given in Schedule I therein and already in practice in the settled districts of the province) were extended to Malakand Division (which includes Swat).[24] The regulation, however, was mainly about procedural law, meaning that it only dealt with the procedures of the courts. This fell short of the expectations and demands of the TNSM, and Sufi Muhammad and his supporters were quick to express their disapproval of the new judicial setup. In June 1995, they began the Jail Bharao Tahrik, the fill the jails struggle. It was one in a series of actions that led to another reform from the Pakistani authorities: the promulgation of a new regulation called the "Shari-Nizam-e-Adl Regulation, 1999" (NWFP Regulation I of 1999). This repealed the Provincially Administered Tribal Areas (Nifaz-e-Nizam-e-Shariah) Regulation, 1994 (NWFP Regulation II of 1994). The new regulation extended and enforced twenty-nine Acts and Ordinances (given in Schedule I and already in force in the settled districts of the province), most of whom were already extended under the now defunct Regulation II of 1994.[25] This regulation was also procedural in nature in that it dealt mainly with the procedures of the courts. One of the reforms of these regulations was that Urdu became the court language and the names of the various officers of the courts were now given in Urdu (for instance, the Civil Judge is now the Alaqa Qazi and the Session Judge is the Zila Qazi). In this backdrop, a step of the High Court was the entry of female judges into Swat. They worked in the Family Courts as Alaqa Qazis. This had not been a demand of the movement and, indeed, given the TNSM's own orientation, it was deeply resented. The Tahrik Taliban Swat emerged during this time, particularly on FM radio. It challenged the role of women in courts.

Concessions from the government came alongside quite brutal treatment of the Swatis by the police. The repressive behavior of the police toward the people (including torture, bribery or *bhata,* collaboration with and assistance to criminals) embittered and alienated most people. In 1994–95, the police insulted and tortured TNSM members arrested during the agitation. The rank and file of the TNSM felt a general bitterness toward the police, and indeed to the state.

The reforms brought no visible change in the procedures of the courts. The scenario was still characterized by prolonged procedures, undue delays, technicalities, high costs, and, in some cases, bribery. The people's grievances were not addressed. TNSM continued with its activism, calling again for a change in the judicial system and the enforcement of Islamic laws. The TNSM and the Tahrik Taliban Swat strengthened their position in the region, with sections of the masses supporting them.

Why did the people of Swat rise up for a change in the judicial system, but not the people of the rest of the country? Nostalgia for a previous state system combined with anger at the current system provided the confidence to fight on to bring order to their laws.

War Making

Swat and the northern part of Pakistan have long been part of Imperialism's Great Game. The long Afghan War (1979 onward) made the people more militant. War-making became a basic part of life, with modern arms and training entering the area. The Pakistani and American intelligence agencies organized and trained jihadi organizations (forerunners of the Taliban) for armed jihad (*qital*) to counter the Soviet Union in Afghanistan.[26] The Pakistani agencies did the same, in the name of jihad, in Kashmir. The various external parties recruited, trained, and deployed the young people of this region to fight their enemies in the name of religion. The Pukhtun people of Pakistan developed close personal and operational ties with the people of Afghanistan as a result of this history, and it is what enables them to work in collaboration and coordination. The Pakistani Taliban emerged out of these experiences.

When the U.S. and NATO invaded Afghanistan in late 2001, the *qital* was further strengthened. The Afghan Taliban were overthrown and the U.S. puppet regime came to rule in Kabul. The Taliban and their supporters in Pakistan felt that Afghanistan, a Muslim country, had to be liberated. The Afghan Taliban and their Pakistani comrades resented the government of Pakistan for its withdrawal of support to the Afghan Taliban under U.S. pressure at a critical juncture in 2001. Provision of logistics, intelligence, and support to the invaders also angered the people of the region. Adding fuel to the fire was the presence of the occupation forces in Afghanistan and later the cross-border raids into Pakistan by U.S./NATO troops (including drone attacks). These factors combined to make the Taliban more stubborn, zealous, and more than eager to stand firm for their cause and make sacrifices to achieve it.

In November 2001, Sufi Muhammad and tens of thousands of his supporters in the TNSM crossed into Afghanistan to fight on the side of the Taliban. Suffering huge losses, Sufi Muhammad and his son-in-law, Fazlullah, made it back to Pakistan, where they were arrested and incarcerated. Sufi Muhammad remained in jail, but Fazlullah was released after 17 months.[27] After his release, Fazlullah began to promote a purity campaign on an FM radio channel. With his father-in-law in prison, he was supported by the TNSM people. He began the construction of a *madrasa* and *markaz* (religious center) in his home village of Mamdherai (also known as Imamdherai). People donated generously to his order, and he was able to personally assemble thousands of people at a short notice for a meeting. He rapidly became "popular among [the] masses, but controversial in [the] media."[28]

Fazlullah's growing power and popularity emboldened him to challenge the government writ on several occasions, due to which the government also had to make a show of force. These situations, however, were brought under control by agreements between Fazlullah and the government. Dissent broke out within the TNSM over Fazlullah's policy, and eventually the TNSM broke with him. Nevertheless, Fazlullah's personal power and popularity continued to increase. In 2007, his breakaway faction became part of the newly established Tahrik-e Taliban Pakistan headed by Baitullah Mahsud.

Both the TNSM and Fazlullah's new group shared the same goal, even as they were divided by strategy. Sufi Muhammad was reported to have told the media that if sharia laws were implemented per his demands, he would go to Swat and disarm Fazlullah's group. Muslim Khan, spokesman of Fazlullah, demanded that the Islamic laws be enforced in toto, per the draft submitted by Sufi Muhammad.[29]

Foreign Hands

Many believe that the Taliban was the creation of Pakistan's intelligence agencies and army. Not only has the government of Pakistan benefited from its struggle in Kashmir and Afghanistan in the past, but it also regards the Taliban as useful for the future.[30] Additionally, the manner and way in which the operations (2007–09) and army action were carried out hint that something is amiss.[31] It is also thought, by some analysts, that the U.S., Afghan, and Indian intelligence services push the

Pakistani Taliban and other jihadi organizations to act inside Pakistan, to divert them from Afghanistan and Kashmir.

In October 2007, Ali Muhammad Jan Orakzai, the governor of the province, claimed that he had proof of the involvement of foreign agencies in the upheaval in Swat and the tribal areas.[32] Pakistan's high-level officials, both at the central and provincial levels, have also repeatedly spoken of the involvement of foreign agencies. Some local people believe that the Indian agents and mercenaries are directly involved and are fighting in the guise of and within the ranks of the Taliban. Even Muslim Khan, spokesman of the local Taliban, alleged the involvement of some external and internal forces in the attacks on the police personnel and girls' school in May 2008. This associate of Fazlullah claimed that these forces do not want to allow peace in Swat.[33] Many people also believe that the U.S. has contributed to this instability to justify its presence in Afghanistan.[34] Against this backdrop an analyst has observed, "The blindfolded reaction of the [Pakistan] government has provided innumerable opportunities to foreign secret intelligentsia to interfere and aggravate the deteriorating situation further."[35]

In the 2002 elections, the Muttahida Majlis-e-Amal (MMA) won the election in the North-West Frontier Province (now Khyber Pukhtunkhwa). To undermine this alliance of religious parties, the federal government, the Pakistan Muslim League (Q) and the Pakistan People's Party (Sherpao) covertly supported Fazlullah. The MMA government was more tolerant to the Taliban, given their common religious orientation. With regard to remaining indifferent and opposing any move against Fazlullah and his supporters, Qari Abdul Bais (MMA's member, National Assembly, from Swat) contended, "Many of the Taliban voted in favor of the MMA in the 2002 elections; we can't annoy them, as they are our vote bank."[36] Such a policy boosted support for Fazlullah and made him and his cause famous in a relatively short span of time.

During the period when Swat was a state, non-Swatis were obligated to sign surety bonds to be able to reside in Swat. This was to prevent them from engaging in unlawful activities.[37] They were also not allowed to purchase land, except with the permission of the ruler or heir apparent, which was granted only in special cases. Bonds were also required of them to run businesses and industries.[38] The dissipation of these sanctions and restrictions, after the merger of Swat State, and the exemption from taxation (since the area was constitutionally a tribal area), caused an influx of outsiders into Swat for business, trade, industry, tourism, labor, services, and other such activities. This migration changed the power structure and led to an increase in the population.

The army wanted to have a new airbase and cantonment. The Saidu Sharif airport (in Tahsil Kabal) was to be converted into a military airbase. New boundary limits were marked, which angered the people of Dherai and Bandai, who would lose some land. The cantonment was to be located in Swat, and some suspected that the entire fracas of 2007–09 was simply a pretext to seize land for the military base (as had happened in the 1980s to build the Panu Aqil cantonment in Sindh and to build the Sui and Dhera Bugti cantonments in Baluchistan in 2000s).

The Armed Struggle

By 2007, Swat was volatile. The government and Fazlullah refused to budge from their demands. The government moved armed forces into the area and provoked clashes with Fazlullah's men. The provincial governor tried to suggest that the army operation was a "last option," this as the army's troops were already in Swat. President Musharraf asked Fazlullah and his men to lay down their arms.[39] Akbar Hussain, Fazlullah's commander, also claimed that they are against arms but would not lay them down unless the armed forces withdrew from Swat, the Pakistan state enforce the Islamic laws, and release Sufi Muhammad.[40]

The clashes continued. Fazlullah and his *shura* (consultative body) asked his fighters to evacuate the roadside bases and go underground. It was not their flight from the fight, they claimed, but a change of strategy.[41] While the situation seemed to have calmed down by January 2008, heavy and indiscriminate shelling and bombardment by the military caused heavy loss of lives and property of innocent civilians as well as the displacement of a large number of people. Losses worth billions of rupees in different forms were also incurred.

In this scenario, the Awami National Party (ANP) emerged as the largest party in the provincial assembly after the elections held in February 2008. The ANP fought the elections on the slogan of restoring peace and order and bringing normalcy to the province. Because of this, it held negotiations both with Sufi Muhammad's and Fazlullah's organizations. They concluded agreements, and released Sufi Muhammad. Promises to enforce Islamic law came alongside the promises to support the government in its righteous endeavors, such as for the restoration and maintenance of law and order.[42]

Differences soon emerged. Each side blamed the other for not honoring the agreements. Armed clashes broke out. The government enforced an unprecedented curfew (it continued for eleven months, sometimes with breaks and sometimes without any break, even during the twenty-two consecutive days during Ramazan). Electricity and telephone lines were severed. The Taliban responded with unprecedented violence: decapitation, targeted killing, and the destruction of governmental installations (educational institutions, bridges, police posts and stations). The government used its full force, including "carpet bombing and massive shelling as invading armies do."[43] Extreme violence became routine. Such violence compelled the people to look at both sides with disdain. The asymmetric force used by the government, however, generated sympathy among the people for the Taliban. Ordinary people considered the security forces "as an occupying force rather than a protector" because it was "the people of the area who [were] suffering as innocent civilians [were] being killed in the army action."[44]

The army's three phases of the Operation Rah-e Haq resulted in spreading the power and authority of the Taliban across the region. The government lost its authority.

Swat was at the crossroads. On February 14, 2009, the provincial government entered a fresh agreement with Sufi Muhammad. The clashes subsided. Sufi Muhammad came to Swat, established his camp, and made peace marches to various areas. Outwardly the situation was moving back to normal and tempers cooled down. It was expected per verbal commitments that Sufi Muhammad would not only restore peace in Swat but also denounce militancy. He, however, instead denounced the state organs, in a public meeting in Swat.

On the surface, the ceasefire held. In truth, both sides were getting ready for a new struggle. The Taliban encroached into Dir and Buner, with the blessings of Commissioner of Malakand Division. The media portrayed this as a prelude to a takeover of Islamabad and so of Pakistan's nuclear establishment. The Prime Minister announced to the nation on May 5, 2009, that the army would start fresh operations against the Taliban, called Operation Rah-e Rast (2009). The indiscriminate bombardments and shelling by jet aeroplanes, gunship helicopters, and artillery, and the brutal use of force targeting mostly the civilians, caused great civilian casualties, destruction of houses and buildings and the infrastructure, and forced displacement of hundreds of thousands of people, bringing distresses to all the Swatis.

By July 2009, as the violence subsided, displaced persons were allowed to return to Swat in small batches. The grip of the Taliban slackened, but Swat and its inhabitants went into the grip of the army. The army, on the whole, behaved like occupying forces. They treated the people in an insulting manner. The Taliban appeared uprooted, but their presence remains. Though the Taliban have been defeated, their ideology, mindset, and goals remain intact despite the army's presence.

The government champions the army's success, but that too is an exaggeration. The army created *lakhkars* (*lashkars*) to fight the Taliban. Swat is constitutionally a tribal area, but it is not a tribal society. *Lakhkars* are typically a phenomenon found in tribal culture. They are alien to Swat, with the last *lakhkar* in Swat taking the field against Buner in 1923. The army also overtly and covertly created and backed bodies in the names of different *jargas*. *Jargas* also are a symptom of, and essential to, tribalism. The army used these bodies as tools for implementing its whims, decisions, and dictates. Thus, the army attempts to foment tribalism in Swat. This is a bad sign.

The core issues that led to the Taliban's emergence have not been addressed. Resentment against the security forces and government remains. People are upset about the manner in which the security forces interact with the masses, with the hurdles they create for the common people in everyday life, with the rudeness of its personnel (who often disregard the sanctity of *chadar* and *chardiwari*—sanctity of veil and privacy of houses—especially at the times of the search operations), disregarding the local values and traditions, occupation and rough use of private residences and other buildings that compel the owners to reside elsewhere in rented houses, the refusal to record all the losses and damages as the consequence of the armed action, and not giving full compensation for all the damages incurred on the civilians in different shapes. These grievances fester. They multiply alongside anger at the foreign forces in Afghanistan and Iraq, the lack of resolution of the Kashmir and Palestine issues, and, of course, the core issues: the lack of development in Swat and the onerous judicial system that continues to oppress people. If these are not tackled, Swat's recent history would once more become its present.

Notes

1. This is a modified version of an earlier paper, "Swat: A Critical Analysis," published by Institute of Peace and Conflict Studies (IPCS), New Delhi, as Research Paper No. 18, January 2009.

2. George Getley, *Swat: Switzerland of the East,* n.p., n.d.

3. For Saidu Baba see Sultan-i-Rome, "Abdul Ghaffur (Akhund): Saidu Baba of Swat: Life, Career, and Role," *Journal of the Pakistan Historical Society* (Karachi) 40:3 (July 1992), 299–308. For some detail about Miangul Abdul Wadud, alias Bacha Sahib, see Sultan-i-Rome, "Miangul Abdul Wadud," in Parvez Khan Toru and Fazal-ur-Rahim Marwat, ed., *Celebrities of NWFP,* vols. 1 and 2 (Peshawar: Pakistan Study Centre, University of Peshawar, 2005), 69–93. For more on the babas and mullahs, see Khushal Khan Khattak, *Swat Nama of Khushal Khan Khattak* (Peshawar: Pashto Academy, n.d.); Khushal Khan Khattak, *Swat Nama da Khushal Khan Khattak* (Pashto) with *Muqaddamah, Tahqiq au Samun* by Hamish Khalil (Akora Khattak: Markazi Khushal Adabi wa Saqafati Jarga Regd., 1986). For some detail about the Sartor Faqir and his role, see Sultan-i-Rome, "The Sartor Faqir: Life and Struggle against British Imperialism," *Journal of the Pakistan Historical Society* (Karachi) 42:1 (January 1994), 93–105. For the Sandakai Baba, see Sultan-i-Rome, *Swat State (1915–1969): From Genesis to Merger. An Analysis of Political, Administrative, Socio-Political, and Economic Development* (Karachi: Oxford University Press, 2008), 54–93; Khurshid, "Sandakai Mullah: Career and Role in the Formation of Swat State, Pakistan," *Journal of the Pakistan Historical Society* (Karachi) 47, part 2, (April–June 1999), 77–81.

4. The full story is told in Sultan-i-Rome, *Swat State.*

5. James W. Spain, *The Pathan Borderland* (Karachi: Indus Publications, 1985), 223.

6. Instrument of Accession executed by the Ruler of Swat on 3 November 1947 and accepted by M. A. Jinnah, Governor-General of Pakistan, 24 November 1947, serial no. 14/Swat, file no. 107–S.St. I., in *Tribal Affairs Research Cell, Home and Tribal Affairs Department, Government of NWFP, Peshawar* [henceforth *TARC*].

7. Naeemul Hadi, personal interview, 5–9 July 1998.

8. Fredrik Barth, *The Last Wali of Swat: An Autobiography as told to Fredrik Barth* (Bangkok: White Orchid Press, 1995), 151.

9. See Abdul Hamid (Joint Secretary, Constituent Assembly of Pakistan), *Memorandum on Federated States of Pakistan* (n.p., n.d.), 2. See also "Supplementary Instrument of Accession, 1954," in *TARC,* book no. 15, 1–3.

10. See *The All Pakistan Legal Decisions* [henceforth *PLD*] 7 (1955), Central Acts and Notifications, 273–74.

11. See *PLD* 8 (1956), Central Acts and Notifications, 88–89, 120–21.

12. See "Constitution of the Republic of Pakistan (1962)" in *PLD* 14 (1962), Central Statutes, 206, 215. See also copy of Memorandum 230/22–C from Additional Political Agent, Chitral, to Political Agent, Dir., Swat and Chitral, Malakand, 25 January 1964, *Files of the Tribal Research Cell (Agencies) in Provincial Archives, Peshawar,* bundle 26, serial no. 687. "The Interim Constitution of the Islamic Republic of Pakistan, [1972]" in *PLD* 24 (1972), Central Statutes, 579–80.

13. See also Sayyad Ali Shah, *Da Shariat Karwan: Manzal ba Manzal* (Pashto) (Lahore: Mukhtar Ahmad Khan Swati, Idara Nashr al-Maarif, 1995), 10–18.

14. See Sultan-i-Rome, "Role of *Jirga* in the Formulation of Laws in Swat State," in Alain Viaro and Arlette Ziegler, ed., *Proceedings of the International Workshop "Urban and Environmental Management: Local Dynamics in Intermediary Cities in the Situation of Centralised Governments"* (Geneva: IUED, 2000), 149–54.

15. For details see Sultan-i-Rome, "Judicial System, Judiciary, and Justice in Swat: The Swat State Era and the Post-State Scenario," *Journal of the Pakistan Historical Society* (Karachi) 49:4 (October–December 2001), 89–100; Sultan-i-Rome, *Swat State,* 195–203, 307–11.

16. Wayne Ayres Wilcox, *Pakistan: The Consolidation of a Nation* (New York: Columbia University Press, 1963), 155.

17. See Regulation I of 1969, Dir., Chitral and Swat (Administration) Regulation, 1969, in *PLD* 22 (1970), West Pakistan Statutes, 2.

18. The chapter of the Pakistan Penal Code was exempted from this change; hence, the cases under this chapter were still to be tried by the judiciary. The same was the case on the civil side but only in the cases in which the government was directly a party or minor(s) or insane(s) were party or any arbitration clause was applicable there. Therefore, the judiciary still existed, side by side, for trial of such cases.

19. *Jargas* here does not mean and refer to the traditional *jargas*. Under the PATA Regulations, the Deputy Commissioner was authorized to refer a case to a group of men, nominated by him and headed by a government functionary—Tahsildar or Naib Tahsildar—so as to see and inquire into the matter and decide. They

were called *jarga*. These *jargas* had no symptom of and hence could not be taken for the traditional one.

20. *PLD* 42 (1990), Peshawar, 51–62; *PLD* 47 (1995), Supreme Court, 281–306.

21. See Shah, *Da Shariat Karwan: Manzal ba Manzal,* 10–19, 24–27.

22. See also ibid., 34–37, 42–53, 129.

23. See also ibid., 137–53.

24. See "Provincially Administered Tribal Areas (Nifaz-e-Nizam-e-Shariah) Regulation, 1994 (N.W.F.P. Regulation II of 1994)" in Ishfaq Ali, *Laws Extended to the Tribal Areas with Jirga Laws,* 2d ed. (Peshawar: New Fine Printers, n.d.), 23–27.

25. See "The Shari-Nizam-e-Adl Regulation, 1999 (N.W.F.P. Regulation No. I of 1999)," ibid., 41–50.

26. See also Muhammad Amir Rana and Rohan Gunaratna, *Al-Qaeda Fights Back Inside Pakistani Tribal Areas* (Lahore: Pak Institute for Peace Studies, 2007), 12, 24–27, 35; Fazal-ur-Rahim Marwat and Parvez Khan Toru, *Talibanization of Pakistan: A Case Study of TNSM* (Peshawar: Pakistan Study Centre, University of Peshawar, 2005), 2; Emma Duncan, *Breaking the Curfew: A Political Journey through Pakistan* (London: Arrow Books Limited, 1990), 280; Christina Lamb, *Waiting for Allah: Pakistan's Struggle for Democracy* (New Delhi: Viking Penguin Books, 1991), 196, 206–42; Khan Abdul Wali Khan, *Bacha Khan au Khudai Khidmatgari* 3 (Pashto) (Charsada: Wali Bagh, 1998); Muhammad Yusuf and Mark Adkin, *Afghanistan—The Bear Trap: The Defeat of a Superpower* (New Delhi: Bookwise, 2007). Jihad has wider meaning and different kinds. Fighting in the way of the Almighty by means of arms (Holy war fought for the cause of Islam against the non-Muslims) is one of its kinds and is mentioned as *qital* in the Holy Qur'an. With the overwhelming purposely use of the word jihad for its *qital* aspect only, its other aspects, kinds, and dimensions remain hidden from the majority of the people around the globe.

27. See Rahimullah Yusufzai, "Inside Fazlullah's Headquarters"; Abdul Hai Kakar, "Maulana Fazlullah, muahiday kay bad," BBC, 21 June 2007.

28. Khurshid Khan, "Exclusive: An Interview with Maulana Fazlullah," Swat, 21 April 2007.

29. For details, see *Roznama Azadi Swat* (Urdu daily, Mingawara, Swat), 18, 20, 22, and 26 October 2008; *Roznama Aaj Peshawar* (Urdu daily, Peshawar), 18 and 22 October 2008.

30. Interestingly, in the backdrop of the Mumbai attacks of 26 November 2008 and the Indian threats to Pakistan, the Pakistan army spokesman termed Baitullah Mahsud and Fazlullah their brothers. See Tanweer Qaisar Shahid, "Musla," *Roznama Express Peshawar* (Urdu daily: Peshawar), 20 December 2008. And in a special interview, Muhammad Alam alias Binaurai—an important figure of the Tahrik Taliban Swat—said that if the government is honest in restoring law and

order it shall enforce Islamic law practically; all members of Tahrik Taliban will become well-wishers of the government and fully cooperate. He asked the government to immediately practically enforce Islamic law in Swat and use the power of all the Taliban against India and America. See *Roznama Azadi Swat* (Urdu daily: Mingawara, Swat), 18 December 2008.

31. For example of such contention, see Ijaz Mehr, "Taqat kay bajayay muzakirat ka mutaliba," BBC, 1 November 2007; Rifatullah Orakzai, "Swat mayn hukumati karwayi mayn dair kyau?" BBC, 15 November 2007.

32. *Roznama Azadi Swat* (Urdu daily: Mingawara, Swat), 30 October 2007. See also pamphlets dropped through the helicopters by the army, captioned *"Fauj kyau ayi hay?"* and *"Swat kay amanpasand awam kay nam paigham."*

33. For Muslim Khan's statement, see "Swat: Muahiday par Amriki tahafuzat," BBC, 22 May 2008.

34. See also Rifatullah Orakzai, "Swat aur Shangla mayn jharpayn," BBC, 18 November 2007.

35. "A call from the Pulpit."

36. Shaheen Buneri, "War on Terror, Taliban and Pukhtun Nationalists," Khyberwatch.com, 6 March 2008. http://khyberwatch.com (accessed 12 March 2008).

37. For such bonds see "Kitab No. 1: Kitab Faisalajat Wali Sahib 16–12–50 Ta 18–9–65," and "Kitab No. 3: Register Faisalajat Daftar-e-Hizur, Az 16–9–58 Ta 4–8–69," in District Record Room, Gulkada, Swat.

38. See *Riwaj Nama-e-Swat,* compiled by Ghulam Habib Khan, n.p., n.d., 174–77. For examples of surety bonds see "Kitab No. 3: Register Faisalajat Daftar-e-Hizur, Az 16–9–58 Ta 4–8–69," and "Kitab No. 5: Register Zamanat Daftar-e-Hizur, Az 19–2–58 Ta 8–11–65," in District Record Room, Gulkada, Swat.

39. See *Roznama Azadi Swat* (Urdu daily: Mingawara, Swat), 30 October 2007.

40. See Abdul Hai Kakar, "Ghair mulki nahi hay, magar aa saktay hay," BBC, 31 October 2007.

41. See Rifatullah Orakzai, "Taliban hikmat amli tabdeel, Matta fauj kay pass," BBC, 5 December 2007; Rifatullah Orakzai, "Swat: lugu mayn adam tahafuz barqarar," BBC, 8 December 2007; Abdul Hai Kakar, "Kharija policy mayn tabdili chahiyayn," BBC, 30 November 2007.

42. For texts of the agreements see *Myashtinai Pukhtu* (Pashto) 3:5 (May 2008), 51–52, and 3:6 (June 2008), 6–7.

43. Khurshid Alam, "The Second Big Game & Pashtoons," Khyberwatch, 15 November 2008. http://khyberwatch.com.

44. "Expats from Pakistan's Swat worry over relatives," Khyberwatch, 26 November 2007. http:khyberwatch.com (accessed 12 March 2008).

Inside Militancy in Waziristan

IQBAL KHATTAK

HEAVY CLOUDS COVERED THE SUN. Rain lashed the hard land of Mehsud. A car carrying a group of journalists made its way to Makeen, the headquarters of the banned Tehreek-e-Taliban Pakistan (TTP) in South Waziristan. Hakeemullah Mehsud, the new face of the TTP and aide to the militant leader Baitullah Mehsud, appeared from the shade to greet the media. "Welcome to our land," he said.

Not long after, on August 5, 2009, a CIA drone struck the region and killed Baitullah Mehsud and his second wife at her father's home. Hakeemullah was crowned the head of the TTP. The Pakistani government had considered the TTP the most dangerous terror network. With Baitullah out of the way, the government pledged to kill both Hakeemullah and the organization he headed. It was hard to believe the Pakistani military spokesperson, Major General Athar Abbas, when he announced on October 17 that it would take not more than six to eight weeks to complete Operation Rah-e-Nijat (Operation Path to Salvation). The "decisive" operation was not long in coming. The inhospitable terrain and the TTP's strong ideological and institutional hold on the population made such brave talk seem ridiculous. What was more shocking than this bravado was the TTP's reaction to Major General Abbas. It began to abandon its base and move to safer havens in other tribal areas. This was the TTP's "strategic retreat."

The military took quite a long time to complete its preparations. It deployed three divisions (some 45,000 soldiers) to plan the three-pronged attacks on the TTP-held areas. These attacks came from Jandola in the east, Shakai in the west, and Ramzak (North Waziristan) in the north. The military first enforced a complete blockade of the Mehsud areas. The civilian population, some half a million, was evicted to avoid collateral damage. When the army advanced, the TTP-held towns of Speenkai Raghzai, Kotkai, Laddah, and Makeen fell like a house of cards. On November 29, 2009, Pakistan Army chief General Ashfaq Pervaiz Kayani spent the second day of Eidul Azha with soldiers in Makeen. His jawans had just defeated and dismantled the "emirates" of the TTP.

The TTP is one of the most vigorous of the Taliban groups in the region. It is a proponent of Takhferi. During the Afghan jihad in the 1980s and 1990s, some Arab mujahideen from Saudi Arabia dissociated themselves from the Wahabbi school of thought. They formed their own school, which they called Takhferi, far more rigid than Wahabbism. (Takhferi comes from the Arabic word *Takhfir*, which is itself derived from *Kafir*, or impiety. To declare someone *Takhfer* is to claim that they are apostates, impure, and so condemned to death.) The Takhferi group formed outfits in Dir district of northwestern Khyber Pakhtunkhwa province of Pakistan and Jalalabad City in Afghanistan. The group is no longer as active as it once was in Pakistan.

In tribal dynamics, local alliances are formed before any major battle takes place. Two particular groups—the Mullah Nazir group in the west of South Waziristan and the Haji Gul Bahadur group in North Waziristan—would have been strategically positioned to make the battles far more difficult, if not impossible for the army. But this time the tribal allies remained neutral, at least during the course of the offensive.

The civil bureaucracy with strong support from the military started building an anti-TTP alliance in favor of the operation. Feuds between tribes are not uncommon. Old rivalries between the Ahmedzai Wazir and the Mehsud tribes provided the government with a golden opportunity. They exploited the situation and kept Mullah Nazir away from Hakeemullah and the Mehsuds. This failure to create a tribal alliance relieved the military of any pressure if they used the western base in Wana, the summer capital of South Waziristan, in their operation against the TTP. The Wana base played a key role in the attack on Laddah from the west.

"Since the Ahmedzai Wazir tribes have traditional rivalry with the Mehsuds we do not want that our areas are also dragged into this operation," an influential Ahmedzai Wazir elder confided to me. "That is why we influenced Mullah Nazir to extend no support to the Mehsuds in this offensive and we are successful in this attempt." He told me this after the military secured the western front against the Hakeemullah-led militants. Mullah Nazir's backing to the operation, however, did not come without concessions from the government.

"Loyalty" from the tribes in critical times does not go unnoticed by the government. It rewards the tribe with cash awards and development projects. The elder confirmed that the government gave "strong assurances" that the area would be developed. In the Wazir–Mehsud rivalry case, the Ahmedzai Wazirs would have stayed away from the battle to let their rivals be crushed by the government force even without any financial help or development fund. The government payoff was an extra.

Keeping the Hafiz Gul Bahadur group in North Waziristan on the government side was equally important. The military used the civilian set-up to woo the Utmanzai Wazirs and win their support. They invited them to a *jirga* of influential leaders and clerics that was attended by the then Khyber Pakhtunkhwa (previously known as the North-West Frontier Province) Governor Owais Ahmed Ghani in Peshawar and held a few days before the operation was launched. The *jirga* was successful. Hafiz Gul Bahadur remained silent as the government forces pounded the TTP positions from their Razmak base in North Waziristan.

Many analysts support the government's deal-making. They contend that the government acts within reason if it makes a deal with one of the two Taliban groups, in this case that of Hafiz Gul Bahadur, to build an alliance against the stronger enemy, the TTP. One government official justified the deals by arguing: "If the United States can fight the Taliban with active support of other Afghan jihadi organizations in Afghanistan then what is harm in using the same experiment on this side of the border."

Others argue that the two Taliban groups have gone mad to allow the government to divide them. As the government dismantles the TTP, it weakens the Gul Bahadur group's position against the government forces. It appears that Pakistan's army will not touch those elements that are mainly interested in fighting the U.S. or NATO forces across the border in Afghanistan, as long as they do not attempt anything inside Pakistan. The military might, however, be pursuing a different strategy: destroying the militants who act inside Pakistan first, and then taking on the ones who are mainly involved in Afghanistan. Their feat is to outfox the enemy in the tribal areas. "Once the bigger threat is removed the smaller threat will be easier to take out," Brig. (Retd) Mehmood Shah told me. "That is what has been followed before the start of the operation."

The rapid turn-around in the battle between the Pakistani military and the Mehsuds is startling. The Mehsuds, historically, have not fled the scene of battle. For that reason the Pakistani media predicted heavy fighting, with high casualties among both sides. By its own account, however, the military lost only sixty soldiers, and killed some six hundred militants (the TTP's spokesman Azam Tariq denies these figures; he claims that more soldiers died, and fewer militants).

"In tribal dynamics, you derive power from the territory you control. I am at a loss to understand what the TTP gained from losing territory," former military officer Muhammad Saad Khan told me at the TTP strategic retreat. Perhaps the military's firm resolve to "finish the anti-Pakistan" Taliban made the TTP decide not to put up any significant resistance. The TTP cannot match the army's firepower in a conventional fire fight. That factor seems to have led to its disappearance into other areas like North Waziristan, Kurram, Orakzai, and Khyber tribal districts.

The government knew how the TTP was going to react to the operation—carrying out suicide attacks and bombings in urban cities and Peshawar, capital of Khyber Pakhtunkhwa province, previously called the North-West Frontier Province. "We knew the militants will resort to suicide attacks and bombings to target innocent civilians," General Kayani told a gathering of police in Peshawar on November 25. That meeting was held to acknowledge the sacrifices of the Frontier Police rendered during the fight against the militancy. During the month following 16 October, a suicide or car-bomb attack took place every other day, killing more than two hundred fifty civilians. Of these attacks, 60 percent took place in the Khyber Pakhtunkhwa, particularly in urban areas such as Peshawar (seven of the fifteen attacks, including one on 28 October that killed around one hundred twenty people), Charsadda and Bannu. It was the revenge of the TTP.

Wazir Background

"Wazir tribes are the most violent among all tribes," said Khalid Aziz, the former chief administrator of North Waziristan. Khalid Aziz compared the Wazir between tribes in seven tribal districts and six Frontier regions. It is quite a large comparison. The Waziris always come up on top. There are many explanations for this. One is that they live in inhospitable terrain, and they lead very difficult lives, in difficult circumstances. "Raiding areas and robbing people used to be their good trade," Khalid Aziz adds. The Waziris also conducted their raids inside Afghanistan.

The link between the Waziris and Afghanistan has a long history. It did not begin when the Pakistanis joined the U.S.-backed "Afghan jihad" in the 1980s. The Waziris have long provided the Afghan king with military service of various kinds. In 1929, when Nadir Khan, the Afghan ambassador to Paris, entered Afghanistan to remove the Tajik brigand Bacha Saqa from Kabul, the Waziris and the Mehsuds helped him along. The Waziris led the campaign for Nadir Khan. Nadir Khan promised the Waziris and the Mehsuds that he would pay them once they took Kabul, but when they entered the capital city it was plain that there was no money for them. For seven days, the Waziris and the Mehsuds were allowed to pillage Kabul, taking what they wanted. Nadir Khan created a Wazir militia and posted them to guard the Afghan side of his border. "There was constant influence of the Afghan government in the Wazir affairs," the former government official recalled. It is very difficult to control the tribal collection of alliances. They make and break by the day.

The United States and NATO have criticized Pakistan's government for allegedly giving al-Qaeda and Taliban safe haven in Waziristan. However, Khalid Aziz argues, "If you look at the dynamics of creation of safe havens it was not because Pakistan encouraged it." He goes on to add, "Belonging to a small subtribe of Zalikhel, a tribal elder gave safe haven to actually gain strength against other tribes. He wanted to use the Uzbek and [other] al-Qaeda militants to sort out feuds with other tribes. And later on, it became a money game, I mean a war industry developed. Instead of staging raids to make money was it not good to manipulate Afghanistan, Pakistan, and the United States?"

Wazirs do not like life without honor. Wazir militant leader Nek Muhammad was sent a message that he should move to a safer place as he would be killed sooner than later. The message received a luke-warm response from the Robin Hood–like Wazir militant leader. "I do not want to pass life without honor and honor, in my opinion, is that I should fight like a Wazir tribesman and history will not forgive me if I do not do what my elders had done," the 28–year-old Nek responded. Weeks later, in June 2004, he was killed in Wana.

The unending Afghan crisis has deeply impacted the tribes living near the border. Simply taking the territory back from the control of the militants will not resolve the complex problem of the border. An incident I experienced from the early spring of 2007 testifies to this intractableness. A friend who works for a foreign radio station and I were embedded by the Baitullah group. They allowed us to spend some time with them, letting us know how they pass time in the absence of combat on both sides of the border. A boy, perhaps ten or twelve years old, with a tray in his hands stood bemused when he spots me in a small room with long-haired and gun-toting Taliban militants. He could not believe that a clean-shaven man could be among the Taliban. "Is he American?" the confused boy asked the militants. "Yes, he is American," joked the militants. "When will we behead him?" asked the boy, who then looked relaxed at seeing that that Talibs had arrested an American. This was just another small example of the everyday brutality of tribal society: a young boy pauses enthusiastically to know that an American might be beheaded before him.

In his 1931 book, *Mizh,* Sir Evelyn Howell wrote of the Mehsuds, "Mehsuds are first Mehsuds and then Muslims." This might have been the case. Now, a version of Islam plays a very important role in the lives of the Mehsuds, governed as they are by the TTP and its rulers Abdullah

Mehsud, Baitullah Mehsud, and Hakeemullah Mehsud. The Mehsud horizon changed the complexion of the ground situation, allowing the Mehsuds to often act as more than a tribe, but as a people willing to make alliances on behalf of Islam against the invaders.

After killing Nek Muhammad, the federal government thought that it was now the appropriate time for the Taliban leadership to take over from the Waziri tribesmen. Former Guantánamo Bay inmate Abdullah Mehsud emerged as the leader after Nek. The government felt that this transition would shift the militancy away from the Afghan border. The new Waziri leadership wanted to reestablish a Taliban-type rule in their homelands rather than threaten the U.S. and NATO in Afghanistan.

The U.S. and Pakistan erred in its judgment regarding Abdullah Mehsud. Why did the U.S. free him from Guantánamo Bay, and why did the Pakistani government release him into the tribal areas, as well as set him up to lead the tribe? A person who has been held prisoner in Guantánamo Bay was not going to remain quiet. He returned angry, offended by his incarceration, and was very radical. The one-legged Abdullah Mehsud galvanized the Mehsuds to militancy. His spur was essential. After him would come Baitullah Mehsud, under whose reign the Mehsuds would do much damage inside Pakistan.

Progressive Forces' Failure?

The issue of Pukhtoonistan came on the table after 1947. The Faqir of Ippi (Mirza Ali Khan, 1897–1960) was the first to call himself the president of Pukhtoonistan, and Khalifa Latif from Northern Waziristan was the prime minister. They refused to be part of Pakistan after 1947. The Afghan government, which refused to support the formation of Pakistan on the grounds that it claimed the lands that straddled the Durand Line (1893), gave material and diplomatic support to Pukhtoonistan. Russia and India, for different reasons, also supported the Faqir of Ippi. The movement was not religiously motivated. It was a nationalist movement that had its roots in tribal independence, the Pashtu language, and the lineage of Khan Abdul Ghafar Khan's Khudai Khidmatgars.

Azizul Hassan, a leader of the Pukhtoon nationalist and secular Awami National Party (ANP), was sure that he had won the National

Assembly seat from South Waziristan during the February 18, 2008, general election. The outside world sees his homeland as the birthplace of the Pakistani Taliban. But Hassan comes from another tradition that remains alive in these borderlands. Hassan felt that he had defeated the candidate of the conservative Jamiat Ulema-e-Pakistan, Fazlur Rehman's group (JUI-F). However, it was not the case. A court had to deliberate over the contested election. Its verdict went against Azizul Hassan and handed victory to the JUI-F. The right-wing JUI-F holds considerable sway in South Waziristan. Only the Awami National Party is capable of mounting a challenge against it. The margin of defeat was thin: the nationalist and secular leader lost the election by only six hundred votes. The ANP has popular support in three tribal districts: South Waziristan, Khyber, and Bajaur. In these three regions, interestingly, the influence of the Afghan government is also high. It is an open secret in these parts that the ANP has a soft corner for Afghanistan, a result of its long-standing Pukhtoon nationalist agenda.

"I would say the progressive forces paid a big price for trying to keep militancy off their areas," Dr. Mehsud Alam, political activist of nationalist Pukhtoonkhwa Milli Awami Party (PkMAP), said. "Why we have not been successful is a different but long story."

In late 2003, Dr. Mehsud Alam visited Nek Muhammad. He advised him to stop his militant campaign. "I told him that what he was doing would not do any good to his people, area, and the Pukhtoons in particular and it will be a wise step on your part if you do not sink Waziristan deeper into anarchy," Alam recounted to me. The progressive-minded nationalist Dr. Mehsud Alam talked to the militant Nek Muhammad, who was unwilling to heed the young, liberal voice.

Farooq Wazir, local leader of the PkMAP, was also present during the meeting between Dr. Mehsud and Nek Muhammad. Farooq was the first progressive Wazir to be target-killed in Wana bazaar in the last quarter of 2003. The assassination of Farooq sent a chilling message in the region. The tribal elders with close links to the government were slowly killed off by al-Qaeda. Some five hundred influential leaders have been eliminated thus far. The bulk of them—some three hundred fifty—were killed in South Waziristan and one hundred fifty in North Waziristan, with the rest killed elsewhere in the tribal areas.

Peace in the Region

It appears the military will repeat the Malakand experience in South Waziristan. By October 2007, Maulana Fazlullah's Tehreeke-Nafaz-e-Shariat-e-Mohammadi forces took command of the beautiful Swat Valley. Small-scale engagements with the Pakistani military did not deter Fazlullah's men. They began to reorder life in the Valley. In 2009, the Pakistani army went into the Valley in force and removed Fazlullah's men from control. At least two million civilians were displaced by this Operation Rahe-Rast (Operation Right Path). Most returned to their homes within three months. "We will repeat the Swat experience in South Waziristan," said a regional spokesman for the army in Peshawar.

The Waziristan situation, however, is not the same as Swat. The tribal system in Waziristan has three pillars: *jirga,* Lashkar, and collective responsibility. The *jirga* or tribal assembly of leaders has been attacked by the Taliban. They send in suicide bombers when the elders sit to discuss issues. This has rendered the *jirga* ineffective. Lashkar, or the army of the people, and collective responsibility have also been surrendered to the army. In the absence of the elders, and these pillars of tribal culture, the institutional connection between the state and the tribal areas is lost. There are no institutional mechanisms for the people to be in touch with the state. As Khalid Aziz put it, "The elders knew how to interact with the state. They knew the rules. They intellectually knew what statecraft is. By killing them the al-Qaeda removed traditional management. And when it is removed then it is very difficult for the chief administrator, locally known as political agent, to control the areas."

Wazirs are known as good fighters, and they used their arms to create territorial spaces for themselves. It was not heard of for a tribe to lose its sovereignty. The TTP was no longer a tribal authority. It substituted a religious political party for tribal leadership. This was an innovation. The military has often allowed parties like the TTP to govern, sometimes because it cannot be bothered to take them on, and at other times as an opportunistic alliance while it clears up other militants.

The people of the region deserve better. They require their state to be rebuilt. For decades, the tribal people were subjugated to inhumane treatment first by the former colonial British power and then by the state of Pakistan. Till now, the Constitution of Islamic Republic of Pakistan does not guarantee fundamental human rights that other citizens of the country enjoy when the military is not ruling the country. The tribal people were given the right to adult franchise in 1997. Political parties cannot operate in tribal areas as the Political Parties Act has not yet been extended to the tribal areas. The tribal people cannot move the High Court or the Supreme Court against their conviction by the political agent, who enjoys immense administrative, judicial, and financial powers. The issue of governance must be addressed if Pakistan wants to eliminate militancy in the tribal areas and for good governance we need to bring democracy to tribal areas.

What about the other side of the border, where the U.S./NATO war continues to bleed an already impoverished country? "For lasting peace it is very important that the border between Pakistan and Afghanistan is regulated," said Khalid Aziz. "Kabul and Washington make the biggest mistake by not recognizing the border and not putting a strong border management authority that is required to defeat the militancy."

Poetic Reflection and Activism in Gilgit-Baltistan

NOSHEEN ALI

POETRY RECITATION HAS A PROMINENT PLACE in the social life of Pakistan, and especially in the northern, mountainous region of Gilgit-Baltistan. In the key administrative city of Gilgit, participants at casual gatherings, cultural celebrations, NGO conferences, or political seminars are likely to quote couplets in Urdu or in one of their local languages such as Shina. Mushairas, or gatherings dedicated to poetry recitation, are often organized in people's homes, at hotels, and in public spaces, and are much valued as a source of pleasure and intellectual stimulation. While mushairas have been part of the Indo-Persian cultural landscape at least since the 16th century, poetic performances have a particularly central place in the cultural and spiritual life of Muslims in northern Pakistan. The ability to use words for poetic, playful, and creative expression is considered the hallmark of intellect, and both the production and reception of poetic performances is deemed integral to Muslim personhood.[1] In Gilgit, I was often told that poetry is truly the *rooh ki giza* or nourishment for the soul. Local poetry that has been put to music is also very popular in Gilgit-Baltistan and is enjoyed both through recordings and in live performances. Hence, a culture of poetry infuses social life in northern Pakistan, similar to what has been claimed for other contexts such as Arab culture.

Poetic expression has been particularly encouraged in Gilgit-Baltistan by the literary organization Halqa-e-Arbab-e-Zauq, which may be translated as the Circle of Literary Fellows. Founded in 1939, Halqa is a prominent Urdu literary forum that promotes literature and poetry through publications and mushairas. The Gilgit chapter of Halqa was established in 1987, at the initiative of a retired army major from "down"—the term most commonly used for Pakistani regions located south of Gilgit-Baltistan—who himself was a poet and was at the time posted in the education department in Gilgit. However, the seeds of a literary organization in Gilgit were already sown in the form of the Karakoram Writers' Forum, a local initiative that preceded the formation of Halqa.

Halqa's poetry in Gilgit combines the traditional themes of self, love, and separation with a concern for social and political transformation. In my individual interviews with Halqa poets in Gilgit, it became clear to me that what motivates their poetry—and often prose as well—is a concern with promoting a progressive vision of humanity and harmony as the essence of faith and politics.

My first encounter with Halqa was at a mushaira that was held at the Karakuram International University (KIU) in Gilgit, as part of the Pakistan Independence Day celebrations in August 2006. Jointly organized by KIU and Halqa, the four-hour mushaira featured the most distinguished poets from Gilgit-Baltistan, as well as a few renowned ones from other parts of Pakistan. It took place in the university garden, in the late evening, against the backdrop of a mountain lit up with *charagan* (fire-lights). No fee was charged for attendance. There were around four hundred people present, all men except for six women: three female poets on stage who were from down-Pakistan and three women in the audience, including myself. We could be there because we taught at the university and were nonlocal. The vast majority of male attendees belonged to the town of Gilgit and nearby areas and came predominantly from an oral culture as opposed to a highly schooled one. The rest were students at KIU. Even among the student audience, female students were conspicuously absent. Thus, the poetic public sphere in Gilgit is essentially a male public sphere. However, women are not entirely absent from the culture of poetry in the region. In the Gojal area of Gilgit-Baltistan, women's poetic songs called *bulbulik* have been traditionally composed and sung by female Wakhi shepherds. Women write poetry in Gilgit city as well, but because of cultural norms are not keen on reciting it in public.

Like several others, I too was completely enthralled by the poetic performances at the KIU–Halqa mushaira. In an Urdu that was both simple and eloquent, and a recitation that was deeply moving, the region's poets attempted to stimulate the audience with their reflections on politics, society, and love. Barring a few Shina poems, most of the poetry that was recited at the mushaira was in Urdu. When I spoke with KIU students and faculty members after the mushaira, they expressed how they relished the poetry for the beauty of words and of thought, and especially for the *dard* and *josh*—feeling and fervor—that it embodied. The performance was thus valued for the way in which it appealed to and nourished the creative, intellectual, and emotional sensibilities of the listeners.

Several poets powerfully captured the political dispossession of Gilgit-Baltistan and criticized the attitude of the Pakistani government toward the region—this, ironically, at a festival that was meant to celebrate the independence day of Pakistan. Sectarian prejudice was likewise a prominent theme, with many verses criticizing the role of orthodox clerics in propagating sectarian hatred. I found it striking that critical poetry pertaining to faith and politics tended to attract the strongest applause from the audience. This applause may be viewed as an endorsement of how the sentiments expressed by the poets echoed the feelings of audience members.

Reimagining Muslim Ethics and Politics

The key theme that dominates Halqa's progressive poetry is a contemplation of Muslim nationhood. Halqa poets criticize the meaning of Muslim nationhood in contemporary Pakistan by exposing the inhuman values and exploitative practices that both Pakistani *Islam* and the Pakistani *nation-state* have come to embody in Gilgit-Baltistan. According to these poets, Muslim nationhood has lived up neither to the ethical values of Islam nor to the legal norms of democratic citizenship. The former is evident in the prejudice that dominates inter-sect relations with Islam, while the latter is exemplified by the absence of a constitutional place and proper political and legal rights for Gilgit-Baltistan in Pakistan. Criticizing such conditions of sectarian prejudice and regional noncitizenship, Halqa poets urge the *ameer-e-waqt* or "Ruler of the Time" to reform state policy, while imploring Muslims to live with respect and humanity toward each other. Here are some examples (I use pseudonyms to refer to the poets).[2]

> Zaban ko mein nay bhi ab be-lagaam chor diya
> Amir-e-waqt! Tira ehtraam chor diya
> Gila baja hai ke aiy doston! Nahin hai baja?
> Nisf sadi say humain kyon gulaam chor diya
> Abhi tak hain qawaneen Dogron kay yahan
> Woh khud to chal diyey apna nizam chor diya

> I've let my tongue loose from now on
> Ruler of the Time! I've stopped respecting you from now on
> Am I right in complaining, or no, my friends?
> Half a century, and we are still in chains
> The laws of Dogras still prevail here
> They have long gone, but their system remains

> —*Anwar Jami*

> Na mera jism apna hai khuda wanda na jaan meri
> Ye meri zindagi kia hai badi kia nekiyaan meri
> Wahan Kashmiriyon pe zulm gairon nay kia lekin
> Yahan apnon nay looti hain sada aazadiyaan meri
> Amir-e-waqt say keh do mujhay aain day warna
> Kisi din ley kay dobein gi isay mehrumiyaan meri

> Neither my body belongs to me nor my soul, oh God
> What is the meaning of my life, my sins, my kindnesses
> Others have committed atrocities, there in Kashmir
> Here, always, my own have robbed me of liberties
> Tell the Ruler of the Time to give me a constitution or else
> Some day he will be drowned by my rightlessness

> —*Shams Zaman*

The tone is both angry and rebellious. The disenfranchisement of Gilgit-Baltistan is paralleled with the historical conditions of Kashmir— when the Dogra rulers of Jammu and Kashmir marginalized Muslim subjects through their Hindu-dominated modes of sovereignty—as well as to the present conditions of Indian-ruled Kashmir where a military occupation continues to oppress Kashmiri Muslims. The irony and tragedy are critical here; what is being highlighted is that fighting to join a *Muslim nation* like Pakistan—as Gilgitis did at the time of partition—has made no difference to their present predicament where their "own" (Muslims) have been responsible for injustice and subjugation.

Along with exposing this hollowness of the Muslim nation, Halqa poetry also emphasizes the poet's understanding of what it means to be a Muslim, and how his interpretation embraces difference and respect, instead of the prejudice and othering that has come to dominate understandings of the Muslim faith.

Mein dastaar-e-fazeelat maangta hoon
Woh kehtay hain tumhaara sar nahin hai
Sabhi momin hain meray deen-e-haq main
Koi mushriq koi kaafir nahin hai

I ask for the crown of goodness
They tell me I don't possess a head
In my true faith everyone is a believer
I see no one as polytheist, no one as non-believer

—*Ali Manzoor*

Taasub say bhara paigaam yeh hai
Bahao khoon darse aam yeh hai
Musalmaanon ka jab anjaam yeh hai
Mein kaafir hoon agar Islam yeh hai

It is a message overflowing with prejudice
"Shed blood!" is being commonly preached
When this is the meaning of being Muslim
I am a non-believer if this is Islam

—*Shams Zaman*

Such verses nurture a pluralistic vision of Islam, one with old roots in the history of Muslims in the region. They stand against a more insular and sectarian vision of Islam that has recently become ascendant in Pakistan, including in Gilgit-Baltistan. These are didactic verses, confronting the inhumanity that has come to prevail in Gilgit. According to the poet Shams Zaman, it is important to be "direct" instead of metaphorical so that the true values of Islam and democratic equality may be cultivated.

Like Urdu poetry elsewhere, Gilgiti poetry also has its fair share of verses that mock the hypocrisies of the *waez, mullah, zahid,* or *sheikh*—titles for pious men, preachers, and religious leaders in Islam. For example, this verse criticizes the bigotry that is often promoted by the local clergy:

Waez ko muhabbat ki fiza raas nahin hai
Anjam-e-taasub ka bhi ahsaas nahin hai
Hoon kaar-e-muhabbat mein hi masroof mein itna
Nafrat key liyey waqt meray paas nahin hai

The Preacher and Love are unknown to each other
He is oblivious to where his prejudice leads him
And I am so busy doing the deeds of love
That I possess no time for hate

— *Dost Faqir*

Another verse exposes the patron–client relation that exists between state officials and clerics in Gilgit-Baltistan. This relation goes back to the early 1970s, when maulvis from both sects were paid by state agencies to incite hatred between Shias and Sunnis, in order to disrupt and divide local secular struggles for political rights in the region.[3] Reflecting this process, the poet suggests that instead of religious guidance, the purpose of the clergy has become one of promoting sectarian conflict at the orders of the ruler:

Kuch hain mazhab ke junoon mein garq kuch zaaton mein hain
Dushmanan-e-qaum har su mukhtalif ghaaton mein hain

Ik bahana hai rasai ka amir-e-shehr tak
Hum ko apas men lara kar khud mulaqaaton mein hain

Some are absorbed in the madness of religion, some are drowned in castes
Enemies of the nation are everywhere hiding in their trenches[4]
It is only an excuse to get to the chief of the city
They make us fight, so that they can sit in meetings with him

—Anwar Jami

In personal interviews, Gilgiti poets spoke to me about this state of sectarian–political intrigue and violence in the region with a profound sense of anguish. Indeed, it is this grief and pain that compels them to write poetry. But this is not their only motivation. Dost Faqir told me that "the path of poetry ultimately meets the path of God," and that he writes poetry as a form of *ibadat* (worship) and *insaniyat* (humanism). Other poets shared similar sentiments. The emphasis on the poetic expression of piety and the values of *insaniyat* is indeed central to folk and Sufi traditions of Islam more generally, and yet remains understudied in anthropological studies of Islam that tend to dwell on *muharram* rituals and *dargah* practices, or more recently on the embodiments of piety in Muslim reform movements. An examination of the poetic thought and activism of Gilgiti poets thus enriches the anthropology of Islam by offering a different lens on Muslim identity, reform, and piety in contemporary Muslim societies.

Moreover, Halqa's poetry demonstrates how Muslims of the Gilgit region grapple with and contest the Islamization of state and society in Pakistan. Gilgiti poetic performances are not just "everyday" forms of resistance as linguistic expressive traditions have often been seen. Even though they are embedded in the rhythms of everyday life, they are neither ordinary nor hidden. The performances help in the very creation of community by both reflecting and reshaping the political consciousness and moral imagination of the public. Ultimately, they help to create the conditions of possibility for peaceful coexistence, and for the achievement of humanistic and democratic values in Gilgit-Baltistan.

The work of Halqa in Gilgit may thus be seen as a form of social struggle and collective action that is as concrete and meaningful as a movement. Indeed, although Halqa is a nongovernmental *tanzeem* (organization), some poets of the organization themselves perceive it as a *tehreek* (movement). In the next section, I elaborate how beyond the usual poetry festivals in which poets recite verses on any theme, Halqa has organized more activist poetry festivals for the explicit purpose of challenging sectarian prejudice.

Poetic Activism

Transformation of attitudes is a fundamental goal that Halqa poets strive toward with their publications and festivals. As key Halqa representative Saqi Jan explained to me: "We have to create religious harmony and local unity to ensure peace. We have worked harder for the promotion of tolerance and peace than for the promotion of literature." Toward this end, Halqa has organized poetry events for the specific purpose of promoting the ethic of respect and tolerance. In October 1999, for example, Halqa organized a mushaira in Gilgit in which poets were specifically asked to write on the topic of *Tark-i-Taasobat* (The Ending of Prejudice).[5]

The role of Halqa was especially critical during the textbook conflict in 2005, when Gilgit was engulfed in the most intense Shia–Sunni violence that the region has witnessed in two decades. Revenge killings had become the norm after the supreme Shia leader in Gilgit, Agha Ziauddin Rizvi, was murdered in January 2005. Twenty days after his murder, a few Halqa poets got together and decided that they must intervene. They were not sure what they could do, as the atmosphere was filled with fear and people tended to remain in their houses. Working toward peace in such a context was considered cowardice, and worse, a betrayal of one's own sect that could result in severe repercussions from other members of one's community. Even as the poets felt that their "creativity was deadened by the violence," they thought that they must strive to write and, at a later point, recite. As one of them said to me, "The *naara-e-ehtiyaat* (the stance of being tight-lipped) had to go. Even if they died, at least they would have died for the noble cause of building peace."

One of the first poems that became popular at this time was "Karbala-e-Jadid" (The New Karbala), authored by the Sunni poet

Rehman Josh, who works as a teacher at a local government school in Gilgit.[6] Some verses from this poem are reproduced here:

Naya ik Karbala hai shehr mein kyon?
Musalmaan be-nawa hai shehr mein kyon?
Usi ka ghar jala hai shehr mein kyon?
Ye matam sa barpa hai shehr mein kyon?
Naya ik Karbala hai shehr mein kyon?

Yeh nafrat ki hawa kyon char su hai?
Bashar matam kuna kyon ku ba ku hai?
Tumharay haath par kis ka laho hai?
Woh ik baccha mara hai shehr mein kyon?
Naya ik karbala hai shehr mein kyon?

Musalmaan ab baraiy deen utho
Badal do uth kay ye aain utho
Utho Iqbal kay shaaheen utho
Bana har ik khuda hai shehr mein kyon?
Naya ik Karbala hai shehr mein kyon?

A new Karbala in the city, why?
Depraved Muslims in the city, why?
His house burns in the city, why?
This air of mourning in the city, why?

A new Karbala in the city, why?
This air of hatred, why, everywhere?
Humans in mourning, why, everywhere?
This blood on your hands, whose is it?
A child has died in the city, why?
A new Karbala in the city, why?

Oh Muslim, now stand up and protect your faith
Stand up to change the constitution, stand up
Stand up, Iqbal's eagles, stand up[7]
Everyone plays God in the city, why?
A new Karbala in the city, why?

—Rehman Josh

Prose along similar themes circulated in the local Urdu newspapers in Gilgit, which were also struggling to play a constructive role in a context of heightened sectarianism. But the most innovative intervention came when Halqa organized a *Gulaman-e-Mustafa* (servants of Prophet Muhammad) recitation conference for the specific purpose of bringing *ulema* (scholars) from different sects together in appreciation of Islamic religious poetry. These were followed by other *seerat* (in praise of Muhammad) and *aman* (peace) conferences.

While showing me pictures of these events, Zaman, a founding member of Halqa, narrated:

> You can see here that we have organized an *aman* conference . . . a *seerat* conference . . . and here's a conference titled *"Hussain sub ka"* (Hussain is for everyone).[8] All to get maulvis from both the Shia and Sunni sects to sit together. They would of course never come to a regular mushaira so we organized events according to their disposition; we talked only about Allah and the Prophet, and compelled them to come. After Agha Ziaduddin's death, there were open killings in Gilgit. Maulvis from the two sects even refused to see each other's faces, and there was only talk of revenge and hatred. We tried on our part to break the tension, by organizing a *naatia* mushaira (poetry evening in praise of Prophet Muhammad) in which the religious leaders of both sects were sitting together for the first time since the sectarian situation went bad. They could not refuse to participate, as it would be seen as *tauheen-e-risalat* (insult to the Prophet). At this event, we also invited progressive-minded *alims* (religious scholars) and intellectuals from down-Pakistan who talked about the need for Muslim unity in the face of larger global challenges.

Such efforts to "break the tension" by creating a space for "sitting together" and recognizing commonality are of profound value in the highly sectarianized context of Gilgit. The poetic veneration of common religious figures—even asserting that they are *common*—and a scholarly attention to the larger global context constitute creative strategies for overcoming sectarian conflict, cultivating social unity, and creating peace. These strategies are all the more significant for securing the involvement of influential local religious leaders, who ordinarily have the strongest stake in maintaining sectarian enmity.

The cultural activism of Halqa in countering sectarian animosity has elicited a mixed reaction from the religious clergy in Gilgit. As Zaman said to me, "There are *ulema*—from both sects—who welcome the work of Halqa members, and say 'Recite!' even when we recite verses that poke fun at their sensibilities. But there are others who dismiss poetry altogether, and view culture as a threat to religion. They want us to forget our history and culture, of which religion is a part."

Gilgit's Sunni clerics have made their displeasure clear in mosque sermons. They accuse Sunni poets, in particular, of *tauheen* (disrespect) of the *ulema*. According to the poet Shafiq Fikri, the clergy have been infuriated by such verses:

> Mullah ka yahan pait nikalta hai musalsal
> Lekin woh samajhta hai kay imaan bauhat hai
>
> The mullah here has a protruding belly
> He thinks he is filled with faith

More tragically, in 2007, a member of an extremist Sunni religious group was caught before attempting to kill a Halqa-affiliated Sunni poet for "organizing conferences" and "uniting sects." This demonstrates the extent to which extremist Sunni organizations feel threatened by Halqa, and also the considerable risk that Halqa poets have taken to bridge the sectarian divide and recover the ethic of religious harmony in Gilgit.

The efforts of Halqa are sometimes dismissed even by members of the secular-liberal left in Gilgit, as they feel that Halqa events are more about "entertainment" than "real change." As journalist–activist Suleman Shah mentioned to me, "The Progressive Writers Movement took on empire. They invited *mazdoor* (labor) and *kisan* (farmer) leaders as chief guests at their events. Halqa poets invite government officials. They are complacent and keen on pleasing officials rather than on boldly challenging them."

Such criticisms overlook the fact that entertaining performances also constitute subversive sites of "real change" and that it is precisely its more mainstream position that enables Halqa to have a wider appeal and reach. More significantly, the majority of poets affiliated with Halqa work for the local government in Gilgit. As government workers, they have severe limitations on political expression, participation, and protest, particularly in a heavily monitored space as Gilgit-Baltistan. Resistance in its directly political form is thus a luxury that they cannot afford given their political and economic circumstances. In such a context, critical poetry affords a creative means of expressing grievance and protest. The abstractness of poetry means that it is not deemed as threatening as, for example, journalistic accounts, which are regularly repressed in the region. Poetry can be performed in a casual and amused tone, so as not to seriously offend—though at one famed Halqa mushaira, the Chief Secretary (highest bureaucratic post in the region), who also happened to be the chief guest at the occasion, felt snubbed and threatened to leave if "guests continued to be respected this way." Thus, Halqa poetry has a history of perturbing both political and religious power in the region.

The work of Halqa also makes us rethink the usual notions of the state, in which bureaucrats are imagined as unthinking agents who simply represent and reproduce state ideas and practices. The poetry of Halqa may be seen as embodying bureaucratic agency, critique, and subversion in the face of coercive state logics. However, the poets are not proposing a radical break from state politics. Their poetry, in fact, evokes the same moral values that historically legitimized the ideal of the Pakistani state—as one that embodied humanity, equality, and Muslim unity, instead of the selfishness and violence of power. Hence, the poets are simultaneously local and national, drawing from the resources of Pakistani nationalism as well as local traditions, and in the process forging creative spaces of poetic reflection and criticism. The parameters of poetic critique, however, are defined by the poets' ideological positions and by the realities of repression in the region. For example, the military-intelligence regime that dominates state power in Gilgit-Baltistan is never directly criticized; indeed, sacrifices of regional soldiers for the Pakistani army are often glorified. The poets also tend to discuss the region's problems as if they themselves exist outside and above them, not as those who are embroiled in negotiating these complex realities. However, these are realities that they are moved by, and which they strive to understand and transform through poetry.

It is also important to note that Halqa-e-Arbab-e-Zauq is one among several literary organizations in Gilgit-Baltistan that seek to bring about progressive change through poetry. Prominent among these is the Bazm-e-Ilm-o-Fann (Bazm) or Society for Knowledge and

Art. While Halqa is dominant in Gilgit, Bazm is more active in Skardu. The motto of Bazm reveals the organization's vision: *adab waseela-e-ittehad, muhabbat waseela-e-aman*—literature is the means for unity, love is the means for peace. As the head of the organization, Jalal Daanish, described to me, "Gatherings that are on party or religious basis tend to create groups, and divide people. But our cultural events are open to everyone. There is no *sarhad* (border) in poetry, and this is the first step toward unity. Of course, polo events are also open to all, and they are important in this respect. But they are just for fun, not for learning and reflection."

When I probed him about what "learning and reflection" Bazm aspires for, he explained:

> Look at the values that have destroyed our region. Like *aksariat aur aqliat ki soch* (the idea of majority and minority). Why should we ever think in these terms? Everyone has the right to live as they desire; once you accept that, why should numbers matter? In our region, we have so much *taasub* (prejudice) and *hasad* (jealousy/competitiveness) that destroys peace and unity. We want others to fail, so that we can succeed. Schools also promote such thinking. That's one reason I think the literate have done more to promote sectarianism than the illiterate. Instead, we should want ourselves to do well, and same for everyone else. In literature, there is neither space for *taasub* nor for *hasad*. We preach *insaniyat*, which is the central message of Islam. We also teach history. At our cultural events, we especially try to target youth aged 15 to 26 and talk about events such as the *jang-e-azadi* (Gilgit war of independence), which is absent from their history textbooks. We try to give the region's youth a sense of local history and culture, which they do not get from schools.

There is thus a "crisis of *insaniyat*" that Bazm and other organizations seek to address through a literary vision for change. Cultural activists in Gilgit-Baltistan link this crisis particularly to school-based education, which is deemed to promote sectarian thinking while also denying a sense of regional identity and history. However, while literary events provide an important antidote, they alone cannot counter the vicious pervasiveness of sectarianism; institutionalized sectarianism itself needs to be rooted out for the recovery of religious harmony in the region.

Final Thoughts

The main banner above the stage at the KIU mushaira carried a line from the renowned progressive Pakistani poet, Faiz Ahmed Faiz:

> Hum parwarish-e-lauh-o-qalam kartay raheingay.
> We will continue to nurture the slate and pen.

Unlike Faiz, however, the reflections of Halqa poets are not grounded in a conscious, socialist sensibility. They are grounded in a specifically regional perspective—that of an ethnically and religiously diverse region that has been silenced and destabilized by the nation. They challenge the coupling of the nation and religion in Pakistani state policy, which has denied Gilgit-Baltistanis equal respect as citizens and as Muslims.

Ultimately, the Halqa in Gilgit is in the midst of building new communities out of the resources that its poets have mined. While its poetic mode of resistance might be accompanied with a sense of disillusionment and bitterness, it rarely resorts to pessimism and cynicism. And this is one of its main strengths as a force of sociopolitical change. Pakistan is an unfinished project for these poets and social reformers. It is out of their regional location in Gilgit-Baltistan that they are trying to work toward a humane and nonsectarian country, nurturing their tablets and their pens, and, in the process, the very soul of society.

Notes

1. Magnus Marsden, *Living Islam: Muslim Religious Experience in Pakistan's North-West Frontier* (Cambridge: Cambridge University Press, 2005).

2. I am immensely grateful to Muhammad Zafar and Asad Ahmed for their help with the translations.

3. Nosheen Ali, "Outrageous State, Sectarianized Citizens: Deconstructing the 'Textbook Controversy' in the Northern Areas, Pakistan," *South Asia Multidisciplinary Academic Journal* 2 (2008). samaj.revues.org/ index1172.html.

4. When I interviewed him, the poet clarified to me that "enemies of the nation" here refers to the *mullahs* (clerics) of both the Sunni and Shia sects.

5. Halqa-e-Arbab-e-Zauq, *Tark-i-Taasoobat* (Baha'i Publishing Trust, Pakistan, 2000).

6. Karbala refers to a battle that took place in 680 A.D. in the city of Karbala in Iraq, in which the Prophet's grandson and the third Shia Imam, Hussain, was brutally murdered along with his followers.

7. The *shaaheen* or eagle is a metaphor for the self-confident, socially conscious Muslim in Mohammad Iqbal's poetry. It is a popular reference in Gilgiti poetry as well.

8. "For everyone" here emphasizes that Hussain is not a revered religious figure just for Shias, but for all Muslims. Hussain has a special significance for Shia Muslims as he is their third Imam, and the yearly commemoration of his martyrdom is a key aspect of Shia identity and devotion.

The Nature of Conservation
Conflict and Articulation in Northern Pakistan

SHAFQAT HUSSAIN

SINCE 1975, Shimshal, a small village of agro-pastoral people in Pakistan's mountainous Northern Areas (now Gilgit-Baltistan), has been embroiled in a conflict with the government Forest Department over the establishment of the Khunjerab National Park (KNP) on traditional grazing grounds. The park was established on the recommendation of the famous American naturalist George Schaller, who in the 1970s visited the region and saw the land use practices of the local people as a threat to Himalayan wildlife and nature. Schaller was especially concerned about the plight of wild sheep and goats, particularly ibex, blue sheep, and the fabled Marco Polo sheep, which he thought had come under threat from the local herders who hunted them and from their yaks, which competed for the grazing areas. The park put a total ban on Shimshalis' use of the area for grazing their yaks, thus threatening their main economic activity.

The people of Shimshal from the start refused to cooperate or give up any land to park management and continued to use the area for grazing. Between 1975 and 1989, the park was a park on paper only. In 1989, the newly opened country office of IUCN (The World Conservation Union) commissioned an international workshop to prepare a management plan for the park. The management plan that came out of the conference and its subsequent versions have all been rejected by the Shimshalis. To date, they remain at loggerheads with the government over the park, and they continue to graze their livestock in the area.

This essay is based on ethnographic research that I conducted during 2005–2006. I will examine how the conflict is articulated both by the Pakistani state and the Shimshali people, and I will use this particular case to show what lies at the heart of such conflicts here and elsewhere. I argue that the heart of the problem is competing and often opposing visions of the landscape where the park is to be established. The idea of the KNP emerged from American ideas of wilderness, as I illustrate through analysis of Schaller's writings, in which he presents landscape as part of pristine nature outside human history. This ideology contrasts with that of the Shimshalis, who view the KNP landscape as part of their economic and social history. These two visions have different implications for conservation policy as the former leads to the threat of or real dispossession and displacement of local people while the latter supports their continued presence and use. This conflict is articulated differently by the Pakistani state and the Shimshalis: the former has often expressed Shimshalis' resistance to the park as antistate, and thus open to the possibility of meeting violence, while the latter sees the imposition of national park status on their land as a continuation of colonialism, thus tantamount to outright theft and deception. Given such an enormous gulf between how the park is seen by, and what it means to, the opposing parties it is unrealistic to expect that the conservation goals of the park will be met.

Part I. The Heart of the Conflict

Shimshalis' Views of KNP Landscape

The village of Shimshal is located in the northeastern part of upper Hunza region in northern Pakistan. The area is generally known as the roof of the world and is renowned for being the point at which the world's mightiest mountain ranges meet. Shimshalis are Wakhi-speaking people—Wakhi is an Indo Iranian language—who trace their origin to the Wakhan region of Afghanistan and Tajikistan. They belong to the minority Ismaili Muslim sect, following a progressive spiritual and religious leader, the Aga Khan. The total population of Shimshal is about 1,000 people.

While crop production is an important element of Shimshali economic and cultural life, it is their livestock, mainly yaks, that are really central to their livelihood, with livestock products including meat, butter, cheese, hides, wool, and carpets all being key elements of Shimshali subsistence. Collectively Shimshalis own the largest herd of yak by a single community in the region, with numbers ranging close to 1,200. It is the Shimshalis' vast high altitude summer pastures that enable them to keep such large numbers of yaks. The economic and material life of the pasture is the bedrock of the Shimshali symbolic and mythical universe.

According to the Shimshalis, the main pasture settlement at Shimshal Pass, the so-called core zone of the KNP, was a divine gift to their community from God. As the Shimshali origin story goes, some seven hundred years ago a man by the name of Mamu Singh, along with his wife, fled his personal enemies in the neighboring state of Wakhan and settled in the location of the present day village of Shimshal. He lived there with his wife for several years, but became increasingly sad as his wife could not bear a child. The couple lived in grief for some years until one day a saint miraculously appeared in the valley and gave the good news to the couple that God would soon give them a son who was destined to become the leader of a great community. The saint instructed the couple that when the child grows up they should send him eastward to look for grazing grounds. Nine months after Shams's departure, a son, Sher, was born to Khadija and Mamu Singh. When Sher became a young man, as instructed by Shams, the couple sent him eastward to look for the grazing areas in the region of Shimshal Pass. According to the story, when Sher arrived at Shimshal Pass he found the area already occupied by the Kirghiz, a group of Central Asian nomadic people. Six Kirghiz men on horses appeared and asked him the reason for his coming to Shimshal Pass. He explained to them that he was following the prophecy of a saint who had foretold about his coming to this area and eventually taking control over it. Upon hearing this story, the Kirghiz told Sher that if he was really assisted by some divine power then he would have to prove this by playing a polo match against them; the winner of the game would become the owner of the pastures at Shimshal Pass. Sher agreed to their suggestion but asked how was he to compete against them when he was on foot and they were on horses. At that point the Kirghiz produced a four-year-old female yak and asked Sher to ride on it. Sher played polo with the Kirghiz men for hours and eventually defeated them. The Kirghiz, true to their word, forfeited their rights to the pasture and rode away from Shimshal Pass, leaving the control of the pasture and the yak in Sher's hands.

According to the Shimshali story, Sher won the polo match pastures for two reasons: first, because he was aided by the divine intervention of Shams, and second, because he played polo on a yak, an animal better suited to the high altitude ecology of the region than his competitors' horses. This narrative of the polo match shows that for the Shimshalis, Shimshal Pass is not only a pasture but also the place from where their yaks originated, and is indeed tied to their cultural identity in which yaks and subsistence practices associated with yaks play a central role.

Schaller's Views of KNP Landscape

I will now examine how George Schaller viewed the same landscape and its implications. Schaller came to the region in the early 1970s to study the Himalayan wildlife, particularly the fabled Marco Sheep. His book, *Stones of Silence,* which is based on his fieldwork in the region, opens with the following:

> At these heights, in this remote universe of stone and sky, the fauna and flora of the *Pleistocene* have endured while many species of lower realm have vanished in the uproar of the elements. Just as we become aware of this hidden splendour of the past, we are in danger of denying it to the future. As we reach for the stars we neglect the flowers at our feet. But the *great age* of mammals in the Himalaya need not be over unless we permit it to be. For *epochs* to come the peaks will still pierce the lonely vistas, but when the last snow leopard has stalked among the crags, and the last markhor has stood on a promontory, his ruff waving in the breeze, a spark of life will have gone, turning the mountains into stones of silence. (1979: 3, emphasis added).

Schaller briefly surveyed some of the valleys adjacent to Shimshal village and Shimshal Pass and found very little wildlife there, especially Marco Polo sheep. He observed people using those areas for grazing their livestock, and concluded that competition between domestic livestock and Marco Polo sheep and uncontrolled hunting by local herders was the reason for the low numbers of wildlife in the area. He writes:

> I had ventured into the mountain naively, thinking that I would be penetrating one of the last greatest wildernesses. But seeing that here, too, man had become a destructive parasite upon the land, I became as much concerned with conservation as studying wildlife. (1979:45)

Schaller further writes disapprovingly of the presence of human beings in what he thought was the last great wilderness:

> To me the most startling discovery was the extent to which the mountains have been devastated by man. Forests have become timber, slopes have turned into fields, grass has vanished into livestock and wildlife into the bellies of the hunters. The future of some animals and plants is now in jeopardy. (1979: 97.)

Schaller recommended that the area should be set aside, protected from disturbance by human activity, so that the "natural" flora and fauna could thrive. He felt so compelled to separate the humans from the natural landscape that he simply brushed away the expected issue of displacement of the Shimshalis. He wrote:

> The fact that several communities graze their livestock for about three months each summer at Khunjerab, Shimshal, and other upland areas poses some problems, for by definition a national park should be free of such *disturbances*. However, I felt that *such details could be resolved later.* (1979: 99, emphasis added)

Dissonance between the Two Views

I will now compare Schaller's vision of the landscape with that of the Shimshalis and argue that a dissonance between the two visions lies at the heart of the contemporary conflict. Comparing the two shows two basic points of divergence.

First, there are two competing visions of time and histories, or ideas about which history or time the area belongs to. In the Shimshali vision the area is the center of origin of *their* community, and is tied to *their* historical narrative and its particular time. In Schaller's vision the area is central to natural history and its universal time. Schaller sees the area as belonging to the undisturbed periods of "Pleistocene," "epochs" or "age of mammals," a much longer and universal time erasing local human history. In the Shimshali view the area is seen as belonging to their own human time, central to which is the origin story of Sher winning the polo match, which animates a particular history of their society. The same landscape is subjected to two different time structures that have different implications for how it is to be used, or not.

The second disjuncture is about whether the area is seen as (sociologically) full or empty. In Schaller's vision the area is an empty land in which yak grazing by the Shimshalis is some kind of moral violation and anthema to nature conservation. In the Shimshal origin story, the yaks are ideally suited to the high altitude ecology of the area. Remember that the Shimshalis won the polo game because the yak was better adapted to the local environment than the horse. Thus what is seen as an integral and natural part of the local landscape and area by the Shimshalis is viewed by Schaller as unnatural, and what was seen by the Shimshalis as adaptation was seen by Schaller as disturbance. In the Shimshali view the area was never empty of people and their domestic livestock as in the Shimshali origin myth story, the area was already under the use of the Kirghiz before them, with their domesticated animals like yaks and horses; it is a sociologically full area. In Schaller's vision the area is sociologically empty and is rather the domain of nature, of wildlife.

Part II. The Articulation of the Conflict

State's Views of Shimshalis

In the mid-nineties a group of educated Shimshalis formed the Shimshal Nature Trust (SNT), a welfare organization that took upon itself the resolution of the KNP problem. Recently they moved to register all

their pastures, that is, land within the National Park, under the ownership of the SNT. Indeed one of the objectives behind the establishment
of SNT was to have it registered as a Trust, under whose name the entire
pasture land could be registered. In 2004 the Shimshalis bribed the local
revenue officer to take out a land deed that showed that the pasture area
had been transferred under the name of the Trust. The government forest department on the other hand argues that because there has never
been any permanent land settlement in Hunza, all common land, known
mainly as wasteland, is de facto government property.

In the summer of 2005, when I was conducting fieldwork in Shimshal, I met the director of KNP and asked him what he thought about
the land claims of the Shimshalis. He told me that in his opinion the
Shimshalis were behaving like the Bugtis of the Northern Areas. On
the surface this was a rhetorical remark, but implicit in it was a threat
of real and material violence against the Shimshalis. The Bugtis are one
of the largest tribal groups in the southwest province of Balochistan and
have long been engaged in an ethnic-nationalist conflict with the state
of Pakistan, which has often exploded in violence. At the time that I
was meeting with the director the situation was particularly tense, and
in 2006 the leader of the Bugtis, Akbar Khan Bugti, was gunned down
by government forces and hundreds of his supporters were thrown in
jail. Comparing the Shimshalis to the Bugtis was also a reminder to the
Shimshalis that by demanding that the management of KNP be handed
over to them, they were challenging the writ of the state. In the current geopolitical milieu in Pakistan when the state is jittery about its
status as a sovereign power, any marginal group resisting state policies
could potentially provoke unrestrained state violence. It was indeed this
veiled threat that the director of KNP was making.

I now turn to a meeting between a delegation from the SNT and
the Federal Minister for the Northern Areas that took place in 2005 at
which I was also present. Meeting with the Federal Minister was a big
deal for the Shimshalis; it was the first time that they had had the opportunity to have an audience with the Minister, who is the most powerful
person in the whole of the NAs. His one line order could change the
status of the KNP to a Community Controlled Hunting Area (CCHA),
which was what the Shimshalis were demanding. Our meeting lasted
only about ten minutes. The meeting opened with the president of SNT

giving a familiar spiel about how their local conservation ethics match the principles of modern scientific conservation and how through SNT they have protected the wildlife and pastures of the area, and how their identity is tied to their unique way of life and continued access to the area, which is now under the national park. As the president of SNT was making these articulations, I could see the minister getting increasingly impatient. After about five minutes his patience ran out, and he said, "I am really fascinated by your culture and history, but tell me the real reason why are you people here, what are your concrete demands?"

Sensing that perhaps their prayers had been answered the Shimshali delegation at once stated their demand to have the KNP redesignated as category four CCHA and its management handed over to the SNT. Hearing these demands the minister snapped and rather harshly said that to him this sounded like a conspiracy to acquire government land. He stated that perhaps the government could relax the rules for the National Park to accommodate local needs, in line with the existing community trophy hunting program, a program started in the late 1990s that seeks to generate revenues for communities from trophy hunting proceeds as an incentive for conservation, but as far as delisting the KNP and handing over its management to SNT was concerned it was not at all possible. He said that the SNT members were day dreaming. After saying this, the minister got up and left the room.

Shimshalis' Views of State

One fall evening in 2005 I was sitting outside my room in the small hotel where I stayed when I visited Shimshal, enjoying the cool air, when I noticed a KNP vehicle entering the village. The vehicle drew up outside the hotel, and a senior park official got out accompanied by some rangers, and asked to see Daud Baig, the numberdar, or head of the village. They were invited into the hotel reception, where I and a number of other Shimshalis gathered. The official told them that he had come on the instructions of higher officials from Islamabad to set up a National Park check post in the village and needed a house to rent for that purpose. Upon hearing this Daud Baig politely told the official that they did not have any house for rent available in the village and even if they did have one they would not allow the KNP officials to establish a post in the village as they do not recognize the park. He then politely asked the official and his men to kindly leave the village and tell the director that he should refrain from sending park officials to Shimshal in the future.

The official and the rangers stood up and started walking out of the room. As they were walking out the official turned and said, "It's a great mistake you Shimshalis are making, and you will have to face the consequences." At this point a few youngsters, including Daud Baig's son, told him to stop threatening the community or he and his men might have to face the consequences. A few harsh words were exchanged, then the official and his rangers drove off. After they left, we sat uncomfortably in silence for some moments; it was clear that at least some of the Shimshalis were extremely anxious about what had unfolded. Daud Baig reassured them that they had done the right thing. "How could we have given them a place to establish their check-post?" he said to the group. "Don't we know what happened to the Mughals when the British first came to India and asked them to grant them a piece of land the size of a skin of horse? We all know what happened next. They cut up the skin of the horse in thin laces and made a long rope and encircled a large piece of land. Just like that, the government will trick us. They will start with just one foothold on our land but will eventually deprive us of all of it."

Two days after the incident with the KNP rangers, a summons arrived in Shimshal, requiring eight Shimshalis, including Daud Baig's son and three SNT office holders, to the district magistrate's office in Gilgit. A First Investigation Report (FIR) had been filed against them by the director of the KNP. The charge: battery and physically abusing the government officials. The leader of the rangers even showed evidence of physical violence inflicted by the Shimshalis, including a torn uniform. The charges carried a maximum sentence of six years in prison and a fine of Rs. 200,000. To date the eight Shimshalis are regularly visiting the court, fighting the case.

The invocation of the historical narrative of colonization of local land by outsiders refers to deception by outsiders, and hence dispossession of local space at the hands of distant players at the helm of political power, such as the colonial and postcolonial states. The expanding horse skin represents the expansion of the state and the military force backing that expansion. The Shimshalis fear that just as the trading post of the merchants of the East India Company expanded into the British Empire, a similar sized check-post space demanded by the Pakistani state will result in a colonial style relationship between them and the Pakistani state.

From the Shimshalis' perspective the environmentalism apparently espoused by today's postcolonial state is not actually about the environment or its conservation. They see the establishment of the national park as having little or nothing to do with conservation and everything to do with outside forces slowly encroaching into their local space. They see the establishment of the national park as a political process in which the state is expanding its control over local people, resources, and space.

Conclusion

During the 1970s, environment emerged as a global concern in industrialized countries resulting in passage of international environmental treaties. The Stockholm declaration of 1972, for example, was one such treaty that young countries like Pakistan eagerly signed and ratified. During this period, nature and wildlife conservation emerged as a legitimate arena of state practice in which Pakistan uncritically adopted international norms and standard for crafting its national conservation policies. Through the adoption of these policies many younger nations like Pakistan sought to announce their arrival on the scene of nation-state, as a mature and civilized country. When implemented in practice these policies perpetuated rather uncivilized response from the state in the form of threats and outright violence toward its own citizens. Such violence more often than not leads to conservation failures, in the face of which states and large conservation institutions seldom revise or review their basic conceptualization of nature, landscapes, and hence conservation. Rather, they usually attribute these failures to the intransigence of the local people, who are represented as stubborn, tradition-bound, and generally not concerned about ethical conservation behavior. Such gulf between state and society in general cuts across other state-led agendas and its discourses, such as education, health, nationalism, religion, etc., and continue to produce both social and ecological failures.

An Art of Extremes

HAMMAD NASAR

NATIONHOOD AND IDENTITY; political tussles between the army, clergy, and politicians; gender roles "fixed" by society and state; a lack of infrastructure for art; the effects of globalization in general, and an India-fueled emerging art market in particular—these are some of the diverse issues that have shaped the course of recent art production and distribution in Pakistan. The "extremes" of the title to this essay refers to the two most vibrant strands of art-making in the country: innovating through tradition, as exemplified by the veritable army of young talent being produced by the miniature department of the National College of Arts, and the art of the everyday, coming from highly divergent sources. This essay discusses some of the issues that contextualize the visual culture of Pakistan, and then focuses on the two highlighted themes as a framework for exploring recent contemporary art practice.

The nation of Pakistan is a young, changing, and unstable construct. Formed in 1947 through the partition of India and its postwar decolonization by the British, Pakistan was initially created in two halves (East and West). But in 1971, with India's help, East Pakistan won independence and emerged as Bangladesh. This split challenged Pakistan's foundational premise of being a home for the subcontinent's Muslims; linguistic, ethnic, and geographic differences proved more potent than the shared Islamic faith. Pakistan has since lurched from crisis to crisis—economic, political, constitutional, humanitarian, and existential. An inability to develop robust democratic institutions has resulted in the country being governed by an alternating group of venal politicians and military dictators, each holding power for roughly half of Pakistan's existence. This toxic politics has seeded a general sense of disenfranchisement and a poverty of expectations among Pakistan's citizenry and has shaped the outlook and artistic output of many artists, young and old.

While a young nation, Pakistan shares a long past with India and, to a lesser extent, Central Asia and the Middle East. These shared histories tap Pakistan into wider narratives of significant civilizations with a considerable "back catalogue" of cultural production. However, cultural production in Pakistan has tended to favor certain past narratives over others: for example, the Mughal miniature over Gandharan Buddhist sculpture. This privileging has often taken the form of state backing, most notably with calligraphy during the regime of military ruler General Zia-ul-Haq in the 1980s. Zia's Islamist agenda and the regressive policies it engendered also gave impetus to the feminist movement, stimulating the focus and zeal of artists such as Salima Hashmi (b. 1942) in mobilizing and promoting the visual arts as a means of resistance.[1]

Like other postcolonial states with uneven access to education and a paucity of opportunities for its growing population, Pakistan has witnessed waves of emigration. The idea of Pakistani art is, therefore, not restrained within national boundaries. Rasheed Araeen (b. 1935), Anwar Jalal Shemza (1928–85), Samina Mansuri (b. 1956), Shahzia Sikander (b. 1969), Iftikhar Dadi (b. 1961), Nusra Latif Qureshi (b. 1973), Faiza Butt (b. 1973), Ruby Chishti (b. 1963), and Khalil Chishtee (b. 1964) are all influential artists from Pakistan who have established careers outside their country of birth. Less obvious but equally important is the role played by artists who moved to Pakistan and worked and taught there for extended periods, including Beate Terfloth (b. 1958), Sophie Ernst (b. 1972), David Alesworth (b. 1957), and Elizabeth Dadi, whose artistic influence has been absorbed by a generation of artists from Pakistan.

At independence from British rule in 1947, Pakistan inherited one major art education institution—the Mayo School of Art in Lahore, later renamed the National College of Arts (NCA). While many other art schools have since been established, the NCA has remained a dominant force in Pakistan's artistic development, its diverse student body finding inspiration from a supply of encouraging artist-teachers over the past four decades, from Shakir Ali (1914–75), Zahoor ul Akhlaq (1941–99), Salima Hashmi, and Naazish Ataullah (b. 1950) to a younger generation including Quddus Mirza (b. 1961), Rashid Rana (b. 1968), and Imran Qureshi (b. 1972). In Karachi, the establishment of the Indus Valley School of Art and Architecture in 1989 generated a burst of energy around what has been called Karachi Pop. Inspired by urban aesthetics, a small group of artist-teachers—Durriya Kazi (b. 1955), David Alesworth, and Iftikhar and Elizabeth Dadi—brought the everyday, and in particular appropriations of popular culture, into the realm of fine art practice in Pakistan, marking a clear break from the experiments with modernism and the contemporary miniature that are closely associated with the NCA. Lahore's recently established Beaconhouse National University (BNU) is the latest institution to register its presence on Pakistan's visual arts production.

In the absence of a museum culture and meaningful state support, art schools have been the primary providers of an art infrastructure, as well as employment for the most promising students. The underdeveloped market and relatively low levels of engagement in art-historical scholarship, critical writing, and curatorial practice have exaggerated this primacy. As an artist, writer, curator, gallerist, and educator, Salima Hashmi's role in nurturing Pakistan's "art scene" has been considerable in this generally inhospitable environment. Over the past decade a number of new initiatives have unfolded: artist collectives such as VASL, and nonprofit organizations such as FOMMA (Foundation for Museum of Modern Art) and VM Gallery have emerged as new platforms for artists to exhibit, and create a dialogue around, their work. The biannual *Nukta* magazine, launched in 2006, and the fortnightly Gallery section of *Dawn*, Pakistan's oldest English-language newspaper, have also begun to lay the foundation for a nascent discourse. The opening of the long-awaited National Art Gallery in Islamabad in 2007, with an ambitious meta-exhibition, "Moving Ahead," presenting individual takes on contemporary art by more than fifteen different curators, promised much. However, by focusing on the physical building rather than the "softer" institutional aspects of running a museum, the vitality of its future program is open to question. This dearth of local infrastructure has resulted in a reliance on and deference to better-funded institutional efforts abroad for artistic validation.

Moreover, as the international art world has looked wider in its perpetual search for renewal, present-day Pakistani artists have found a more open international audience than their predecessors. Their art has enjoyed increasing visibility over the past decade, through participation in international exhibitions (public and commercial) and appearance in art fairs and auctions. Notable survey exhibitions that have informed this greater interest include *Pakistan—Another Vision* curated by Timothy Wilcox for Asia House, London, in 2000; *Threads Dreams Desires, Art from Pakistan* curated by Salima Hashmi for Harris Museum and Art Gallery, Preston (UK), in 2002; *Playing with a Loaded Gun,* curated by Atteqa Ali for apexart, New York, and Kunsthalle Fridericianum, Kassel (Germany), in 2004; *Beyond Borders,* curated by Quddus Mirza and Saryu Doshi for the National Gallery of Modern Art, Mumbai, in 2005; and *Beyond the Page: Contemporary Art from Pakistan,* curated by Hammad Nasar for Asia House, London, and Manchester Art Gallery in 2006.[2] The growing Indian art market, itself a reflection of structural changes in the Indian economy and demographics, has been significant in this development. With a common art history, shared visual languages, and concerns, Indian galleries and collectors have been quick to recognize the opportunity of acquiring significant works from Pakistan for a fraction of the prices enjoyed by comparable work in India.

Nowhere has the increased popularity of art from Pakistan been more visible than in the practice of the contemporary miniature, with numerous exhibitions accompanied by well-researched catalogues and a pipeline of forthcoming books. The survey exhibition, *Contemporary Miniature Paintings from Pakistan,* curated by Virginia Whiles for the Fukuoka Asian Art Museum in Japan (2004), featured the work of nineteen artists and proved to be a landmark. Another exhibition that marked the international arrival of contemporary miniature art was *Karkhana: A Contemporary Collaboration,* a project conceived by artist and teacher Imran Qureshi. (*Karkhana* was realized as an exhibition for the Aldrich Contemporary Art Museum in Ridgefield, Connecticut, and the Asian Art Museum in San Francisco in 2005–6, and was curated by Jessica Hough, Hammad Nasar, and Anna Sloan.) *Karkhana* was a series of collaborative paintings by six artists who trained in the NCA's miniature department—Aisha Khalid (b. 1972), Hasnat Mehmood (b. 1978), Imran Qureshi, Nusra Latif Qureshi, Talha Rathore (b. 1969), and Saira Wasim (b. 1975)—but were based in five cities on three continents. The project was inspired by the cooperative nature of miniature painting during the Mughal era (early 16th–early 18th centuries) in India and catalyzed by a series of correspondences between the artists in Pakistan and those who had moved abroad discussing the aftermath of the attacks on the World Trade Center on 11 September 2001 and the invasions of Afghanistan and Iraq that followed. Each artist started work on two new pieces of *wasli* paper, and then sent the paintings by courier in succession to the five other artists in the group, each of whom added a layer of imagery, marks, or other processes (Figure 1). The process and its end results marked a groundbreaking collaboration, an "improvisational act involving creative destruction, semiotic play, and dynamic adaptation."[3]

Karkhana and the Fukuoka survey exhibition helped establish the idea of the contemporary miniature as a "movement." Larry Rinder, the Whitney Museum of American Art's contemporary art curator, recognized this when he invited Imran Qureshi and Saira Wasim to participate in his landmark *The American Effect* exhibition (the only exhibition of non-American artists in the history of the Whitney, featuring nearly fifty artists from over thirty countries) at the Whitney in New York in 2003: "I had put my finger inadvertently on a scene by choosing these two people, two very different manifestations of a tendency of an old tradition . . . it suggests to me that this is a very healthy and vibrant part of the culture."[4]

While miniature art was taught at the NCA for decades, the establishment of the college's miniature department as a "major" happened only in the early 1980s under the encouragement of artist Zahoor ul Akhlaq, who was exploring the conceptual framework underpinning miniature painting in his own practice. He persuaded a promising student, Bashir Ahmed (b. 1954), to head the miniature department and

FIGURE I. Imran Qureshi, Hasnat Mehmood, Aisha Khalid, Nusra Latif Qureshi, Saira Wasim, and Talha Rathore, *Untitled*, 2003. Gouache and mixed media on *wasli*, 18 cm × 23 cm. Photograph courtesy of the artists and Green Cardamom.

bring academic rigor to an art form formerly taught through apprenticeship. Ahmed remains in this post.

Shahzia Sikander, who observed Akhlaq deconstructing the miniature just as she was learning to "construct" it under Ahmed's tutelage, can be seen as the pioneer in bringing the miniature firmly into conversation with the postmodern; in particular, through her experimentation with new media and almost theatrical installations. Her success in the United States, with numerous museum exhibitions and the prestigious MacArthur Fellowship has been an inspiration to more recent alumni of the NCA.

It is, however, Imran Qureshi who has arguably been the most influential practitioner in this field. Qureshi's practice has systematically deconstructed the many characteristics of the miniature, often, as the American academic Anna Sloan has noted, "confronting the preciousness associated with the historical miniature, while retaining the aesthetic qualities of its base materials."[5] He has also taught miniature painting for over a decade at the NCA, representing what Virginia Whiles describes as the "experimental" strain that creates a productive creative tension with Ahmed's more orthodox focus on the rigors of technique. Qureshi's students include Saira Wasim, Muhammad Zeeshan (b. 1980), Hasnat Mehmood, and Khadim Ali (b. 1978)—artists who have all made a name for themselves internationally in their own right. Under his influence, these artists (and others) have developed an approach characterized by improvisation, wit and irony, and a visual language that deploys pictorial strategies of mimicry, pastiche, punning, and iconoclasm. The contemporary miniature is also marked by a critical engagement that varies from Qureshi's own gentle provocations to Wasim's "stage for human drama . . . that approaches the grandeur of Cecil B. DeMille and the glamour of Bollywood."[6] Another key characteristic that these artists share is their defining vernacular frame of reference—not always true for many contemporary artists in Pakistan, especially those who received at least part of their training abroad.

Other significant and influential artists include Nusra Latif Qureshi (based in Melbourne) and Aisha Khalid, who share an approach that has moved from narrative (albeit fractured) structures toward more abstract explorations of line and space. Qureshi, a formidable draughtswoman, favors small, sparely painted surfaces that are "on closer examination, very crowded places, teeming with complex layers of imagery from the past, meanings from the present, and methods from both."[7] Her long-term project has been the exploration of the idea of historical truth as it applies to the subcontinent and the cultural legacy of colonialism.

Khalid began her practice with thinly veiled narratives on the claustrophobic conditions of female domesticity, often depicted through walled spaces, curtains, and veiled figures ("veil" and "curtain" both translate as "purdah" in Urdu), a continuation of the feminist explorations that Hashmi and others, such as Lala Rukh (b. 1948) and Summaya Durrani (b. 1963), had initiated in the 1980s. From this narrow base have grown a formal complexity and experimentation with media and scale that embrace video, site-specific installations, and objects using textile and ornamental decorations.

In fact, Khalid and Imran Qureshi (who happen to be a couple) are probably the foremost exponents of the move of the miniature beyond the page, a subject explored in the exhibition *Beyond the Page* (Asia House, London, and Manchester Art Gallery in 2006) and examined with great insight in the accompanying catalogue by Anna Sloan. She argues that the miniature's status as a hybrid—where paintings were often executed to illustrate manuscripts, as opposed to the medium-specific tradition of Western painting—and its tendency to "revel in the dialectic tension between the second and third dimensions" encourages artists to adapt "the multiple perspectives embedded in architectural depictions in classical miniatures into three-dimensional installations." Khalid and Qureshi's installations as part of the "Living Traditions" exhibition at the historic Bagh-e-Babur in Kabul (2008) demonstrate the critical and formal elegance of this approach, where their work on the floor, walls, and windows and its interaction with the light and views from the exhibition site bear silent witness to the changes that brutal times have brought to Afghanistan (Figures 2 and 3).

The history of the other "extreme" in Pakistan's art-making, the art of the everyday, can be traced, at least in part, to another husband-and-wife team, Iftikhar and Elizabeth Dadi. Returning from graduate studies in the U.S. to live in Karachi in 1990–91, the Dadis struggled with the disconnection between "the realities of a mega city like Karachi and accounts of it via artistic means." "None of this seemed to fit what we were observing, a city that experienced an unimaginable expansion from about 500,000 to well over 10 million in a period of only fifty years, characterized by giant slums, breakdowns in planning, ethnic violence, massive growth of privatized institutions such as hospitals and schools,

FIGURE 2. Aisha Khalid, *Viewpoint*, 2008. Watercolor, glue, and paper. Site-specific installation view at "Living Traditions," Queen's Palace, Bagh-e-Babur, Kabul, 2008. Variable dimensions. Photograph courtesy of the artist and Corvi-Mora, London.

FIGURE 3. Imran Qureshi, *Time Changes,* 2008. Site-specific installation view at "Living Traditions," Queen's Palace, Bagh-e-Babur, Kabul, 2008. Variable dimensions. Photograph courtesy of the artist and Corvi-Mora, London.

but a very active and performative contestation via texts, icons, spatiality, and performativity deploying all sorts of media such as print, lights, vehicle decoration, billboards, political slogans, etc."[8]

The Dadis' individual responses to this disjuncture between art and life built on their distinctive practices of photography and conceptual sculptural installations. They developed an extensive archive of photographs of the city, which Iftikhar had started in the mid-1980s. One of the projects that emerged from this archival exploration, *Urdu Film Stills,* took the form of a series of photographs taken of Urdu language films shown on television. The project examined the use of the television as a way of imagining and disseminating modern urban ideas and, in particular, the shaping of collective ideas of "success" as exemplified by the interiors, personae, and gestures of the films.

This critical engagement with the visuality of the everyday was also reflected in Elizabeth Dadi's conceptual serial works in cast brass and aluminum. Based on popular plastic items such as baby rattles and toys, they were informed by "gender issues, minimalism-conceptualism, and an opening toward the popular." This was reflected in the choice of materials (recycled scrap metal) and thematic references to popular, inexpensive plastic toys. These works were early precursors to what has since become well-covered territory between the sculptural object and the museum artifact, explored by numerous South Asian artists, including Subodh Gupta (b. 1964), Huma Mulji (b. 1970), Adeela Suleman (b. 1970), and Hema Upadhyay (b. 1972).

In a more recent work, *They Made History* (1999–2002), the Dadis present a series of ten light boxes displaying portraits of historical figures ranging from Gandhi and Malcolm X to the Mehdi of Sudan and the King of Siam (Figure 4). With the exception of one character—a local Punjabi film hero with the unlikely stage name of Jan Rambo—the personalities chosen had all been the subjects of Hollywood biopics; the figures that we see, though, are not, for example, Gandhi or Malcolm X, but their filmic depictions by Ben Kingsley and Denzel Washington. In this staging, the Dadis argue, "the events of history are recuperated most effectively in the imaginary of the electronic media."[9] They unpack the role of the global media in framing perception: even Punjabi stage names are not spared its hegemonic effects (Figure 5).

The work and practice of the Dadis, as well as that of artist-teachers Durriya Kazi and David Alesworth, who were active in Karachi at the same time, served as a source of inspiration for a slightly younger group of artists in Lahore and Karachi who were intrigued by the immediacy of their strategies, the critical distancing from any essentialist narratives of belonging, and the development of a visual language that moved away

FIGURE 4. Iftikhar and Elizabeth Dadi, *They Made History—Jan Rambo,* 1999–2002. C-print photograph in circular backlit frame, 45.7 cm diam. × 12.7 cm. Photograph courtesy of the artists and Green Cardamom.

FIGURE 5. Iftikhar and Elizabeth Dadi, *They Made History,* 2002. Photograph courtesy of the artists and Green Cardamom.

from the modernist tropes that had dominated Pakistan's art history into the 1980s. The Dadis' use of what literary critic Roland Barthes described as "thinking photography" can be seen to have directly influenced an approach to art-making that has been adopted by a number of younger artists, most notably Rashid Rana, Bani Abidi (b. 1971), Huma Mulji (b. 1970), and Farida Batool (b. 1970).

In Rashid Rana's *Non-Sense* (2000) series of assemblages, he re-creates depictions of masculinity from popular Urdu and Punjabi cinema. In *Face to Face* (2000), for instance, he juxtaposes a larger-than-life image of the Punjabi film legend Sultan Rahi (1938–96) (known for playing the angry young man who rails against injustice), painted in photorealist style as the image would appear in a black-and-white negative, with a black-and-white framed childhood photograph of the artist stuck to the patterned fabric of a dhoti or Punjabi men's tunic. This encounter of gender expectations being consumed through popular media continues the critical dialogue that the Dadis initiated with filmic depiction in *Urdu Film Stills,* but adds multiple layers covering narrative—of self, gender roles, and visual reinforcement; formal features—the heroically large canvas with a small photographic portrait; and artistic production—the painting was executed by assistants under Rana's instruction.

Rana went on to work with the often dramatically scaled composite photographic works that have made him a superstar on the international art fair and auction circuit. Using the simple conceptual device of composite images, borrowed from the visual language of advertising (but also found in classical miniature painting), Rana constructs multiple narratives by exploring the relationship between the thousands of small individual images and the larger image they help create. For instance, in *I Love Miniatures* (2003), Rana mirrors the emperor Shah Jahan (r. 1628–58) as depicted in a famous portrait in the Victoria and Albert collection in London. But in Rana's work, the portrait has been built up with tiny photographs of billboards from the streets of Lahore. In a later work, *All Eyes Skyward during the Annual Parade* (2004—a large-scale work displayed on two walls at right angles to each other), he shows a seemingly banal image of a flag-waving crowd celebrating the ritual fly-past of jet fighters. As one approaches, the large image of the crowd dissolves into thousands of stills from Bollywood films (Figure 6),

FIGURE 6. Rashid Rana, *All Eyes Skyward during the Annual Parade*, 2004. Digital print, 250 cm. × 610 cm. Collection of Lekha and Anupam Poddar. Photograph courtesy of the artist and Green Cardamom.

Below: Detail.

officially illegal but unofficially the most popular mass entertainment in urban Pakistan. This instance of "constructing an image of Pakistan self-identity from images of the 'Other'" is witty and insightful, and is an iconic work in the long trajectory of Pakistani visual artists' persistent attempts to address the "identity issue."[10]

Bani Abidi poignantly examines the phenomenon of shaping identity, as well as the Arabization of Pakistan's cultural history under Zia-ul-Haq's Islamization efforts in the 1980s, in *The Boy Who Got Tired of Posing* (2006). This series of studio photographs features young boys posing as Muhammad bin Qasim (695–715), the Arab general responsible for the first Muslim entry to the subcontinent in the 8th century, and points to the process of cultural conditioning, whereby Pakistanis have been encouraged to privilege "Muslim" aspects of their history.

Abidi's other persistent concern has been the issue of "power and servility" in human society.[11] In the two-channel video *Shan Pipe Band Learns the Star-Spangled Banner* (2004), she commissioned a brass band (a leftover from the British Raj, complete with bagpipes and kilts) to learn the U.S. national anthem in one day. One screen records the earnest efforts of band members to listen and learn through trial and error, while the other shows the small, crowded, incongruous Lahore street where this rehearsal takes place. The work layers ideas of history and tradition in the postcolonial context onto the general notion of servility. The fact that it is now "traditional" to have a band in Scottish dress play Indian songs at Punjabi weddings is ironic. However, one feels a great empathy for the Shan Pipe Band as they learn the notes of "The Star-Spangled Banner," and in that human story is a reflection of the postcolonial narrative, from the British Empire to the United States.

The Address is a photograph that Abidi took of a studio set (which she commissioned) for the televised presidential address in Pakistan (Figure 7). The setting, comprising a blue background curtain, a portrait of Mohammed Ali Jinnah (the founder of the nation), and the Pakistan flag, is the one consistent feature in every announcement of a coup or change of government. Abidi arranged to play a still image of this work on television screens throughout Karachi, and produced a series of photographs documenting the process. The work captures the duality of waiting—suggesting that the fact the nation is still standing, given all that it has been through in its 61 years, is something to celebrate, but also lamenting that the nation appears to be standing still. It is an incredibly prescient work, realized months before the latest shift in administration from military dictator to politician, itself triggered by the killing of Benazir Bhutto in December 2007.

FIGURE 7. Bani Abidi, *The Address*, 2007. Digital print, 76 cm. × 101 cm. Khanna Family Collection, India. Photograph courtesy of the artist and Green Cardamom.

Hammad Nasar

Within this politically engaged cultural production, it is worth briefly considering the fact that so many other artists, including Lalarukh, Naiza Khan (b. 1968), Summaya Durrani, Adeela Suleman, Aisha Khalid, and Ruby Chishti, have followed Salima Hashmi's lead in creating a vernacular feminist discourse. Khan's *Henna Hands* (2003) and Chishti's *Armour* (2006) are two recent works in this trajectory that have reached iconic status. *Henna Hands* is a series of public interventions, where Khan stencilled female silhouettes in henna on the graffitied and bill-posted streets of Karachi, introducing an ephemeral and uneasy female presence into the predominantly male urban space (Figure 8). Chishti's *Armour* is a delicate soft sculpture of a baby cast from sanitary napkins, a material used by Chishti in a series of works exploring societal pressures on women's fertility.

Innovating tradition and the art of the popular/everyday are impulses in Pakistan art that may have started as extremes but have begun to overlap and at times seem to have merged into each other. Rashid Rana's *I Love Miniatures,* where he questions the factors underlying the privileging of the miniature in contemporary Pakistan art, is one example of this phenomenon. Another is Imran Qureshi's series of missile paintings, where he treats the missile (often garlanded) as the subject of Mughal-style portraits, critiquing the fetishization of missiles that came with the successful testing of nuclear weapons in 1998.

But perhaps the poster-child for the convergence between these two streams is the work of Hamra Abbas (b. 1976). Abbas trained as a sculptor, with a minor in miniature painting, at the NCA. In a ten-year

FIGURE 8. Naiza Khan, *Henna Hands,* 2003. Henna pigment on wall. Installation view of site-specific project at Adam Road, Cantonment Station, Karachi; variable dimensions. Photograph courtesy of the artist.

peripatetic artistic career, she has established a practice quite stagger-
ing in its scope. Her recent work has included a series of 99 exquisitely
painted miniatures from photographs she took of children in *madrassas*
(religious schools) in Pakistan, installed in a room with a large-scale
photograph (*God Grows on Trees*, 2008); a wood labyrinth suspended
from the ceiling, the sides of which conceal speakers playing the scram-
bled sound of the same children reciting the Quran (*Read*, 2007); two–
meter tall letters made from intricately "woven" paper collage making
"Islamic" patterns and spelling out "Please Do Not Step" on the floor
of the ARTIUM de Álava art center in Vitoria, Spain, that required
the audience to step on them to see the rest of the show (*Please Do Not
Step 2*, 2008); a video documenting the last-day crowds queuing for the
exhibition of a selection from MOMA's collection on tour in Germany
(*MOMA Is the Star*, 2004); an animation made from photographing
passersby on the streets and parks of London posing as figures from the
depiction of a battle scene in a manuscript in the V&A collection (*Battle
Scenes*, 2006): the list goes on.

For the 2007 Istanbul Biennial, she created a series of three larger-
than-life figures of couples, referencing depictions of the *Kama Sutra,*
in brightly colored Plasticine. Clutching weapons while making love,
these couples cut playful, almost absurd figures, with their stern counte-
nances. In *Lessons on Love,* Abbas transforms the two-dimensional classical language of the miniature into contemporary sculpture (Figure 9):
an artistic strategy that closely mirrors Takashi Murakami's (b. 1962)
sculptural exploration of manga comics.

In her most recent sculptural work, a fiberglass figure more than
two meters tall of a voluptuous female holding a staff and extending
her middle finger (*Woman in Black*) (Figure 10), Abbas has drawn on
visual references from Indian temple sculpture (one of Pakistan's mostly
ignored historic narratives) to comic-book superheroes (think Wonder
Woman or Supergirl), and a specific contextual reference to the infamous Red Mosque siege in Islamabad in 2007, where burqa-clad, staff-
wielding female seminary students were involved in a stand-off with
security forces.

This work also serves as a conclusion for this essay, returning us
to where we started—to considerations of identity, political/religious

FIGURE 9. Hamra Abbas, *Lessons on Love* (detail), 2007. Resin (originally Plasticine), 230 cm. × 170 cm × 140 cm. Vanhaerents Art Collection, Brussels. Photograph courtesy of the artist and Green Cardamom.

FIGURE 10. Hamra Abbas, *Woman in Black,* 2008. Fiberglass, 210 cm. × 79 cm. × 99 cm. Photograph courtesy of the artist and Green Cardamom.

struggles, globalization, and gender roles. This pillar of female strength (physical and sexual) seems like a fun-house mirror reflection of the Mother India figure and suggests a visual metaphor for Pakistan: a nation whose extremes can combine to form something very potent.

Notes

1. For further study of women artists in Pakistan, see Salima Hashmi, *Unveiling the Visible: Lives and Works of Women Artists of Pakistan* (Islamabad: ActionAid Pakistan, 2002).

2. Hammad Nasar, *Beyond the Page: Contemporary Art from Pakistan* (London and Manchester: Shisha, 2006).

3. Jessica Hough, Hammad Nasar, and Anna Sloan, "Introduction," in Hammad Nasar, ed., *Karkhana: A Contemporary Collaboration* (London and Ridgefield: The Aldrich Contemporary Art Museum/Green Cardamom, 2005), 8.

4. Larry Rinder in conversation with Hammad Nasar, "Same Planet, Different Worlds," *Herald* (Karachi), February 2004, 97.

5. Anna Sloan, "Embodied Space: Miniature as Attitude," in *Beyond the Page,* 37.

6. Anna Sloan, "A Divine Comedy of Errors: Political Paintings by Saira Wasim," in Anita Dawood and Hammad Nasar, eds., *Transcendent Contemplations: Paintings by Hasnat Mehmood and Saira Wasim* (London: Green Cardamom, 2004).

7. Hammad Nasar, "Disturbing the Order of Things," in Anita Dawood, ed., *Acts of Compliance* (London: Green Cardamom, 2005), 8.

8. Iftikhar Dadi, "Iftikhar Dadi and Elizabeth Dadi's Art Practice in Karachi during the 1990s: A Self-Assessment," n.p., 28 October 2008.

9. Iftikhar Dadi and Elizabeth Dadi, "Artists' Statement," n.p., n.d.

10. *Beyond the Page,* 18.

11. Francesco Cincotta, "Featured Artist: Interview with Bani Abidi," in *Naked Punch* 10 (Spring 2008), 93.

Will You Not See the Full Moon
Kya Tum Poora Chand Na Dekhoge

FEHMIDA RIYAZ

Should I call this the day of enlightenment and hope?
When the kite circles the burning sky
And in the web of highways
The traffic begins to growl like a wounded animal
In the marketplace
The lust for imported goods awakes and rubs her eyes
Purchasing power!
The interrogator's favorite whore
See how shamelessly she moves around
While dirty, dried-up mothers
Scavenge for bones in garbage heaps
To silence their sobbing children.

On the molested bodies of cities
Mansions and shopping plazas have begun to erupt
Like boils
Declaring the decisive victory of the black market
You can see their advertisements in tomorrow's paper
Scoffing at your poverty:
You can beat your head against the wall, in fact, cut it off and
Throw it away

Into the graveyard of your murdered desires
We'll make a minaret of your skulls
And give it some trendy name
Like "The Garden of the Prophet"
Or "This is the Benevolence of God"
Or some other piping hot name
Because business is brisk
Why is this business flourishing?

It is a horrible secret
Which everyone knows but none mentions

We are grinding humans to produce dwarves
O Sheikh, praise our achievements!
Alms! O Brother!
I swear by your hallowed petrodollar!

Translated by Saadia Toor, Ali Mir, and Raza Mir

Contributors

Mahvish Ahmad is an independent journalist and political science lecturer in Islamabad, Pakistan.

Nosheen Ali is a lecturer in South and South East Asian studies at the University of California, Berkeley. Her research in social anthropology focuses on the cultural politics of citizenship, religion, and development in Gilgit-Baltistan (Pakistan/Kashmir). She is a founding member of the international network GRASP (Group for Research in the Anthropology, Sociology, and Politics of Pakistan) and serves on the editorial board of the South Asian journal *SAMAJ*.

Qalandar Bux Memon is the editor of *Naked Punch,* a philosophy, art, and politics platform run by a collective of writers and activists. He is a lecturer of politics at Forman Christian University, Lahore, and cofounder of Café Bol, an intellectual café in Lahore.

Shafqat Hussain is a professor of anthropology at Trinity College in Hartford, Connecticut. He obtained a PhD from the School of Forestry and Environmental Studies and the Department of Anthropology at Yale University. He is from Pakistan and worked in the Gilgit-Baltistan region of northern Pakistan for the Aga Khan Rural Support Program in Skardu and IUCN–Washington as a Ford Foundation policy fellow. He is interested in how geopolitical and intellectual changes affect the perception of nature and human society's relationship with it.

Humeira Iqtidar is a lecturer in politics at King's College London. Her research explores the contours of social and political theory related to state, market, religion, secularism, and citizenship. She is the author of *Secularizing Islamists? Jamaat-e-Islami and Jamaat-ud-Dawa in Urban Pakistan.*

Habib Jalib (1928–1993) was a Communist poet who was frequently imprisoned in Pakistan. He is best known for his landmark poem "Dastoor," written to pillory the military dictatorship of Ayub Khan, and for his revolutionary anthem for the film *Zarqa,* "Raqs zanjeer pahan ker bhi kiya jata hai."

Amina Jamal is assistant professor of sociology at Ryerson University. She investigates the ambivalent positioning of women citizens through the intersection of Islamization and feminism at diverse sites; most recently her research focuses on the politics of Jamaat-e-Islami women in Pakistan.

Hafeez Jamali is an anthropologist based in Pakistan and the United States. He is a PhD candidate and assistant instructor of anthropology at the University of Texas at Austin. His research is on anthropology of globalization and development, history of Indian Ocean trade, and politics of place in Balochistan, Pakistan. His writing has been published in *Anthropology News, Cultural Dynamics,* and the *Middle East Report.*

Iqbal Khattak began his career as a journalist in 1989 at *The Frontier Post,* then went to the *Friday Times* in 2001 before founding the *Daily Times,* for which he is the Peshawar bureau chief. He has been the representative in Pakistan of Reporters Without Borders since 1999 and is a contributing editor to *Himal South Asia.*

Zahra Malkani is an artist and activist from Karachi, Pakistan.

Hammad Nasar is a curator and writer. He cofounded the arts organization Green Cardamom and the arts advisory firm Asal Partners.

Vijay Prashad is the George and Martha Kellner Chair in South Asian History and professor of international studies at Trinity College in Hartford, Connecticut. He is the author of several books, including *The Darker Nations*; *Arab Spring, Libyan Winter*; and *The Karma of Brown Folk* (Minnesota, 2001). He is coeditor of *Dispatches from the Arab Spring: Understanding the New Middle East* (Minnesota, 2013).

Junaid Rana is associate professor of Asian American studies with appointments in the Department of Anthropology, the Center for South Asian and Middle Eastern Studies, and the Unit for Criticism and Interpretive Theory at the University of Illinois at Urbana–Champaign. He is the author of *Terrifying Muslims: Race and Labor in the South Asian Diaspora.*

Fehmida Riyaz is a feminist progressive poet. She lived in exile in India during the Zia years, then returned to Pakistan and wrote of her disillusionment with the land that germinated Hindu nationalism. Her collection *Badan Dareedah* (1973) was the first feminist poetry published in Pakistan.

Maliha Safri is assistant professor at Drew University. She teaches political economy and migration, and her work has been published in *Signs*, *Rethinking Marxism*, and *Middle East Journal*. She participates in popular education seminars and economic literacy work with activists with the Center for Popular Economics and in worker cooperatives in New Jersey and the New York metropolitan area.

Aasim Sajjad Akhtar is a political activist associated with the People's Rights Movement, a confederation of working-class struggles. He teaches colonial history and political economy at the Lahore University of Management Sciences (LUMS).

Ayesha Siddiqa is the author of two books on defense decision making and the political economy of the military, *Military Inc.: Inside Pakistan's Military Economy* and *Pakistan's Arms Procurement and Military Buildup, 1979–99: In Search of a Policy*. She has extensive experience with public sector projects and research related to defense decision making, defense economics, arms procurement and production, and revolution in military affairs in South Asia.

Sultan-i-Rome is assistant professor of history in Government Jahanzeb Postgraduate College, Swat, Pakistan. Originally from Hazara village in Swat, he received degrees in history from the University of Karachi and the University of Peshawar. He is a life member of the Pakistan Historical Society and sitting member of its Executive Committee and a life member of the Council of Social Sciences Pakistan (COSS). He is the author of *Swat State, 1915–1969*.

Madiha R. Tahir is a multimedia and print freelance journalist based in Karachi, Pakistan. Her work has appeared in *Foreign Affairs*, *The National*, the *Columbia Journalism Review*, *The Herald*, and the *Friday Times*, as well as on *Democracy Now!*, Public Radio International's *The World*, and *Global Post*.

Saadia Toor is assistant professor at Staten Island College. She is author of *The State of Islam* and an active member of Action for a Progressive Pakistan.

Index

Burki, Shahid Javed, 37, 85
Burson-Marsteller, 73
Bush administration, lobbying, 71–72
Butt, Faiza, 239
Butt (DJ), 96

capitalism, 50; global neoliberal project and, 28; land reforms encouraging capitalist exploitation, 48–49; Pakistan as laboratory of neoliberalism and spread of, 8–9; patterns of social and political exchange changed by, 5–6, 13; self-image of Pakistani, 42; wage labor identified as a capitalist relation, 45. *See also* Gwadar, Balochistan; megaprojects under Musharraf
Carter, Jimmy, 76
Cassidy and Associates, 72–73
casual labor, 44–45
Central Asian Republics (CARS), Gwadar as "hub port" for transfer of oil and natural gas from, 171–72, 183n4
chadar and *chardiwari* (veil and privacy of houses), sanctity of, 198
Chagai, atomic waste deposited in, 163
Chagai-I (underground nuclear tests), 150
Chamalang Coal mines (Lorelai and Kohlu), 162, 163
Chaman (Balochistan), underground economy on border at, 7
Chatterjee, Partha, 128, 177
China: copper and gold mining sites leased to, 161–62; partnership with Pakistani military, 62
Chishtee, Khalil, 239
Chishti, Ruby, 239, 251
Christian Science Monitor, 81
CIA, 68, 203
Cincotta, Francesco, 254n11

civilian bureaucracy: changing class composition of, 9–10; politics of patronage and, 13
civilian rule (democracy), periods of: of Zulfiqar Ali Bhutto (1971–77), 54; elections of 2008 and, 53; "Rule of Troika" (1988–99), 56
class: changing class composition of bureaucracies, 9–10, 12; cricket and class politics, 85. *See also* commercial class; elite, Pakistani; middle class
clergy: mixed reaction to poetic activism in Gilgit, 222–23; patron–client relation between state officials and, Halqa poetry exposing, 218–19
Clinton, Hillary, 65
Clinton administration, 72
coal mines, 162, 163
Coastal Highway linking Gwadar to Karachi, 160
Cohen, Stephen P., 9, 17n11
Cold War, 76, 107
Collective of Social Science Research, 46, 47
collective responsibility (pillar of tribal system in Waziristan), 211
colonialism: cultural components of, 85; damage of, Imran Khan on, 85, 103; feudalism created under British, 125; Shimshalis' view of Pakistani state in light of history of, 236–37
commercial class: economic modernization of 1960s and, 11; "nativised," 11, 12; political economy of war and, 6–7, 11, 13; symbiotic link with religio-ideological establishment, 11; Zia's patronage politics and, 13
Communist Party of India, 132n1, 136
Community Controlled Hunting Area (CCHA), 234–35

drug smuggling, 6, 7, 16n5
Duncan, Emma, 201n26
Durand Line (1893), 209
Durrani, Mohammad Ali, 94
Durrani, Summaya, 244, 251
Durrani, Tasneem, 115

earthquake of 2005, relief organizations after, 17n16
East Bengal, 122
East India Company, 237
economic protection of women (*kifalat*), Jamaat women's work for, 115
economy: capitalism and changing patterns of social and political exchange, 5–6, 13; dependence of growth on foreign aid, 75; informal, 6–7, 11, 12, 13, 16n3; military's domination of, 25–27, 59–60; during Musharraf period (1999–2008), 8; political economy of war, 6–7, 11, 13, 14; unfairness of economic development in Balochistan, 159–63. *See also* Gwadar, Balochistan
education: art schools, 239–40; crisis of *insaniyat* (humanism) and school-based, 225; investment in Punjabi institutions in early years of Pakistan's formation, 123; of Jamaat women and Pakistani feminists, similarity in, 117; military's penetration into academia, 60–61; postcolonial modernization project of higher, 111
education NGO, state's social welfare responsibilities taken over by, 29
18th Amendment, 159
elections, military subversion of, 57–58, 63n6
electoral power, feudalism and, 47–48
elite, Pakistani: alienation of, 10,

17n13; Bhutto's alliance with, 80; interconnected with large patronage network, 140–41; Jamaat women's criticism of feminists from Western-educated, 113–18; Imran Khan's criticism of, 87; in Lahore, 129; leaders of Islamic movement among, 116; lifestyle politics of, 91; Mohajir, 121; in private corporate sphere, 17n12; pro-business lobby work in U.S. favoring, 74; rift in, meteoric rise of Bhutto and emergence of PPP and, 125; secular liberal, view of military of, 61; strategic alliances with military, 58–59; urban intelligentsia's lack of recognition of lower middle class intellectuals, 130–31; Westernized liberal, erosion of influence of, 10, 12–13; Westernized liberal, support of Musharraf, 32–33
emigration from Pakistan, 239
Emirates Investment Group, 23
English language, as language of elite youth in global cities, 129, 133n6
entrepreneurial class, dependence on official patronage, 59. *See also* commercial class
environmentalism. *See* Khunjerab National Park
Ernst, Sophie, 239
Establishment of the West Pakistan Act (1955), 188
ethics, Halqa poets reimagining Muslim, 215–20
ethnocentrism, 4
ethnonationalists, 14, 15, 234
Export Processing Zones, 171
extractive megaprojects, 160–61

Face to Face (Rana), 248
Faisalabad, Punjab, workers of, 135–49;

Halqa-e-Arbab-e-Zauq (literary organization), 214–25, 226; government workers, poetry as resistance for, 223–24; mocking hypocrisies of local clergy and religious leaders, 218–19; motivation for poetry of, 214; poetic activism of, 220–25; poetry as form of *ibadat* (worship) and *insaniyat* (humanism), 219; reimagining Muslim ethics and politics, 215–20

Hamid, Abdul, 200n9

Hamid, Zaid, 91

Haq, Ikramul, 16n2

Haqqani, Hussain, 17n14, 70–71

haris (sharecropper tenants), 43–44

Harris Museum and Art Gallery, Preston (United Kingdom), 241

Harrison, Selig S., 155, 157, 158, 166n6, 183n1

Harvey, David, 13–14

Hasan, Arif, 16n1, 16n6, 17n13, 113

Hashmi, Salima, 239, 244, 251, 253n1; role in nurturing Pakistan's "art scene," 240, 241

Hashtnagar, military crackdown on peasantry in (2002), 33

Hassan, Azizul, 183n4, 209–10

Hassan, Parvez, 97, 99

hatian system (sharecropping), 43–44

Hazara Democratic Party, 158

Henna Hands (Khan), 251

heroin trafficking, 7

Herring, Ronald J., 48

hijra communities, bonded labor in, 46, 51n4

Hilali, A. Z., 16n5

Hoodhbhoy, Pervez, 63n16

Hoti, Khwaja Khan, 99

Hoti, Omar Farooq, 99

Hough, Jessica, 242, 253n3

Howell, Sir Evelyn, 208

Hudood Ordinance, 33, 89, 105, 112

human rights: transnational activism, 112; universal human rights discourse, 28

Human Rights Commission of Pakistan, 164, 167n16

Human Rights Watch, 23, 40n3; report on Balochistan, 164, 167n15

Hurricane Katrina, xii

Hussain, Akbar, 196

Hussain, Qatrina, 63n15

Hussain, Sayyad Munir, 187

Hussain, Shazreh, 43

Hussain (third Shia Imam), 227n6, 227n8

Hussein, Chaudhury Shujaat, 164

Hussein, Maliha, 43

Hyderabad Trials, 157

Hyperion Protective Consultants, 68

I Am Alive (Faraz), xii

ibadat (worship), poetry as form of, 219

identity: Baloch, resurgence of, 170; phenomenon of shaping, 249; Rana's *All Eyes Skyward during the Annual Parade* constructing image of Pakistan self-identity from images of "Other," 248–49

ideology, military's self-promotion as defender of country's, 61–62

I Love Miniatures (Rana), 248, 251

independence: desire in Balochistan for, 152, 153, 154, 179, 181; of Swat, 185–87

independent television channels, 106

India: art market, 241; Chatterjee on future of Indian political dynamics, 128; informal economy in, 16n3; partition of, 107, 122–24, 238

Indian Communist Party, 132n1, 136

Indian Literature (magazine), 136

India–Pakistan war: first (1947–48), 54; in 1965, 76

Indus River: floods of 2010, 124–27; planned breaches in embankment along, 126; and tributaries, 1, 3. *See also* floods of 2010

Indus Valley School of Art and Architecture, 240

inequality, ever-increasing, 48–50. *See also* commercial class; elite, Pakistani; middle class; military, Pakistani; poverty

informal economy: emergence of "nativized" commercial class rooted in, 6–7, 11, 12; in India, 16n3; politics of patronage symbiotic with growth of, 13

insaniyat (humanism), poetry as form of, 219, 225

Instrument of Accession, 186, 199n6

Interim Constitution of the Islamic Republic of Pakistan, 1973, The, 188

international financial institutions (IFIs), radical financial liberalization enforced by, 6, 8

International Labour Organization (ILO), 43

International Monetary Fund (IMF), 8, 24, 42, 49, 78, 132; Pakistan's default on loans from, 77; privatization imposed by, 37–38

Inter-Service Public Relations (ISPR), 60

Inter-Services Intelligence (ISI), 53, 57, 94; penetration into academia and media, 60–61; surveillance by, 150

Iqbal, Muhammad, 87, 103, 227n7

Iqbal, Walid, 99

Iqtidar, Humeira, 133n1, 133n4

Iran, "Islamic Feminists" of, 110

Islam: anthropology of, 219; cynical use of, by oligarchy, 9, 10, 14; Halqa poets exposing inhuman values and exploitative practices of Pakistani,

215–20; as ideological bulwark against communism, U.S. funding to develop, 108; Imran Khan's pious turn to, 86–87, 88; Maududi's reframing of, into system of practices linking religious energy to Muslim politics, 107; military's use of, 10, 14, 17n14, 25; pluralistic vision of, in Halqa poetry, 218; Zia's blend of modernity and, 108–9. *See also* feminism and "fundamentalism" in Pakistan

Islamabad: development plans (*see* Gwadar Port Project; Shimshal, Gilgit-Baltistan); Lawyers Movement and, 34; PTI rally in, 101–2; Quaid-e-Azam University in, 61; Red Mosque Siege (2007), 252; resistance toward attempts at provincial autonomy, 159–60; transformation of real estate in, 17n8; workers meeting at PTCL headquarters in, 38

Islamic law: Muslim Family Laws, 105; Shariah Bill, 31, 41n11; Swat insurgencies in 1994 and 2007–9 calling for enforcement and implementation of, 189, 191–93, 202n30

Islami Jamhoori Itihad (Islamic Democratic Alliance), 57, 63n5

Islamization, 9–10; Arabization of Pakistan's cultural history under Zia-ul-Haq, 249; articulation of Women-in-Development (WID) programs with state project of, 112–13; Halqa's poetry and Muslim grappling with, 219–20; insidious effects of, 108. *See also* religious right

Ismaili Muslim sect, 230

Istanbul Biennial (2007), 252

IUCN (The World Conservation Union), 228

migrant permanent workers, 44
military, Pakistani, 53–63; anti-Musharraf movement and movement against, 34, 35; armed struggle in Swat (2007–9), 35, 196–99; in Balochistan, 24–26, 80, 174; central role in establishing neoliberal security state, 22–24; changing class composition of, 9–10, 12; control of narrative, 60–63; crackdown on peasantry in Hashtnagar in 2002, 33; defense budget, 24, 54, 59; economic empire, 25–27, 59–60; expenditures on, 50, 51n8; foreign benefactors of, 62; grievances in Swat against, 198–99; image as an alternative institution, 54, 62–63; instability produced by, 27; instrumentalizing Islam, policy of, 10, 14, 17n14, 25; intelligence network (ISI), 53, 57, 60–61, 94, 150; intervention of, 54–55; Imran Khan and, 80–81, 94–95; land takeover by, 22, 23–24, 40n4–5; militarization of Mekran Coast, 174; Musharraf's coup, 30, 31–33, 49, 183n2; new airbase and cantonment in Swat, desire for, 196; Operation Rah-e Haq, 197; Operation Rah-e-Nijat (Operation Path to Salvation), 203–6; Operation Rah-e-Rast (Operation Right Path, 2009), 198, 211; paramilitary (Pakistan Rangers) crackdown in Okara district in Punjab and, 19–24, 28; patronage politics and, 23–24, 27, 57, 59; perception of, after Musharraf's rule, 53–54; politics of, 55–59, 63n6; predatory nature of, 22–24; religious right and, 57, 61–62; stranglehold on Gwadar, 178–82; strategic alliances with political elite, 58–59

military aid, 71, 72, 76, 77
miniature art, practice of contemporary, 241–45; convergence between art of the everyday and, 251–53; influential artists, 242–45; miniature's status as a hybrid, 244; as a "movement," 242
Minimum Wage Board, 140
mining sector, debt bondage throughout, 45–46
minority rights, Musharraf and, 31–32, 33
Mirani Dam, 160, 161, 169
Mirza, Quddus, 240, 241
missile paintings of Qureshi, 251
Mizh (Howell), 208
mobile phone revolution, 8
modernity: economic development and (*see* Gwadar, Balochistan); founding of Jamaat-e-Islami and, 107; invoked by Jamaat women, 117, 118; Progressive Writers Movement championing workers' rights and, 136; struggle of Islam and, Said Khan on, 116; Zia's blend of Islam and, 108–9. *See also* feminism and "fundamentalism" in Pakistan
Mohajirs, 121, 166n11
Mohamad, Dr. Mahathir, 87
MOMA Is the Star (Abbas), 252
Movement for Enforcement of Islamic Law. *See* Tahrik Nifaz-e-Shariat-e-Muhammadi
Movement for Justice. *See* Pakistan Tehrik-i-Insaaf
Mubarik, Sindh, military takeover of, 40n4
Mueller, Robert S., III, 72
Muhammad, Nek, 208, 209, 210
Muhammad, Prophet, Imran Khan on, 86–87
Muhammad, Sufi, 191; armed struggle in Swat (2007–9) and, 196, 197;

fighting in Afghanistan for Taliban, 193–94

Mulji, Huma, 246, 248

Mullah Nazir, tribal group in South Waziristan, 204, 205

mullas, elite position of, 116

Mumbai attacks (November 26, 2008), 201n30

Mumtaz, Kahwar, 105, 108

Murakami, Takashi, 252

Murree, Sher Muhammad, 156, 157

mushairas (poetry recitation gatherings), 213, 220; at Karakuram International University in Gilgit, 214–16, 226; *naatia*, 222

Musharraf, Pervez, 24, 27, 50, 57, 174; armed struggle (2007–9) with Fazlullah, 196–99; co-option of media figures, 61; Corporate Farming Ordinance under, 23; coup d'etat in 1999, 30, 31–33, 49, 183n2; defense budget under, 59; "devolution plan" of, 29–30; dismissal of Chief Justice of Supreme Court, 34; economy under, 8; "enlightened moderation" of, 32; Imran Khan and, 94–95, 97; liberal lifestyle of, 32; megaprojects for Pakistani economy under, 159–63, 169; minority rights and, 31–32, 33; national reconciliation ordinance and, 58; NGO support of, 29–32; plans for developing Gwadar, 169, 170, 171–75; PML-Q, 99, 100; progressive anti-Musharraf movement, 33–34; rule from 1999–2008, 54; terrors unleashed by, 32–33; U.S. policymakers support of, since 9/11, 41n10; women's participation in public politics under, 106; working class dissent suppressed under, 37–38

Mushtaq, 105

Muslim ethics and politics: Halqa's progressive poetry reimagining, 215–20; poetic activism against sectarian conflict, 220–23. *See also* feminism and "fundamentalism" in Pakistan; Islam; religious right

Muslim Family Laws, 105

Muslim League, 121

Muttahida Majlis-e-Amal (United Assembly of Action; MMA), 11, 33, 57, 63n5, 106, 195

Muttahida Qaumi Movement (MQM), 95, 96

narrative, military's control of national, 60–63

Nasar, Hammad, 241, 242, 253n2–4, 254n7

Nasir, Gul Khan, 165–66

Nasir, Mir Gul Khan, 173

Nasr, Seyyed Vali Reza, 107, 109

Nation, The, 88

National Art Gallery (Islamabad), 240–41

National Association of Pakistani Americans, 74

National Awami Party, 156, 157

National College of Arts (NCA), 238, 240; miniature department, 242–44

National Finance Commission Award meeting in Gwadar (2009), 175, 183n5

National Gallery of Modern Art, Mumbai, 241

nationalism: ethnic Baloch, 179–80, 181, 183n2; Fisherfolk's Movement and, 180–82; Pukhtoon, 209–10

National Party (NP), Baloch, 151, 153

national reconciliation ordinance (NRO), 58

national security state, military's

influence linked to development of, 54–55. *See also* neoliberal security state

National Students' Front, 124

National Trade Union Federation, 142

National Workers Party, 32

nation-state, Halqa poets exposing inhuman values and exploitative practices of Pakistani, 215–20

natural resources of Balochistan, leasing for investments in, 161–63, 171–72, 179. *See also* Balochistan, Pakistani betrayal of; Gwadar, Balochistan

Nawazabad in Bahawalpur, eviction of peasants in, 40n4

Naya Adab (New Literature), 136

Nazir, Malik, 137, 138

neoliberalism: emerging consolidation of global neoliberal project, 28; Pakistan as laboratory of, 8–9; shared stakes in, 14

neoliberal security state, development of, 19–41; corporate control of agriculture and, 23–24; debt burden and, 24; military occupation of Balochistan, 24–26; military's central role in establishing, 22–24; Musharraf regime, 37–38; paramilitary crackdown in Okara district in Punjab, 19–24, 28; proliferation of "security-talk" and, 36; state of progressive politics and, 28–39; U.S.–Pakistan alliance and running neoliberal War on Terror, 65, 66, 67–70; U.S.'s new war in Afghanistan and, 24–25. *See also* Musharraf, Pervez

Nisar, Atiya, 112, 114–15

Nizamani, K.B., 166n6

non-governmental organizations (NGOs): activists, 28, 29–30;

feminist, 110; Jamaat women's Islamic, 110–11; NGO-ization of liberal politics, 29–30; NGO movement, 112, 113; revolution, 14; support of Musharraf's coup, 30, 31–32; support of Musharraf's "devolution plan," 29–30

Non-Sense (Rana), 248

Noor, Mian, 186

Northern Areas. *See* Gilgit-Baltistan

North-West Frontier Province. *See* Khyber Pakhtunkhwa; Swat

nuclear ambitions, 76–77

nuclear tests, 25–26; Chagai-I, 150

Nukta magazine, 240

Obama, Barack, Kerry–Lugar bill signed by, 64–65, 72–73

Oda, Hisaya, 17n7

Ogilvy Public Relations Worldwide, 73

oil and gas fields, 161, 163

Okara district in Punjab, peasant rebellion in, 69, 124; violent crackdown by paramilitary Pakistan Rangers in, 19–24, 28

oligarchy, erosion of, 9

One Unit Plan, 155, 156

Operation Rah-e Haq, 197

Operation Rah-e-Nijat (Operation Path to Salvation), 203–6

Operation Rah-e Rast (Operation Right Path, 2009), 198, 211

Orakzai, Ali Muhammad Jan, 195

Orakzai, Rifatullah, 202n31, 202n34, 202n41

Pakhtuns, 7, 16n5

Pakistan: accounting for voices of multitude, xiv; administrative areas, 1, 2; current problems, 22; defense budget in, 24, 54, 59; formation of

contracting as strategy in, 68; U.S.–
Pakistan alliance and, 65, 66, 67–70
*Warrior Race: a Journey through the
Land of Tribal Pathans* (Imran
Khan), 87
Waseem, Muhammad, 97–98
Washington, Denzel, 247
Washington Consensus, 28
Wasim, Saira, 242, 243, 244
Wazir, Farooq, 210
Wazir, Nek Muhammad, 93
Waziristan, militancy in, 203–12; al-
Qaeda and, 207–8, 210; Operation
Rah-e-Nijat against TTP, 203–6;
peace in region, need for, 211–12;
progressive forces and, 209–10;
tribal dynamics, 204–5, 206, 211;
Wazir background and, 207–9
Weiss, Anita M., 108
Whiles, Virginia, 241, 243
Whitney Museum of American Art,
242
Wilcox, Timothy, 241
Wilcox, Wayne Ayres, 200n16
wilderness, conservation of. *See*
Khunjerab National Park
Will You Not See the Full Moon (Riyaz),
255–56
Wirsing, R.G., 183n3
Woman in Black (Abbas), 252–53
women: in AMP's struggle, 21; artists,
239, 244–45, 251, 253n1; culture of
poetry in Gilgit-Baltistan and,
214–15; female judges in Swat, 192;
Islamization and formation of idea
of modern Muslim woman, 108–9;
Jamaat, 105–7, 109–11, 113–18;
Khalid's miniature art depicting,
244; participation in public politics,
106–7; piety movements, 105,
109; social transformations, 104;
working-class struggle and, 145. *See*

also feminism and "fundamentalism" in Pakistan
Women-in-Development (WID)
programs, 112–13
Women's Commission, 110
women's movement. *See* feminism and
"fundamentalism" in Pakistan
Women's Protection Bill, 32
women's rights: ministers appointed
by Zardari and violence against
women, 35; Musharraf and, 31–32,
33; Nawaz Sharif government and,
31, 41n11
working-class struggle: demonstrations, 146–48; in Faisalabad,
Punjab, 137–49; J'afri's support
of, 136; Labour Qaumi Movement and, 39, 138–42; Mustansar
Randhawa and, 141–42; organization in Jhang, 140–41; radicalism,
36–39; Rana Muhammad Tahir and,
142–46; trade union movement,
36–39; workers' pay and conditions,
145–46, 147; workers' status in
relation to social security cards,
140, 141
World Bank, 24, 42, 49, 50, 78, 112, 117,
132; breakdown of civil bureaucracy facilitated by "devolution"
sponsored by, 126; grants and aid
through non-governmental organizations, 113; non-governmental
organizations promoted by, 28, 30;
Pakistan's default on loans from, 77
World Conservation Union, The
(IUCN), 228
World Drug Report 2010, 7
World Food Programme, 77
Wright, Lawrence, 78n2

yaks, centrality to Shimshali livelihood
and culture of, 230, 231, 233

INDEX   287